T0355681

THE REAL POPULATION
BOMB

ALSO BY P. H. LIOTTA AND JAMES F. MISKEL

A Fevered Crescent: Security and Insecurity in the Greater Near East (2006)

ALSO BY P. H. LIOTTA

The Graveyard of Fallen Monuments (2007)

Gaia's Revenge: Climate Change and Humanity's Loss
(2007, with Allan W. Shearer)

The Fight for Legitimacy: Democracy vs. Terrorism (2006, with
Cindy R. Jebb, Thomas Sherlock, and Ruth Margolies Beitler)

*The Uncertain Certainty: Human Security, Environmental Change,
and the Future Euro-Mediterranean* (2003)

Diamond's Compass (1993; 1995)

ALSO BY JAMES F. MISKEL

Disaster Response and Homeland Security: What Works, What Doesn't (2006)

Buying Trouble? National Security and Reliance upon Foreign Industry (1993)

RELATED TITLES FROM POTOMAC BOOKS

Population Decline and the Remaking of Great Power Politics
—Susan Yoshihara and Douglas A. Sylva, eds.

*Fighting Chance: Global Trends and Shocks in the National Security
Environment*—Neyla Arnas, ed.

MEGACITIES, GLOBAL SECURITY
& THE MAP OF
THE FUTURE

THE REAL POPULATION

BOMB

P. H. LIOTTA AND JAMES F. MISKEL

POTOMAC BOOKS
WASHINGTON, D.C.

Library of Congress Cataloging-in-Publication Data
Liotta, P. H.
  The real population bomb : megacities, global security & the map of the future / P.H. Liotta and James F. Miskel.—1st ed.
     p. cm.
  Includes bibliographical references and index.
  ISBN 978-1-59797-551-3 (hardcover)
  ISBN 978-1-61234-107-1 (electronic edition)
 1. Urban density. 2. Cities and towns—Growth. 3. Security, International.
4. Overpopulation. I. Miskel, James F., 1946– II. Title.
  HB2161.L56 2012
  304.6'2—dc23
                                                    2011041805

Printed in the United States of America on acid-free paper that meets the American National Standards Institute Z39-48 Standard.

Potomac Books
22841 Quicksilver Drive
Dulles, Virginia 20166

First Edition

10 9 8 7 6 5 4 3 2 1

for our children's children

This squalid brawl in a distant city is more
important than might appear at first sight.
—George Orwell, *Homage to Catalonia*

There are too many of us.
—Philip Caputo, *Ghosts of Tsavo*

Work on this book began at Villa Aventino in Rome, Italy,
and ended at Miti Mingi House in Nairobi, Kenya.

CONTENTS

ILLUSTRATIONS

AUTHORS' NOTE

This book is about where and how geopolitics will play out in the twenty-first century. Cumulatively it represents three decades of work from authors with seemingly dissimilar backgrounds: one is a poet, novelist, and translator; the other is a security analyst and expert in disaster response and management who has worked for two presidential administrations. Both were colleagues at the U.S. Naval War College in the early 2000s.

We have traveled widely and conducted fieldwork in places as disparate as the Altiplano of Bolivia; Caracas, Venezuela; Guayaquil, Ecuador; the autonomous Altai Republic in deep Siberia; and the massive slums of Egypt, India, Kenya, South Africa, and Brazil. What we share from this experience is the recognition that the world has changed before our eyes. Terms such as the "developed" and "developing" world—phrases that were always dangerous and loaded with false value—no longer have the relevance they seem to have had once. Concepts such as "first world" and "third world" are stubborn relics of Cold War thinking—just as our "mental maps" are grounded in the often difficult but known past. We must change our ways of seeing the world.

Traditionally there have been two general approaches to understanding societies and states. One is the humanitarian or ecological perspective in which the focus is on society—how people live and are affected by war, pollution, and economic globalization. The other is a realist perspective in which the focus is on the economic, political, and military relations among major powers such as the European Union, the United States, China, and Russia. What these traditional approaches underemphasize is the overlap and natural alignment between them. To understand the map of the future, we need to critically appreciate how astonishing population growth in cities—particularly fast-growing megalopolises in weak or failing states in Africa, the Middle East, and Asia—impacts ecology and ecosystems, human security, *and* the national security of Western states, as well as allies and trading partners.

For both better and worse, globalization and urban population growth have changed political and economic dynamics in ways that previous conceptions of how the world works cannot do justice. In this book we examine how developments below the nation-state level—at the municipal level—affect how we must see the world of the future.

While this work is anything but a travelogue, we do visit some of the most alarming locations on the earth. Often these places have been viewed in impressionistic terms, as distant locations where "Others" live—with whom "we" have little interaction. But we are far more connected than we think; whether Nigeria or Pakistan, Bangladesh or Egypt, their future is also ours. The odds seem stacked against those who live there. In the dense, overgrown neighborhoods and shantytowns of Lagos, Kinshasa, Cairo, Karachi, Lahore, or Dhaka, government authorities have failed to provide infrastructure and public services. We need urgent, collective, and innovative actions to help critical megacities weather the gathering storm.

But there is hope and strength. Though time is running short, solutions are still possible. In the end, this book is about the power and resilience of the human spirit.

1

INTRODUCTION

Welcome to the Urban Century

> We live in the age of the city. The City is everything to us—
> it consumes us, and for that reason we glorify it.
>
> —*Onookome Okome*[1]

There was a time when the city was the dominant political identity. Centuries and even millennia ago, the most advanced societies in the Mediterranean, the Near East, and South America revolved around cities that were either states in themselves or were the locus of power for larger empires and kingdoms. The time of the city is coming again, though now in a considerably less benign way.

With the rise of massive urban centers in Africa and Asia, cities that will matter most in the twenty-first century are located in less-developed, struggling states. A number of these huge megalopolises—whether Lagos or Karachi, Dhaka or Kinshasa—reside in states often unable or simply unwilling to manage the challenges that their vast and growing urban populations pose. There are no signs that their governments will prove more capable in the future. These swarming, massive urban monsters will continue to grow and should concern the world.

By 2015 there will be six hundred cities on the planet with populations of 1 million or more, and fifty-eight with populations over 5 million. By 2025,

according to the National Intelligence Council, there will be twenty-seven cities with populations greater than 10 million—the common measure by which
an urban population constitutes a "megacity." If measures are not taken soon,
some of these megacities will pose *the* most significant security threat in the
coming decades. They will become havens for terrorists and criminal networks, as well as sources of major environmental depletion. They will serve
as freakish natural laboratories where all the elements most harmful to international and human security are grown. If crowded masses within these
unaccommodating spaces are left to their own devices by inept or uncaring
governments, their collective rage, despair, and hunger will inevitably erupt.
And when inhabitants tire of the lawlessness, poverty, and instability of the
megacities, they will leave—those that can—bringing violence with them. In
the face of rising expectations that globalization inevitably entails, these petri
dishes of despair and danger will spill over municipal boundaries and international borders with rapidly spreading contagion.

Although there are significant differences in the cultures and histories of
emerging megacities, from the dangerous streets of Karachi to the sprawling
shantytowns of Lagos, basic similarities are dramatic. All have experienced recent and rapid population booms during unsettled periods in national histories, driven in large part by internal migration from depressed or chaotic rural
districts. In each, municipal and national governments failed to either govern or provide for exploding urban populations. Continued failure seems preordained without some form of external assistance.

LIFE IN THE 10/40 WINDOW

A number of megacities of greatest concern are located in or situated close to
the so-called 10/40 Window—the area in Africa and Asia between 10 and 40
degrees north latitude.

A term both human geographers and Christian missionaries use, the 10/40
Window demarcates regions of the world where socioeconomic challenges are
the most daunting, where two-thirds of the world's population and four-fifths
of the world's poor live.[2] This "window" is a veritable stew of competing religious identities and ethnic groups. Preponderant faiths are Hinduism, Islam—

THE 10/40 WINDOW

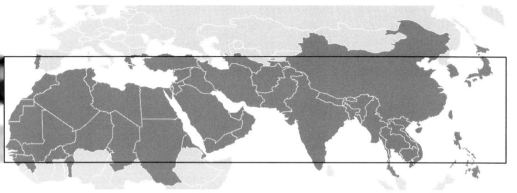

in its various sects—and Buddhism, Christianity, Judaism, and tribal animism. As journalist Robert Kaplan's *The Arabists* points out, people in much of this part of the world have been resistant not only towards Christianity but to Western political and social culture in general—yet mass media and the Internet have made them aware and desirous of at least some of the materialism associated with Western modernity.

The friction between the thesis of traditional beliefs and the antithesis of Western modernity (better hospitals, longer life spans, healthier children, and more comfortable homes, among other things) has yet to yield a synthesis in many parts of the 10/40 Window. Until it does, chaos and carnage will persevere. Some of this violence will be internationalized; it already has been, as the 2008 terrorist attacks in Mumbai in India, repeated attacks on the World Trade Center, and the bombings of European mass transit systems demonstrate.

These megacities have become Leviathans—in biblical terminology the name for an uncontrollable entity. The political philosopher Thomas Hobbes used the term as the title for his classic text; for him, the Leviathan was the state that supervised or managed the city (and the rest of the territory claimed by the state). The Leviathan-state in Hobbes's view may itself be uncontrollable; it was nevertheless all that ultimately stood between the individual citizen and a life that was "solitary, poor, nasty, brutish, and short." Hobbes argued that the citizen essentially had to relinquish individual rights to the state in return for state protection against the violence and chaos of the world. Tragically, that bargain is not holding for the people living in many of the world's largest cities—particularly those cities in the 10/40 Window where Hobbes's Leviathan-state has ceased to perform its protective function. Residents of these cities are largely condemned, as his fellow Englishmen may have been in the early seventeenth century, to poor, nasty, brutish, and short lives precisely because the Leviathan-city is beyond the control of non-Leviathan states.

This work focuses on the dramatic effects that these massive, underserved, and undergoverned cities will have on international stability, human security, and environmental degradation, as well as offers strategies for mitigating those effects. We specifically examine the impact of crime, inequality, and violence in some of the largest cities in the world. We show how developments in these cities threaten to destabilize entire states and regions—and plunge the entire world into cycles of crises, conflicts, and wars that will do little to resolve underlying issues. We compare these cities to other densely populated areas of the globe, from the violent "mini-megacities" in Gaza to the new million-plus cities of China and India. We also look for lessons in the history of the great metropolises of the past (New York, Los Angeles, London, and Paris), which in their early days also teemed with slums and unrest. Each, nonetheless, overcame the challenges of growth and proved capable of delivering public services and maintaining order in the face of mushrooming expansion—something that few of the cities we examine here will be able to do.

WELCOME TO THE URBAN CENTURY

In 1905 only 10 percent of the world's population lived in cities. Today over 50 percent does. By 2030, likely much sooner, two out of three will live in cities, and 90 percent of population growth will occur in cities of the developing world—what we should properly call the "majority" world. This massive shift to urban landscapes has never occurred on such scale before in human history. Citizens flock to the city for opportunity, employment, health care, and education. Today one in six lives in cities with unhealthy air quality; one in fifteen has inadequate sanitation; one in thirty lacks access to safe drinking water.

According to the United Nations, by the year 2025 there will be at least twenty-seven cities with populations greater than 10 million. In 1950 there was only one: New York. In 1975 there were only three: Tokyo, New York, and Mexico City. Tokyo and New York are located in economically advanced nations with governmental institutions and economic infrastructures able to effectively manage urban growth.[3] Less well supported by its government and economy, Mexico City has nonetheless been a relative success, though it remains to be seen whether that will still be the case in 2025 when its population reaches 21 million.

There are, naturally, significant differences in the cultures and histories of the world's largest cities. One of the most important differences is the timing of their growth spurts. Paris and London, despite the challenges faced during their emergence as major cities, never experienced the wrenchingly sudden growth spurts that new megacities have recently experienced and will continue to suffer. The population of Dhaka, for example, will have virtually exploded by more than 5,400 percent between 1950 and 2015. (If New York had grown at such a pace, its population would now be a staggering 684 million.)

In the nineteenth century, London grew by seven times. By contrast, projected population growth from 1950 to 2015 is significantly more dynamic—and frightening—for megacities in the 10/40 Window. Kinshasa will grow by a factor approaching *fifty times*, Lagos by a factor of twenty-five, and Karachi by 2,000 percent during the same period.

The population of New York City will have grown only 30 percent between 1950 and 2015—and in 1950 the city already had a capable government and healthy public infrastructure of schools, hospitals, water and sanitation systems, roads, mass transit, and communications. New York City also began the 1950s with a robust housing stock that could be easily expanded to accommodate its population growth. Los Angeles, as another example, grew as a direct result of a preexisting and relatively effective national economic, transportation, and legal infrastructure. Its growth spurts also occurred long after the United States had secured its borders and solidified citizens' perception of a common national identity.

By contrast, some of the states that house the new megacities had to spend their first decades establishing and defending their national sovereignty, at the evident expense of building governmental and economic infrastructure.

URBAN POPULATIONS, 1950–2015

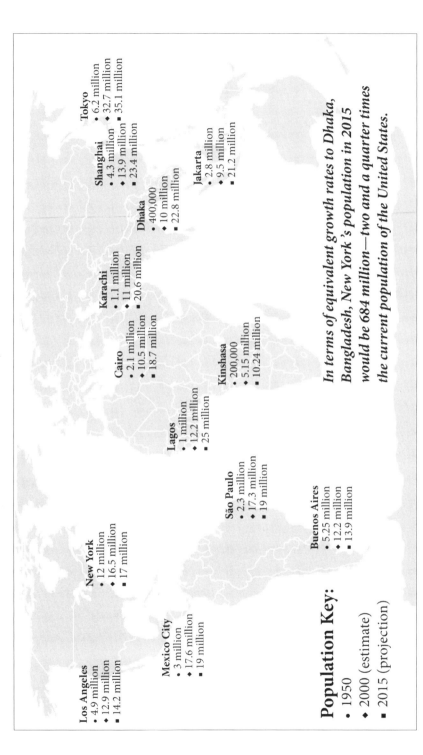

Los Angeles
- 4.9 million
- 12.9 million
- 14.2 million

New York
- 12 million
- 16.5 million
- 17 million

Mexico City
- 3 million
- 17.6 million
- 19 million

Cairo
- 2.1 million
- 10.5 million
- 18.7 million

Karachi
- 1.1 million
- 11 million
- 20.6 million

Dhaka
- 400,000
- 10 million
- 22.8 million

Shanghai
- 4.3 million
- 13.9 million
- 23.4 million

Tokyo
- 6.2 million
- 32.7 million
- 35.1 million

Jakarta
- 2.8 million
- 9.5 million
- 21.2 million

Lagos
- 1 million
- 12.2 million
- 25 million

Kinshasa
- 200,000
- 5.15 million
- 10.24 million

São Paulo
- 2.3 million
- 17.3 million
- 19 million

Buenos Aires
- 5.25 million
- 12.2 million
- 13.9 million

Population Key:
- 1950
- 2000 (estimate)
- 2015 (projection)

In terms of equivalent growth rates to Dhaka, Bangladesh, New York's population in 2015 would be 684 million—two and a quarter times the current population of the United States.

Pakistan fought a civil war that dismembered the country, as well as several wars and near-war skirmishes with its larger neighbor, India, in the decades after independence in 1947. Similarly, the Democratic Republic of the Congo's independence in 1960 was followed by secessionist civil wars in the 1960s and again in the 1990s and 2000s. All the while, both Pakistan and the DRC's major cities kept growing ever more rapidly and ever more uncontrollably.

Megacities that have emerged in the last half-century have passed the tipping point. They have become overwhelmed, dangerous, ungovernable, and, remarkably, still grow. Compared to urban centers of the West, they are unlike anything the earth has ever seen. They pose major threats to global security as they become both platforms and havens for extremists and criminal networks, which recent events in Gaza, a much smaller but densely populated and uncontrolled city, amply demonstrate.

If we seek to understand the world of tomorrow, a good place to start is in Gaza—an entity that has for years been functioning in defiance of its parent "national" government and has provoked a war with Israel and launched hundreds of cross-border terror attacks. It has also tried to undermine its parent government in the West Bank through violence and the intimidation of its representatives. Unlike Gaza—which even in the best of times exported little, and in recent years has been effectively isolated—some of these "new" megacities are intimately connected with the rest of the world through trade and easily available transportation for businessmen, diplomats, and ordinary citizens, as well as criminals, weapons dealers, terrorists, and insurgents.

THE NEW ALIGNMENT: MEGACITIES AND SPLINTERED STATES

The end of the Cold War precipitated the search to comprehend the best responses to an increasingly fragmented—and increasingly dangerous—world. That search continues today, with no clear answers revealed. What pundits once considered the benchmarks for integration and global peace and security—privatization, deregulation, and globalization—are recognized today as imperfect solutions, even in advanced states. Moreover, unlike during the Cold War, with its clearly articulated threats, we have moved into a world defined by "entangled vulnerabilities," where disproportionate population growth;

disease; climate change; depletion of water and other natural resources; decline in food production, access, and availability; soil erosion and desertification; and rapid urbanization, pollution, and infrastructure decay in megacities form one part of the new problem set.

All these vulnerabilities are interwoven—with complex linkages, interdependence, and often unpredictable and chaotic causes and effects. In many instances, these effects have led to conflict and bloodshed. We have only begun to appreciate the truths that many of these negative outcomes came from the "the City" and grievances within them. Twenty-first-century warfare, after all, did not begin on September 11, 2001. It began with the death of Yugoslavia in 1991, the Battle of Mogadishu in 1993, the siege of Sarajevo, and the genocide in Kigali that spread throughout Rwanda, with the bombings of U.S. embassies in Dar es Salaam and Nairobi in 1998 and the attack on the USS *Cole* in 2000.

And while much has been written about the notion of "failed states," little attention has been given to the concept of "failed cities." Certainly when the *Foreign Policy* "Index of Failed States" proclaims (in comments that senior State Department officials echo) that there exist between thirty to fifty failed or failing states in the world today, insufficient focus centers on cities within such states that are driving forces for deterioration—and are the locus of the greatest trials ahead. Similarly, in works such as Thomas P. M. Barnett's *The Pentagon's New Map: War and Peace in the Twenty-First Century*, the notion that those most disconnected from the flows of globalization are where we will be most likely to intervene is simply wrong.

We mean to change the conversation. All of the emerging powers of the twenty-first century—Brazil, India, China—are intimately connected to globalization. But they face extraordinary obstacles and (unlike Western Europe or the United States during their periods of emergence) will drag these impediments alongside as they become twenty-first-century powers. These are the pivotal "splintered states."

These states are not disconnected from globalization; to the contrary, they are *intimately* connected to it. Both prominent and deficient, these new great powers share more in common with the splintered states of the rest of the majority world—where the consequences and human impacts of climate change, resource scarcity, disease, demographic shifts, declining productivity, trans-national criminality, and terrorism as factors that lead to destabilization and potential conflict and will define the human landscape. Unquestionably, the locus of all these intensely concentrated critical uncertainties will be in one place: the City.

On the positive side, the emerging megacities of Brazil, India, and China offer lessons that can be shared across boundaries and borders. From the un-easy but acknowledged acceptance of Rio de Janeiro's *favela* slums to Mumbai's civil society arrangement of community-police cooperation for local gover-nance known as *panchayat*, new methods of adaptation and accommodation may emerge.

OLD AND NEW WORLDS

A handful of new megacities should be of particular concern because of their size, strategic locations, roles in the global economy, or their environmental vulnerabilities. As illustration, Lagos, Kinshasa, Cairo, Dhaka, Karachi, La-hore, and Rio de Janeiro will each have populations in excess of 10 million in 2025. Five of these seven (Lagos, Karachi, Kinshasa, Dhaka, and Rio) will have populations of 15 million or more. All are located in states that have largely proven incapable of providing the scale of law enforcement, public health, education, and social services that such large populations require. And all are located in states that are strategic pivots in their respective regions and impor-tant to global stability.

While terrorism, homelessness, poverty, and failure of any effective gover-nance to provide support are not one and the same, they often coexist and col-lectively are symptomatic of a severe "dis-ease" within the system—one with which the system in many countries is demonstrably unable to cope. There are practical applications that the larger international system can and should take on to strengthen governance in states where megacities present the greatest direct challenges.

DANGERS THAT THE LEVIATHANS POSE

Life in megacities will deteriorate as populations surge beyond carrying capac-ity. The teeming populations of Lagos, Karachi, Cairo, and Dhaka have few options. In Lagos one could almost say that the rule of law does not exist. Police are corrupt and government services close to nonexistent. Residents in most neighborhoods have to provide transportation for officers in order for local crimes to be investigated. Urban "bustle" is not a lively scene of pedestrians enjoying the streets or shops. Rather, jostling street gangs and militias fight each other while nudging aside overmatched and all-too-often exploitive government agencies—peeling away whatever thin layers of protection the state provides and setting the stage for the eventual storming of a by-then hollowed-out Bastille. In Lagos life expectancy is less than forty years. Thirty-eight percent of Lagos' children under five suffer from malnutrition stunting; 50 percent have never received an inoculation; only 60 percent attend school. Fishing is a main livelihood for many—in a place where raw sewage is routinely dumped in the same waters. As conditions in Lagos deteriorate, a stampede of refugees into nearby Benin (a half-day's walk from the city) could result and would unsettle an already fragile West African region.

One result of municipal failure in emerging megacities is "contagion effect," which will swallow host states and entire regions in whirlpools of collapse—and bring about cycles of military intervention by the United States or by the UN, the European Union, or other coalition to restore peace after collapse and to reestablish order. Such costly interventions, however, never have appreciable effect on underlying social circumstances. As our experiences in Iraq, Afghanistan, and elsewhere illustrate, military interventions address symptoms, not diseases. Unless underlying diseases in megacities are cured, violence will recur after peacekeepers withdraw. Even as military action will not solve the problem, the costs of intervention will remain exorbitant.

Another result entails environmental catastrophe. Bangladesh nestles in the most ecologically vulnerable delta in the world. With a population half the size of the United States squeezed onto territory roughly the size of Iowa, 60 percent of its land floods each year—and drought is now a major threat during nonmonsoon seasons. At the heart of this explosive and yet decaying ecosystem, residents of the capital, Dhaka, have experienced the most rapid urban growth ever known. Preoccupied with and overwhelmed by the need to placate the huge population of the capital, the government failed and continues to fail to provide meaningful assistance to desperately needy rural communities.

The delta is vulnerable to even the slightest climatic variations. Ten million people will be stranded or driven off the land if sea levels rise by a mere twenty centimeters in the Bay of Bengal. Seawater is creeping ever northward, replacing precious freshwater resources the huge population depends on. With the effects of climate change more evident, declining freshwater runoff of snow from the Himalayas in the north and rising sea levels in the south only exacerbate an already dangerous, destructive feedback loop. Recognizing the likely outcome of Bangladesh's plight, India in 2007 completed a four-thousand-kilometer, three-meter-high barrier separating the two states—a Maginot Line supposedly designed to keep illegal immigrants and militants out (as well as thwart the smuggling of weapons and narcotics). In reality, it will seal off what could be the world's first massive wave of environmental refugees, bringing anomie, violence, and desperation in their wake.

Conditions in megacities in many states have already created fertile recruitment grounds for terrorist, criminal, and extremist organizations. In Cairo and Karachi, urban poverty and chronic instability leave populations with few options for a better life. Is it any surprise that these cities, with their crumbling services, poverty, and basic unfairness, rank among the world's top sources of Islamic extremism? Moreover, some of what we term indigenous "non-state actors" and nongovernment organizations (NGOs) have the potential to become so powerful within megacities as to be virtually invulnerable to the power of the governments of their respective states.

Others may actually seize control of the state. This is what happened in the Gaza Strip, a place so densely populated it qualifies as a mini-megacity, sharing many of the same problems of larger urban masses. Wretched living conditions and an unresponsive government led to Hamas' victory in the 2006 parliamentary elections and, portentously, to its success since then in violently driving out rival elements of the parent Palestinian Authority government.

At the same time, the strain of attempting to manage fast-growing cities will force some national governments to make a Faustian bargain to maintain control over urban turbulence. In terms of politics, it makes sense for governments to concentrate energies and spending on megacities—where, after all, problems are most immediately threatening and the need for public services is quantitatively greatest. In so doing, remote, underpopulated rural areas are inevitably written off. As a result, ungoverned rural areas will proliferate and become havens for terrorists, insurgency, and criminal organizations—not un-like what took place in the tribal agency areas of Pakistan, the cradle of Al Qaeda—and the remote valleys of eastern Colombia. As Al Qaeda's attacks on 9/11 made clear, in the modern, globalized economy even small terrorist outfits in isolated havens can target the United States and other economically advanced states at a time and place of their choosing. They can achieve horrific destruction.

In some states the consequences will be bitterly ironic: undergoverned ru-ral areas, remote from metropolitan (and ineffectively governed) centers, will engender parallel universes of insurgency, violence, and crime. While much has been written about extremists setting up camps and training bases in un-governed rural areas, the reality is that they also operate—often freely—out of undergoverned cities. With hydra-headed networks that know no borders, along with access to Internet and digital communications technology (as well as rail connections, airline hubs, and seaports), sprawling cities—themselves concentrated, high-value targets—offer extremists the perfect place to export violence, as well as recruit and maintain networks, and yet remain invisible.

The time for action is short. We are *already* in a race against time. Cities such as Karachi and Lagos may boil over as civil distemper permanently fouls relationships among economic, ethnic, and religious groups and between the population as a whole and governments. If cities descend into complete anar-chy, vicious consequences will include an increase in more powerful terrorism, violence against U.S. interests here and overseas, new havens for international criminals, the potential mass exodus of peoples, and dramatic increases in smuggling, drugs, and other forms of criminal activity.

The human impact and human toll are in themselves staggering. With the world's population now well past 7 billion, there are 1 billion "squatters" on the planet, with their density rising daily. As investigative reporter Robert Neuwirth writes in *Shadow Cities: A Billion Squatters, A New Urban World*, two hundred thousand people daily leave their rural areas and move to cities—1.5 million a week, 70 million a year.[4] By 2030, if conditions and social support systems do not improve, the number of city squatters may well double to 2 billion, almost one in four people on the planet.

OUR ROAD MAP

There have, of course, been environmental studies that predicted dire consequences from overpopulation in general. These predictions have proven untrue in part because they underestimated the impact of technology on agriculture and discounted the likelihood of decreased fertility in Europe, Russia, and other parts of the world. The most notable book, written in 1968, was Paul Ehrlich's bestseller, *The Population Bomb*. Warning of mass starvation that would come in the 1970s and 1980s due to overpopulation, Ehrlich suggested a premise similar to that Thomas Robert Malthus put forward in 1798: the world's population would outstrip food production and securing of critical natural resources. Nonetheless, thanks to innovations such as Norman Borlaug's "Green Revolution," agricultural initiatives that increased production around the world beginning in the 1960s, as well as declining general world fertility rates, the worst of Ehrlich's warnings never came to pass. Despite his dire tone and unfulfilled predictions, he stands by his central argument to this day. And what he predicted for the globe may well prove true for some of our largest cities.

With the rapidly increasing concentration of human populations within cities, we are witnessing a *real* population bomb. The urban growth of the twenty-first century, however, results from human migration as much as higher birth and lower death rates—and there are no quick technological fixes for the problems of cities because they already have grown too large, too fast. This may well be the central challenge of our times.

Perhaps the most significant academic work to address the new urban challenge remains Joseph Tainter's concept-driven *The Collapse of Complex Societies*—a work that influenced Pulitzer Prize–winner Jared Diamond's widely popular *Collapse: How Societies Choose to Fail or Succeed*. Just as Diamond successfully incorporated highlights of intense archaeological studies to present powerful portraits, in this work we follow a similar strategy. While we cull from recent data and demographic projections, as well as draw on historical examples, our central focus is to present a human face—through human narratives—in this unfolding and enormous global drama. Our goal is to present the political, economic, social, and environmental contours and contexts as we "map" the new megacity terrain.

We identify emerging problematic megacities, examine why their populations continue to surge, and explain how conditions there often lead to terrorism, war, criminal violence, human rights abuses, and flagrant pollution. We further address why many states fail to manage urban challenges and analyze the dire implications for international efforts to suppress terrorism and promote international relations and peace and security in strategically critical regions. We discuss why the UN, along with the United States and other economically advanced states, have not taken effective action to offset looming disasters. We examine specific challenges in critical cities. We conclude with policy recommendations that we must adopt to help better manage challenges that have already emerged as populations skyrocket.

There is no widely circulating work available on the rise of the twenty-first-century megacity—despite its rapid emergence on the global stage and its attendant global security implications. While specific case studies do exist of some megacities—such as James Pick and Edward Butler's *Mexico Megacity* and Christopher Silver's *Planning the Megacity: Jakarta in the Twentieth Century*—these works are not accessible for a larger reading audience and retain a highly specialized focus on landscape design and environmental impact. One of the few works to consider the broader implications of urban growth is Norman Myers' *The Gaia Atlas of Future Worlds: Challenges and Opportunities in an Age of Change,* published in 1991. He particularly recognized the "termite queen phenomenon," in which urban centers, acting as a kind of supernest, attract resources—both positive *and* negative—from rural centers, including human capital and labor, skills, food, water, and raw materials. Myers' projections, while fascinating, are now decades old. New events, trends, effects, and phenomena have emerged.

What we offer are hardly panaceas for what may seem to be insurmountable problems. Moreover, actions we offer cannot be taken in isolation from each other. As practical means to achievable ends, they should be synergistically applied to deal with specific environments as well as common symptoms within the megacities of Lagos, Kinshasa, Cairo, Dhaka, Karachi, Lahore, and Rio.[5] Notably, as a number of pundits have focused on Southeast Asia as the next "hotbed" of foment and instability, any reasonable reader may ask why we do not focus on Manila or Jakarta (in the world's largest Muslim state, with a population of 250 million).

Jakarta is an example. With over 25 million residents in the extended Jakarta-Bandung megalopolis, it is the fourth largest urban area in the world. Jakarta suffers—as do most megacities—from "urbanization overload." Growing from a population of slightly over 1 million in 1960 to 9 million in 2004, Jakarta's government is unable to meet basic infrastructure needs for residents. Air pollution and garbage mismanagement create severe problems. With a population that doubles on weekends with the influx of residents to markets and access points, coupled with the lack of adequate transportation systems, massive traffic congestion is constant. The urban financial, economic, and environmental challenges facing Jakarta reflect the obstacles all megacities will have to confront: proliferation of slums, high disease rates, unchecked industrial growth, poor air quality, high pollution, and almost nonexistent sanitation and waste disposal.

Much like Indonesia itself, Jakarta remains a critical pivot largely ignored except in times of crisis.[6] While many remember the massive impact of the Sumatra tsunami in 2004, fewer recall that U.S. Treasury Secretary Robert E. Rubin declared in 1997 that Indonesia "was critical to the national security and economic interests of the United States."[7] Despite the dire predictions of the late 1990s that centered on Indonesia as a pivotal state on the verge of collapse, however, present realities are quite different. In contrast to Pakistan—which *is* in danger—Indonesia today, as Steve Coll of the *New Yorker* writes, is "a comparably bland, democratic archipelago."[8]

REDRAWING THE MAP OF THE FUTURE

In attempting to address the present and future trials that megacities present, the international community has already begun to prepare itself to mitigate at least some negative consequences. After all, one could argue that this is really what the "long war on terror" is about. Still, no state, international regime, or organization has directed sufficient strategic attention, planning, or investment to reversing trends that created challenges in the first place. One reason is that statesmen continue to think in terms of states, not subordinate polities. Perhaps there is good reason for this: states have improved security globally but not universally. Secondarily, national governments in states in which ungoverned megacities are located are averse to acknowledging their failures to others, for fear of undermining their own claims of national sovereignty and calling into question their political legitimacy in the eyes of constituents.

By calling attention to these challenges, and to opportunities that exist, we hope to provide ideas, means, and methods for addressing problems that megacities of the developing world—and through them, the rest of the world—face as the new Leviathans arise. The time to act is here.

2

TOO FAR, TOO FAST

The Real Population Bomb

Think of a stretch limo in the potholed streets of New York City, where homeless beggars live. Inside the limo are the air-conditioned post-industrial regions of North America, Europe, the emerging Pacific Rim, and a few other isolated places, with their trade summitry and computer-information highways. Outside is the rest of mankind, going in a completely different direction.

—*Robert D. Kaplan*, The Coming Anarchy

We live in an age of extremes. Today, more than half the global population resides in cities and, by 2030, two out of three humans will be city dwellers. Of the seven billion-plus who inhabit the earth, nearly one in six has no property rights at all. Overall these numbers of the dispossessed are growing in ever-increasing pockets of urban agglomeration.

Favela, barriada, kijiji, gecekondu, aashiwa'i, mudukku, johpadpatti, kampung, penghu—depending on whether one lives in Rio, Lima, Nairobi, İstanbul, Cairo, Colombo, Mumbai, Kuala Lumpur, or Shanghai—these terms all mean one thing: slum. The word itself ought to be neutral in its description of an overcrowded city neighborhood—but it is not. Robert Neuwirth is far more accurate in his assessment of the mental imagery and baggage we bring to the term: "laden with emotional values: decay, dirt, and disease. Danger, despair, and degradation. Criminality, horror, abuse, and fear."[1] Today the slum is where the cities of the future are being born.

But this does not constitute a crisis. After all, as geographer Jared Diamond notes, the average rate at which people consume resources (oil, metals) and produce waste (plastics, greenhouse gases) is thirty-two times higher in the "developed world" (admittedly an arrogant term) than in the "majority world." And the trend for these emerging states is to move toward ever-increasing high-consumption lifestyles. Per capita consumption in China is still eleven times below the United States, but if India and China were to catch up with the developed world, world consumption would triple. At the same time, living standards are not tightly coupled to consumption. Per capita U.S. oil consumption, as Diamond observes, is twice that of Western Europe, yet Western Europe's standard of living is better in life expectancy, infant mortality, medical care access, retirement security, vacation time, quality of public schools, and support for the arts.

OUT OF CONTROL? CHANGING LIFESTYLES AND LIFESPANS

In the most successful emerging states of the "majority world," there is a move toward lifestyles that echo the excess of the developed world. More and more people are adopting high-protein diets richer in animal products, which deplete both water resources and arable land. In India (a place not known for meat consumption), animal product consumption rose by 5 percent over slightly more than a decade; in China this increase was 10 percent.

The United States today expends ten calories of fossil-fuel energy for one calorie of food. Eighty percent of the grain produced in the United States— wheat, rice, corn—goes to livestock. Much of the emerging world is following America's example. In 1960 Mexico fed 5 percent of its grain to livestock; today the figure is 50 percent. Egypt went from 3 percent to 31 percent over the same time period. China, with a sixth of the world's population, has gone from 8 percent to 26 percent. The explosion in the use of water for agricultural purposes, agriculture that largely feeds urban centers, rose by 700 percent in the twentieth century. (In the nineteenth century, the increase in water use for agricultural purposes—even with populations that nearly doubled—was less than 100 percent.) Today, with a global population eleven and a half times more than three centuries ago, we collectively use fifty times more water.

The figures are stunning for car ownership as well. There are nine personal vehicles per thousand eligible drivers in China and eleven for every thousand Indians, compared with 1,148 for every thousand Americans. The United States has 140 million personal vehicles on the road. In China there are 20 million personal vehicles, and in India there are 10 million. Incomes in both China and India, as twenty-first-century megapowers, are rising rapidly. Both economies are expected to continue impressive growth. Millions of families without automobiles will soon be in a position to buy them, especially with the accessible Tata Nano in India—the "People's Car." Soon, hundreds of millions in China and India will own cars. Were these states to match American ownership rates, there would be an additional one *billion* more vehicles on the world's streets and highways.

The United States alone consumes almost one-fourth of the world's oil produced daily. Total global oil use is 86 million barrels a day, and the United States consumes seventy thousand barrels more a day than can be produced.[2] Were China and India to increase their rates of car ownership to the point where per capita oil consumption reached just half of American levels, the two countries would burn through a hundred million additional barrels a day. Yes, what you've just read is correct: We are sucking ourselves "dry"—and have been doing so for over five decades. This is one reason why some of us obsess over "Peak Oil" as the End of Days.

People are living longer—and cities may well play a role in extended lifespans. In 1900 the average life expectancy for an American male was forty-seven years. At the same time, in the largely rural Balkans and agricultural-based Spain, life expectancy was less than thirty-five years. Today, according to the Central Intelligence Agency, the average life expectancy in Spain is eighty years; in Bosnia and Herzegovina, seventy-nine; and in the United States, seventy-eight. For the emerging world, in China the life expectancy is seventy-four years, and in India, seventy. In states with cities that we consider in this work (with the exception of Egypt), life expectancy hovers in the second tier: Nigerians have life expectancies of forty-six years; the Democratic Republic of the Congo and Kenya roughly fifty-four years.

What does this mean for the large cities and megacities that are the Leviathans rising? One answer, which *New Yorker* critic and urban architect Paul Goldberger offers, is that cities are "inherently sustainable."[3] And indeed that is true, when urban planning, design, and persistent renewal are primary emphases—and when we recognize these factors as the most important aspects to create security in this century. But, all too often, urban planning and investment are not priorities—or are beyond the capacity of municipal governance. For those one in six globally who have no property rights and no viable chance to enter a more prosperous existence, inherent sustainability is not a matter of design but of survival.

HAVE WE BEEN HERE BEFORE?

Cities offer hope—the chance for better jobs, health care, education—as well as severe inequities. According to the World Resources Institute, "Millions of children living in the world's largest cities, particularly in developing countries, are exposed to life-threatening air pollution two to eight times above the maximum World Health Organization guidelines."[4]

It is fair to ask: have we been here before? To some extent, the answer is yes. While Japan, the major countries of Western Europe, and the United States have somewhat mastered the challenges of fast-growing urban environments, their practices cannot be grafted onto the governmental structures in the so-called developing world. In the eighteenth century, William Hogarth gave us grotesque prints of gin-soaked London squalor, and in the nineteenth Karl Marx vented outrage at working-class exploitation. And even as we mythologize the violence of the infamous Five Points slum in *Gangs of New York,* the hazards for new megacities are far more lethal.

When we contrast the growth of urban populations in nineteenth-century Europe in particular, we see trends and patterns that replicate themselves in twenty-first-century Leviathans. Today such effects have accelerated in terms of both growth and impact. During the nineteenth century, industrial cities expanded at the highest rate. Essen, Germany, for example, grew by 300 percent between 1800 and 1900. The great preindustrial centers—Paris and Vienna, say—expanded by three times during the century. In Europe, more than 75 percent lived in cities, a percentage exceeded only in North American urban centers. Cities became magnets of money, power, and creativity—as well as harbors of festering and pestilential slums.

This may seem difficult to accept as we know these modern and (mostly) thriving European cities today. Yet London, one of the world's first megacities to emerge in the twentieth century, was in the mid-nineteenth century a nightmare. The novels of Charles Dickens reflect these wretched conditions in the leading city in what was the world's most industrialized state. In *Bleak House* he describes one London thoroughfare as

> a black, dilapidated street, avoided by all decent people; where the crazy houses were seized upon, when their decay was far advanced, by some bold vagrants, who, after establishing their own possession, took to letting them out in lodgings. Now, these tumbling tenements contain, by night, a swarm of misery. As on the ruined human wretch, vermin parasites appear, so these ruined shelters have bred a crowd of foul existence that crawls in and out of gaps in walls and boards; and coils itself to sleep, in maggot numbers, where the rain drips in; and comes and goes, fetching and carrying fever, and sowing more evil in its every footprint.

Residents of any major city in Europe or the United States today would undoubtedly offer similar—if less evocative—descriptions of local slums or rundown neighborhoods where unemployment and crime are prevalent, drug abuse abounds, the roads and streetlights are ignored, and the schools fail to give students the rudimentary skills and knowledge necessary to survive in the contemporary economy. Every major city has these places, ones "avoided by decent people." First-time visitors to these cities learn from tourist guidebooks and the advice of concerned acquaintances to avoid these neighborhoods, at least after nightfall. Certainly, the urban riots in Paris during 2005 and 2007 and the 2011 UK unrest remain vivid reminders that decayed and despairing neighborhoods exist in the most economically advanced states.

We know that pockets of enduring poverty and crime exist in American and European urban centers. Apart from periodic and geographically limited attempts at urban renewal—essentially concentrated economic aid to finance the improvement of the public infrastructure or to subsidize the renovation of existing housing stock—municipal governments have almost always attempted containment. National and municipal governments work more to limit the spread of crime, drug abuse, and infrastructure erosion into neighborhoods where the problems are less significant (specifically, wealthier or more politically active neighborhoods) than they do in eradicating the problems in the "black, dilapidated" streets of the worst neighborhoods.

This form of containment is reasonably successful, although urban riots do occur and no part of any city is ever completely free of criminal violence. This success is based on the capacity of the national and municipal governments to deliver law enforcement and public safety services, albeit unevenly in poorer city neighborhoods. A form of dependency is created: minimum levels of economic opportunity for "contained" neighborhoods are heavily reliant on governments to maintain order necessary for daily commerce, as well as provide social transfer payments and access to health care for residents of contained neighborhoods.

That there might be city neighborhoods in which there is a considerable amount of crime, decaying infrastructure, and inadequate public services is not peculiar to the twenty-first century or to municipalities in the developing world. Providing the necessary levels of economic opportunity and governmental assistance to the poorest neighborhoods and effective law enforcement and public safety services to all neighborhoods (but especially to the neighborhoods that are not the poorest) can be difficult and expensive—yet the number of places where these tasks must be performed will only grow.

To be blunt, nineteenth- and twentieth-century Europe and North America also demonstrated that the basic target of attention in urban planning and development was not the underprivileged, but the sources of middle-class prosperity. Unlike the careful planning of Venice or Florence in earlier periods, nineteenth-century planners gutted urban districts for the sake of real estate development, often seeking to locate new sites for rising economic sources (upwind) of former ancient city centers. In 1858 in Vienna, work began on the Ringstrasse, with its elegant cafés and opera, which resulted in the destruction of the old city walls. As historian Robert O. Paxton notes, perhaps the least carefully planned development took place in the construction of Berlin's commercial venues such as the Kurfürstendamm, with its massive villas and fashionable shops, houses, hotels, and restaurants, which caused the destruction of wooded areas and potato fields west of the capital.[5]

Certainly, the most determined urban development took place under Napoleon III with the construction of Paris's *grands boulevards* in the 1860s. The self-titled civic planner Baron Georges-Eugène Haussmann is credited with the creation of the Paris we most associate with today. But by retaking urban space for the sake of real estate owners, foreign investment, and wealthier interests, Haussmann fanatically displaced the urban poor from their ancient *quartiers* and left them to fend for themselves.[6] In the words of urban and community studies scholar Richard Stren, such populations become "human encumberments" to social control and private profit.

Tragically most of the growth that will take place in the twenty-first century will occur in cities that are not equipped to perform even the most basic—and necessary—urban planning and support tasks. The new Leviathans are capable of far less than what Paris and Berlin undertook in the mid-nineteenth century. Municipal authorities in Cairo and Karachi (and many other twenty-first-century new megacities) have already demonstrated the brutality of clearing slums and evicting residents but not the foresight to keep neighborhoods clear for growth, promote infrastructure, or build factories and sorely needed schools.

There will be certainties, nonetheless. We can be certain that in almost any one of these cities, sources and residences of conspicuous consumption will be located (often virtually looming over) neighborhoods of evident poverty, separated by barbed wire or electrified walls and gates. We can be certain that every year thousands and even millions of urban poor, whether legal tenants or resident squatters, will be forcibly removed from their neighborhoods. We can be certain that, as urban planner Tunde Agbola characterized the plight of many in his native Lagos, such urban citizens will be "transients in a perpetual state of relocation."[7]

For all their early flaws, so-called first world megacities expanded at a more manageable pace and, today's fastest growing megacities, did so after their parent nation-states—and their governing structures—had been firmly established and the population had more or less settled on a common national identity. Further, past megacities took shape before the communications revolution raised their residents' expectations and before globalization integrated them as deeply into the international economy as Cairo, Rio, and Lagos today.

More than anywhere else, megacities suffer from a catalog of environmental perils. All face major freshwater challenges, and many inhabitants live without access to clean running water. Today, 90 percent of population growth occurs in majority world cities; one in six lives with unhealthy air quality; one in fifteen lacks adequate sanitation; one in thirty has no access to safe drinking water. There are gross inequities as well. In Kenya's capital, Nairobi, its richest neighborhood is Karen, with 360 inhabitants per square kilometer; in Kibera, the poorest neighborhood, there are 80,000 inhabitants per square kilometer. Yet potable water in Nairobi can be exorbitant for the poorest neighborhoods and is virtually free in the richest ones.[8]

Consider what we term "defecation rights" as a basic human right. In 1998 in the Laina Saba slum in Kibera, there were ten working toilets for forty thousand people; in Mathare 4A, another major Nairobi slum, there were two working toilets for twenty-eight thousand.[9] In Kinshasa and Kigali there are no waterborne sewage systems.[10] It is out of these extraordinary contradictions—between frightening consumption and horrifying deprivation—that we concern ourselves here. In that sense, the Robert Kaplan epigraph we drew on for this chapter is not hyperbolic. Rather, it describes our current reality.

These trends have been building since the latter half of the twentieth century in majority world cities. P. H. Liotta recalls witnessing, as a college student visiting his family in Tehran, an appalling sprawl of poverty that fell away from the Elburz Mountains and stretched on seemingly forever. Shortly after that visit, the revolution that established the Islamic Republic of Iran exploded. Though poverty, inequities, and the lack of basic rights may not have been the main drivers in the people's revolt, they were unquestionably influences.

Urban populations in many locations have ruptured; projected population growth seems now largely irreversible. Thus, to conclude this chapter, we offer considerations of three unique urban centers—the *gecekondu* of Tür-kiye, the sprawling Dharavi slum in Mumbai, and Kibera—with an extended review of the challenges that Kenya faces (and, in some cases, has created).

THE GECEKONDU

"Ne mutlu Türküm diyene"—"Happy am I to call myself a Türk." Mustafa Ke-mal Atatürk, the father of modern Türkiye, did actually say these words, and these same words embellish the mile-wide, sixteen-story Atatürk Dam. The dam was completed in 1990 as part of the Southeast Anatolia Project—which includes twenty-two major dams and irrigation systems—collectively im-pounding the waters of the Euphrates River. Ninety percent of its annual flow originates in Türkiye.

Though they may be taken for a cliché today, Atatürk's words nonetheless spell out a sense of belonging, even community, that is perhaps rare in other locations throughout the 10/40 Window. Visiting the shantytown of Altındağ, or "Golden Mountain," in Ankara, Robert Kaplan describes in *The Coming An-archy* how he was immediately struck by its order and nonthreatening pres-ence. Unlike slums he had visited in Africa, which could "terrify and repel the outsider," Altındağ left quite a different impression.

With its more than four hundred thousand residents, it was one of the first *gecekondu* developments in Türkiye and sprang up from the hillside that was once part of the ancient Ottoman city of Ankara. Beginning in the 1970s, residents built illegal one-bedroom cottages on small plots of land. In the 1980s and 1990s, these plots were sold to developers who often replaced the cottages with apartment buildings—a pattern repeated in other *gecekondular* in İstanbul as well. Such "development" plans, according to some observers, were linked to corruption as well. In her chapter in the edited volume *Illegal Cities*, urban planner Ayşe Yönder described conditions this way:

> By the mid-1960s squatting in the traditional sense of the term had disappeared in İstanbul. Settlers had to pay local strong men for the right to occupy even public land. In the mid-1970s, entrepreneurs with underground connections started controlling public lands in certain districts . . . selling land and monopolizing all construction activity.[11]

Gecekondu is taken from the combination of two Türkish words: *gece,* which means "at night," and *kondu,* from the verb *kondurmak,* "to happen" or "to appear." Thus, the term *gecekondu* means "to appear overnight"—and a *gecekondu bölgesi* is a community made up of these *gecekondular.* Taking advantage of Türkish law, which stipulates that if one is already moved into a residence and its structure is sound, a *gecekondu* dweller cannot be evicted without being taken to court.[12] As the original settlers of *gecekondular* built quickly and in such sheer numbers with the most available construction materials (such as quick-drying concrete or plaster), these communities literally *did* appear overnight.

The shift in population from rural to urban did not happen by accident. Post–World War II Marshall Plan aid, agricultural modernization, and improved manufacturing all contributed to this demographic shift. (Even today, rural residents disembarking at Haydarpaşa Garı train station can be heard to remark, "İstanbul'un taşı, toprağı altın" ["Move to İstanbul, the land of gold"]. According to the Marxist sociologist Çağlar Keyder, between 1955 to 1965 *gecekondu* populations soared from 5 percent to almost 23 percent of the total urban population in Ankara and İstanbul—a figure that has not changed significantly since. Many of the residents of these *gecekondular* follow the pattern of moving from rural locations to urban centers for jobs, education, even as a place of anonymity to escape to. Yet we have noticed in conversation with Türkish friends and colleagues that those outside the community do not entirely trust *gecekondu* residents. One colleague, for example, mentioned that Kaplan perhaps felt "too safe" walking through Altındağ simply because he was *not* a Türk. Similarly, Robert Neuwirth, who spent several months living in the *gecekondular* of İstanbul, was warned to be careful, describing the thriving community of Sultanbeyli as "strange, separatist, dangerous . . . that it was *kuyu Musselman* ('deep or dark Muslim')"—an intentional reference to the *hijab* many observant Muslim women wear.

And it is true that many *gecekondular* are more traditional. As one college student resident of Sultanbeyli noted in Neuwirth's *Shadow Cities,* "Sultanbeyli is a mirror for Türkiye."[13] People from every region have migrated there even as Türkiye itself is a rich cultural soup of Europe and Asia, modern and traditional. As Neuwirth emphasized (and Kaplan did before him in the

1990s), walking the hillsides of the *gecekondular bölgesi* of İstanbul, people were "amazingly open" and encountered little of the hesitation or hostility that outsiders predicted.

Sultanbeyli best reflects Türkiye's *gecekondu* of the future. As with Altındağ in Ankara, Sultanbeyli boomed in the 1980s with Türkish economic stagnation. Many rural dwellers were forced to leave ancestral villages and seek opportunity in cities. From 1986 to 1989, "residents" built twenty thousand homes inside İstanbul's city limits—and the local government collected fees from each family that built a home. Today its population approaches three hundred thousand—triple its size in 1990—and in many ways resembles a true, albeit impoverished, downtown environment with banks, travel agents, and even real estate offices. Sultanbeyli is a small city within the larger one. (Under Türkish law, communities with more than two thousand residents can apply to the federal government to organize as a quasi-independent municipality.) Residents are actually citizens of two elected governments—one for the *büyük şehir* ("big city") and one for the *belediye* ("municipality")—and have two mayors, one for the big and one for the small.

PARADISE OF HEAVENS, PARADISE OF HELLS: THE MEGASLUM WITHIN A MEGACITY

Two Academy Award–winning films, *Slumdog Millionaire* and *Born into Brothels,* respectively portrayed the slums of Juhu in Mumbai and Sonagachi, Kolkata's red light district, through often startling visual images and direct confrontation of daily realities. Gaining such attention brought the world the recognition of life for residents of these *johpadpatti* and exposed a mark of shame for many Indians. The Bollywood film hero Amitabh Bachchan criticized *Slumdog Millionaire* for projecting "India as [a] Third World, dirty under belly [*sic*] developing nation and causes pain and disgust among nationalists and patriots, let it be known that a murky under belly exists [*sic*] and thrives even in the most developed nations." While true, the realities of conditions in numerous slums of India also depict—as with Türkiye—the pull of the city and a sense of identity.

Once a fishing colony of seven collective islands, Mumbai has grown to be not only the most populous city of India but its economic engine as well—

with the highest gross domestic product (GDP) of any location in South and Central Asia. Mumbai, in a term that is not yet in the global vernacular, is an "alpha city," meaning it represents a critical node in the world economic system. With more cell phones per capita of any city on the subcontinent, Mumbai generates more than one-sixth of India's GDP.

Mumbai also suffers from major urbanization problems all megacities face: widespread poverty, unemployment, and poor public services for its population. With the highest real estate prices in Asia, residents reside in cramped, expensive housing far from workplaces. Half the city lacks adequate running water or electricity. Belching smoke from thousands of open cooking fires, combined with the high-decibel screech of traffic, create a lethal combination of constant noise, constant pollution, and constant struggle. By some estimates, breathing Mumbai's choked air is equivalent to smoking twenty cigarettes a day. According to a 2000 Mega-Cities Project report, three-quarters of women in Mumbai slums suffer from malnutrition, anemia, gastroenteritis, or helminthic infections caused by parasitic worms. Paralysis is a common form of death.

Yet the pressures to migrate to Mumbai are enormous. From 1991 to 2001, 55 percent (1.1 million) of those who came to live in Mumbai were from outside the state of Maharashtra. As Nobel laureate V. S. Naipaul writes in the opening sentence of *India: A Thousand Mutinies Now,* "Bombay is a crowd."[14]

The slums of Mumbai, nonetheless, are also the most literate in India—approaching 70 percent. Dharavi, one of the world's largest slums in one of the world's largest cities, is of particular interest.[15] Asia's second largest slum is located in central Mumbai and houses more than one million people.[16] In a city with some of the most expensive rents in the world, Dharavi residents sometimes survive on as little as four dollars a month—though that is increasingly less common. While Dharavi is a shadow city of Mumbai, where many look on it as an eyesore, residents call it "home."

As in many slums, Dharavi is divided by a railway line—and, yes, it matters which side of the rail you live on. (Many live far too dangerously close to railway lines, and news reports frequently detail vehicles backing over or running down children or rows of sleeping residents.) This is not to say there is complete deprivation: many have televisions with cable connection and a sense of access to the "outside." Dharavi is home to a cottage industry of tiny manufacturing entities (more than fifteen thousand small factories) producing embroidered garments, export-quality leather goods, pottery, and plastic for national and international markets—and profits approaching $700 million a year. For better or worse, the slum is the recycling center for industrial waste. Although government plans to transform Dharavi into a modern township, such plans have been on the books for years. Bluntly, Dharavi may be better off as it is.

In concept at least, Dharavi's redevelopment would assist residents. Most residents, predominantly Hindu (with a 20 percent Muslim population), are Dalits, of the *Dalit*—sometimes referred to as "Untouchables"—or "Outcast" system. Though the caste system may be illegal in India, it remains much in evidence. Government regulations would limit new residences to 225 square feet (often smaller than current homes for many residents and families), and many small businesses now fear relocation due to new development areas. Certainly, improved sanitation conditions—most are currently atrocious— would save lives. Many residents urinate and defecate in the water source of Mahim Creek, which brings us back to the essential "human right to shit."

In what emerges as a common theme for megacity slums, Dharavi's water supply is critically lacking. As Neuwirth offers in *Shadow Cities,* in stark terms:

> I never realized how tough and dehumanizing life can be for some of these squatters until I took the bus early one day, around 6AM. As we traveled down the access road along the Western Express Highway, I saw a dozen men lined up, squatting by a drainage ditch. They were spread out at various points, along the ditch. I wondered what they were doing. Then I noticed the buckets.
>
> I realized then that in a country of one billion people, in a city of 12 million [*sic*], toilets are a major issue, perhaps even the most important issue. . . . Living without toilets can be dangerous. People actually die because of the lack of toilets.[17]

Given the positives and negatives of life in this thriving slum, things were not always as they are today. Once an island in the eighteenth century, Dharavi was predominantly a mangrove swamp that employed Koli fishermen. When the swamp filled with coconut leaves, rotten fish, and human excrement, Kolis were deprived of their fishing grounds, and they turned to bootlegged liquor. But others came, and they built: Kumbhars came from Gujarat to establish pottery works; Tamils opened tanneries; thousands traveled from Uttar Pradesh to work in the textile industry.

During the violent Mumbai riots (detailed in *Slumdog Millionaire*), life became uncertain for many. From 1992 to 1993, more than a thousand residents were killed in what has been described as "the Hindu-Muslim riots." Such characterizations as springing solely from religious conflict or ethnic difference—as with the explanations for the slaughter in former Yugoslavia or the genocide in Rwanda—are simplistic. While true that conflict erupted after the detonation of the Babri Masjid (mosque) in Uttar Pradesh, the initial Muslim backlash was followed by Hindu reprisals—with widespread arson, killings, and the destruction of property. Eventually, many Muslim and Hindu slum dwellers migrated to their "majority" areas within the city of Mumbai. At the same time, underlying causes for these disputes were economic: too many people for too few opportunities. Efforts to transform Mumbai in January 2005 into a South Asian Shanghai further aggravated this reality. Government forces attempted to evict more than three hundred thousand from their homes and keep them outside city limits.[18]

Dharavi today has a population density twice that of New York City's horrific nineteenth-century days. In *Rediscovering Dharavi: Stories from Asia's Largest Slum,* Kalpana Sharma declares that more than eighteen thousand people live in less than one acre, crowding residents into ten-by-fifteen-foot rooms squashed one of top of each other. Yet the urban geographer Arjun Appadurai suggests that 6 million Mumbai residents live on 8 percent of the land, while the wealthy own 90 percent of the land and live in oblivious comfort.[19]

Despite all this, Dharavi—and the resident slums of Jogeshwari, Pydhonie, Dongri, Agripada, Gamdevi, V. P. Road, Byculla, Bhoiwada, Nagpada,

Kherwadi, Nehru Nagar, Ghatkopar, Kurla, Deonar, Trombay, Bandra, and Vakola—continue to grow, even prosper. The slum itself is described as an experiment in neoliberal growth without any form of regulation. Despite odds, which lead to prosperity or chaos, Dharavi tends toward the former rather than latter.

One could ask: why would people want to come to Mumbai, to struggle for an opportunity? Perhaps the best—certainly the most eloquent—answer comes from an American-born Indian himself, Anand Giridharadas, writing in the *International Herald Tribune:*

> If the elite live in virtual exile, seeing Mumbai as a port of departure, the city teems with millions of migrants who see it in exactly the opposite way: as a mesmeric port of arrival, offering what is missing on the mainland, a chance to invent oneself, to break with one's supposed fate. . . . They arrive from the 660,000 villages of India. Perhaps the monsoon failed and crops perished. Perhaps their mother is ill and needs money for surgery. Perhaps they took a loan whose mushrooming interest even cow-milking and wheat-sheafing cannot repay. Perhaps they are tired of waiting for the future to come to them. . . . The longer you remain, the less you notice what Mumbai looks, smells, sounds like. You think instead of what it could be. You become addicted to the companionship of 19 million other beings. Surrounded by hells, you glimpse paradise.[20]

KENYA AND KIBERA'S CHALLENGE

At first glance, Kenya would not be a state of major concern for chaos or failure—or even disruption. Since its break from British colonial rule in 1963, Kenya (even during the often dictatorial rule of Daniel arap Moi) was most often considered a stable, even prosperous, example for other African nations. With its population approaching 40 million people and with over forty-one different major ethnic groups, Kenya seemed a kind of prosperous example where—as was once true in former Yugoslavia—national identity could overcome religious, ethnic, cultural, and historic differences. As one native describes to Liotta, his country, Kenya, with "its Anglicized urban population, modern cities, and relatively well-developed infrastructure, epitomized everything positive about Africa."

Things Fall Apart

The disastrous December 2007 presidential elections, sharply illustrated that Kenya's stability was a fraud. In the election's wake, a national crisis ensued that resulted in political stalemate between the two contenders: President Mwai Kibaki and eventual prime minister Raila Odinga. Protests escalated into sectarian violence and destruction of property. Almost a thousand people died (often by machete mutilation or by burning, when tires were put on victims and set afire) and six hundred thousand were displaced. International mediation, with significant assistance from the United States, was necessary. Despite major constitutional reforms in 2010, rumors persist that weapons are being brought into divisive regions of Kenya in anticipation of the 2012 elections.

The claims above are not simply the opinions of two *wazungu* authors. They are realities honest Kenyans recognize and attempt to redress. Perhaps the Kenyan we most admire for his efforts to right wrongs is John Githongo, the former journalist who fled to Britain in 2005 after claimed threats to his life prevented him from effectively investigating political maneuverings and corruption. Githongo's story is best told in Michela Wrong's *It's Our Turn to Eat: The Story of a Kenyan Whistle Blower*, which details how Githongo's inquiry into a contracting scandal resulted in personal attacks, ostracism, and death threats.

After Kibaki took office in 2002, Githongo was appointed permanent secretary for governance and ethics. His corruption investigations exposed deeper problems in Kenya's patronage system, which exploits state coffers as if personal booty. Worse, this dysfunctional system promotes—rather than proscribes—ethnic patronage, providing deep pockets for tribal parties in power. Resulting graft and discrimination—which Wrong suggests helped fuel the communal slaughter of Kenya's 2007 and 2008 postelection violence—reinforces both the poorest and the richest Kenyans' view of their own personal existence "as a merciless contest, in which only ethnic preference offers hope of survival."

Githongo, now CEO of the Inuka Kenya Trust and head of the nongovern-mental organization Twaweza in Kenya, wrote in *Foreign Affairs* that the 2007 elections exposed a "far deeper rot" in the country—where there is a distinct danger of the "Pakistanization of Kenya" that would cripple the state with stark economic inequalities while retaining an easily corruptible elite, and where general national sympathies would grow for policies and ideas inimi-cal to U.S. interests. Moreover, this could occur despite Kenya and the United States sharing basic global interests: commitment to democracy (with all its flawed forms) and desire for a strong private sector with overall general eco-nomic growth, as well as support for efforts to stem international drug trade, Islamic extremism, and terrorism.

How could things have gone so wrong and been so deeply exposed in 2007 and 2008? Too many political, economic, and social injustices had been ignored or overlooked for far too long. Perception and reality, essentially, merged: unless one were a member of the Kikuyu tribe, the largest and his-torically most ethnically dominant group, there was little to expect in terms of life improvement following the election of Kibaki to his first term in 2002. Certainly with ethnic Kikuyu gluttony bonding around the Kibaki adminis-tration, the poor were virtually ignored, witnessed only inflation as change, and lost all confidence in government. Some came to prefer the iron rule of Kibaki's predecessor, Moi.

Violence that emerged also exposed the truth that such protests could prove effective in bringing change. In a state where over 70 percent of the population is under the age of thirty, protestors recognized that government was no longer an institution to be feared.[21] Postelection violence became an empowering event for many poor, disaffected Kenyan youths, who succeeded in controlling wide swaths of the country that lost control. In their aggressive expression, Kenyans found their first form of having a true democratic voice.

Notably, on December 15, 2010, the International Criminal Court (ICC) in The Hague sought indictments for six prominent Kenyans—collectively known as "the Hague Six"—including the country's deputy prime minister, Uhuru Kenyatta—son of Kenya's first president, Mzee Jomo Kenyatta—as suspects for their actions in ethnically fueled violence in the wake of the disputed presidential election.[22] Prosecutor Luis Moreno-Ocampo of the ICC stressed that this action was an effort to put Kenya back on its feet and help regain international recognition. Ocampo, nonetheless, sought these indictments for what he named as crimes against humanity in an orchestrated campaign to displace, torture, persecute and kill civilians. Others named include William Ruto, Kenya's fiery and most divisive political figure—and the minister for higher education until late October 2010, when he was suspended for corruption. Accused of directly instigating violence, Ruto remains a hero within his ethnic community, the Kalenjin. Some of the worst episodes of violence, including the burning of a church with women and children inside, occurred in predominantly Kalenjin areas in the Rift Valley. A group calling itself "Friends of Hon. William Ruto" chillingly called those who testified at The Hague "moderate Tutsis"—referring to victims of the 1994 Rwandan genocide—and who would be dealt with "ruthlessly."

Fear and Loathing in Nairobi

While some might think that this postelection uprising was simply an unfortunate speed bump in Kenya's history, we suggest otherwise. If one views Kenya's capital of Nairobi (the fourth largest, and one of the fastest growing cities in Africa) and its massive megaslum of Kibera as a case example of how cities can grow too far, too fast, it should be no surprise to witness frightening human outcomes as events boil over and erupt during a growth process.[23] Nairobi has become a port of migration. Whereas 24 percent of the population lived in urban centers in 1990, that figure had grown to one in three by 2000, with Nairobi now growing by 7 percent each year. Most residents live in what are called "informal settlements," 50 percent of the population lives below the poverty line, and most residents must find informal-sector activities (ranging from small trade to casual labor) to survive.

Garnering international attention and shock, genocidal violence in late 2007 and early 2008—along with acts of blood revenge and corrupt politics—spread from the capital to the rest of the country. General opposition rallies bred further violence, including rape, looting, and brutal murders. President Kibaki's failure to provide effective leadership or to engage in dialogue (which effectively showed his refusal to let go of power or admit wrongdoing in the election process) was the real driving force that unleashed endemic urban—and rural—violence. The country further endured massive food and fuel shortages that crippled East Africa as supplies lay dormant in Kenyan shipping ports.

Kenya has grown by a factor of three in four decades—without solving its sense of identity, offering a true sense of democracy for all, or providing a sound economic foundation for its citizens. If Nairobi were to collapse (and Kenya along with it), the contagion effect would be a mineshaft cave-in for East Africa. Nairobi illustrates the difficult challenges that "nonresilient" cities face. Suffering from the "million-plus" dilemma, the engine fueling ongoing decay in Kenya stems from the rampant corruption of government officials and politicians, who refuse to assist honestly in development or to refrain from personal enrichment.

Although British ambassadors to Kenya in the past were reticent to express direct criticism of Kenyan government failures, former British High Commissioner Sir Edward Clay, in a speech to the British Business Association of Kenya in 2004, was quite blunt:

> We never expected corruption to be vanquished overnight. We all implicitly recognized that some would be carried over to the new era [after the time of Daniel arap Moi]. We hoped it would not be rammed in our faces. But it has. Evidently, the practitioners now in government have the arrogance, greed and perhaps a desperate sense of panic to lead them to eat like gluttons. They may expect we shall not see, or notice, or forgive them a bit of gluttony because they profess to like OXFAM lunches. But they can hardly expect us not to care when their gluttony causes them to vomit all over our shoes. Do they really expect us to ignore the lurid and mostly accurate details conveyed in the commendably free media and pursued by a properly curious Parliament?[24]

High Commissioner Clay's remarks spurred howls of indignation from the government. Yet according to a World Bank study, exorbitant funds (in excess of $1 trillion, by some estimates) are spent annually on bribes; in Kenya, corruption allegedly accounts for 8 percent of its GDP. Estimates for 2006 claimed that Kenyan members of parliament awarded themselves an average of $169,625 a year in salaries and allowances, while the average Kenyan annual income was $400.[25]

High Commissioner Clay later apologized—with a twist. Claiming regret for failing to speak out earlier and for the "moderation" of his earlier language, he stated that he had underestimated the scale of the looting, after which the Kenyan government referred to him as an "incorrigible liar." The United States, doubting the Kenyan government's credibility, abruptly cancelled a multimillion-dollar package to assist in rooting out corruption. High Commissioner Clay subsequently handed over a dossier detailing twenty corruption scandals involving ministers. According to the then U.S. ambassador, William Bellamy, the money that disappeared in these cases could have provided funding for every HIV-positive Kenyan in the country for the next decade.

There is an alarming human element here. While there are sections of Nairobi of undeniable beauty, much of the city and its outlying regions are overused and exhausted. At an altitude of 1,660 meters, the high charcoal burn rate and traffic belching exhaust fumes, the atmosphere is dense—almost impenetrable, with gray-black fog in the mornings. The streets are wedged with traffic, especially the ever-present and always treacherous *matatu* public vehicles.[26] Insanely overcrowded, driven by seemingly lunatic drivers, these fragile minibuses and pickups teeter in and out of asynchronous traffic chaos, heading towards inevitable disaster.

Police are seen as uniformly corrupt and more interested in bribes for beer than in any sense of order.[27] During a recent field visit to Nairobi, Liotta learned from one colleague how a purse thief was "collared" by an enraged mob at the scene of a crime. He was seized moments after a petty theft, bound, and, with a rubber tire around his torso, set aflame. Another incident, in which police chose not to intervene, involved the thugs of a real estate developer who were sent to clear squatters off his property. In this case, squatter women attacked the thugs, doused them in kerosene, and set them on fire. The squatters remained.

The most personal and disturbing incident came on visiting the home of a senior official in an exclusive residential neighborhood not far from the

American embassy.[28] Winding through the switchbacks on the hillsides of rows upon rows of coffee plants, the official remarked, "We never take these roads at night. Too dangerous. Thugs—kids, really—step out of the coffee rows with AK-47s or pistols planted square in your face. They mean to rob you blind or hijack you. They'll shoot you if you resist. They still might shoot you if you don't."

Topping a ridge, we looked across a slight depression to his home. The official proudly declared that he loved to watch eagles soar up and down this minor valley during the day. Yet on the other slope the entire hillside had been deforested. His explanation was clear: "This makes gangs moving up from the slums on raids more noticeable. Easier to spot." Given that walls of concrete surrounding the entire residential section were at least four meters high in many sections, his words were staggering.

As we arrived home, his *askari* security guard and one house assistant greeted us. The home was a modest English cottage, which snugly accommodated him, his wife, and their young children. The home nestled on five acres of land—almost unthinkable luxury for many Kenyans. He described neighborhood break-ins where gunfire spilled over into neighboring resident properties. On more than one occasion, bullets grazed their home.

He related one harrowing incident. Details were in retrospect, after a young domestic was interrogated following the incident. She revealed she had been "dating" a resident of the Kibera slum for two weeks. He asked her about the residence she worked at, the hours when security was and was not present, the state and location of alarm systems on premises. He also beat her. The official and family admitted they had seen signs of domestic violence but believed her explanation that she had been mugged.

The night of the break-in was orchestrated. Five thugs targeted the one door without sensor alarms and smashed the locks with sledge hammers and entered the home. The official and his family, fortunately, had been woken by the fracas and had barricaded themselves in the home's "safe zone," behind a gridded security gate.[29] The official, nonetheless, furious and a bit foolish, stood behind the barrier and heard the lead thug spit out four precise words as he entered the house: "We will kill you."

Remotely alerted security forces arrived minutes later, but the thieves had fled, taking little more than a stereo system, cameras, and personal items.

The official remembered looking at the thief and hearing those words, while his wife, crying in terror, huddled with their children. This example, as frightening as it was, is typical of what even affluent urban dwellers face in cities with massive populations, where the government offers little and is no longer in control.

Where the People Are Trees

One in four residents of Nairobi live in slums. Kibera, Africa's oldest and largest slum, is a massive community of mile after mile of mud construction and corrugated roofs where one can dimly see the Nairobi city skyline in the distance. The 2009 Kenyan census claimed Kibera's population to be only 170,000 residents, whereas previous estimates ranged as high as 1 million.[30] There is a likely explanation for such widely disparate population estimates. Unlike the *gecekondular* of Türkiye or the *johpadpatti* of India, Kibera's residents lack any squatter property rights. Residents neither built their homes nor have community control. Instead, they pay rent to often wealthy landowners; in theory, at least, they do not exist. Robert Neuwirth, during his time living in Kibera, heard the clearest, cruelest, and most ironic description of this dilemma from a local resident: "The problem here is land. The government claims the land is forest. When they come to ask for votes from the forest, we are suddenly changed from trees to people. But, legally, we are just trees."

Piles of trash line every street and alley; sewage sluices run alongside water pipes, where the latter exist. Many residents spend half their meager monthly incomes to travel to "the city" to hawk their goods. Unlike the hillside *favelas* of Rio, Kiberan mud homes are built in valleys, and in many cases you must walk down to enter houses. Although Nairobi ecotours bill Kibera as "the world's friendliest slum," it can be a dangerous place. While some still insist the slum is safe and secure, with over 50 percent unemployment, crime is rife—with high levels of rape and violence. (And, as we have seen, with gang action that spills over into other communities.) Many members of the banned occult, political-religious, criminal Mungiki sect live in Kibera (with its largest base in the Mathare slum) and carry out violent acts with near impunity. The Mungiki were particularly active in the 2007 and 2008 postelection violence.[31] Compounding levels of violence and crime are the widespread use of cheap drugs and the drinking of the high-methanol local hooch known as *changaa*. Glue sniffing, which causes severe brain damage and death in many cases, is widespread among children.

Kibera, as with many slums in critical urban centers, is a point of arrival for many. Comprising almost twenty separate subcommunities split neatly in half by railroad tracks, Kibera represents the first "taste" of the capital. Among its youth, more than half have migrated from other regions, especially rural areas. Sixty percent of young girls claim they fear being raped, 50 percent of youths describe living in fear of someone in their neighborhood, and young women have far fewer safety networks in their neighborhoods compared to boys.

Kibera reeks of colonial legacy. The king of England gave the area to the King's African Rifles (KAR)—a corps of mostly "Sudanese" (a term loosely applied) Muslims—formed in 1891 to guard the new railway line flowing into Nairobi, for use as a firing range. Inevitably, soldiers retired and settled in Kibera, from the term *kibra*—which in Nubian means "forest" or "wilderness." In 1953, as the Kikuyu Mau Mau rebellion was just beginning to fight back against British colonial rule, police moved through slums that had grown throughout the Mathare River valley and left seven thousand people homeless; eventually, of course, they returned. Shortly after taking office in 2002, Mwai Kibaki announced plans to "restore order" by privatizing Kenyan Railways and evicting people in a two-hundred-foot-wide swath alongside the tracks in Kibera, which had the potential to affect up to a third of a million residents. During demolitions, armed police told residents they had two hours to evacuate their homes.

A place known for cholera and other excrement-related diseases, Kibera is not just home to impoverished Kenyans. Its inhabitants also include middle class and civil servants; even the wealthy choose to live there. One resident Liotta spoke with, originally from Uganda, confirmed that people live in Kibera because it is cheap—after all, you do not pay for electricity or water—

and because there is a true sense of community. At the same time, you belong to a specific "group" for purposes of security. But there are other problems as well. Taxis, many of which have false plates, are often run by criminal gangs and control commutes to Nairobi proper (that is, for those who can afford the fare). HIV/AIDS rates are high, and many Nairobi prostitutes are residents of Kibera. It can sound like a nightmare.

To the Kenyan government's credit, under an initiative from the United Nations Human Settlements Programme (commonly known as UN-HABI-TAT), attempts were made to eliminate current slums and replace them with high-rise apartment housing. Almost universally among Kiberans, this is unacceptable: they do not trust the government (which closed down and blocked off Kibera in the 2008 violence) and do not believe they can afford the costs of such housing, essentially turning "horizontal slums into vertical ones."[32] For many, though, Kibera is a place to make a stand—emblematic of slums in major urban centers of Africa and representing deep, enduring challenges that lie ahead.

WHO ARE WE?

Of the urban centers we considered here, all but one have one great advantage: a sense of national identity. This factor may augur well in helping India and Türkiye overcome the numerous trials they face as they emerge as significant states. Kenya confronts a different challenge, which is the burden of denying the socially constructed myth of ethnic identity as ethnic predominance. For too long, the domination of one tribe (the Kikuyu, say) over another (such as the Luo) has led to division, stalled progress, and outright violence (as occurred after the 2007 elections).[33] Yet even with the 2010 popular mandate to change the Kenyan constitution, many obstacles remain—and blaming Kenya's faults on the sins of colonialism becomes increasingly a less sufficient causal explanation.[34]

Without a national sense of identity or an economic cushion to soften the rough edges of tribalism, political consensus and long-term strategies for urban growth and economic development are simply not feasible. Several "splintered states" have had serious, unresolved border issues with neighboring states that diverted too much national treasure and energy toward defense or attempted conquest and away from domestic infrastructure issues. To be sure, these deficiencies are enormous and daunting—causing a state and its people to ask "Who are we?" and "Why, as a nation, do we exist?"

BRAVE NEW WORLD

In an article titled "The New Population Bomb: The Four Megatrends That Will Change the World" written for *Foreign Affairs,* Jack A. Goldstone emphasized some of the shifts we note here.[35] While many might still hasten to hyperemphasize that Paul Ehrlich's *The Population Bomb* did not bring about mass starvation predicted for the 1970s and 1980s, technological innovations such as the Green Revolution helped stem such worst fears from coming to pass. Equally, valid strategic recognition of looming challenges helped societies prepare and adapt before disaster struck.

The four trends Goldstone described are: Over the next four decades, developed countries' relative demographic weight will decline by 25 percent, shifting economic and demographic power to the emerging world. In the developed world, labor forces will age as well as decline in numbers, hindering economic growth and raising the need for immigrant labor. Much of the world's population growth will occur in some of the poorest, youngest, and most heavily Muslim states, which lack education, capital, and employment. Finally, for the first time in history, the world's population will become urbanized, with many megacities located in some of the world's poorest states, where policing, sanitation, and health care are in short supply.

Richard Manning's essay for *Harper's,* titled "The Oil We Eat: Following the Food Chain Back to Iraq," is also the most provocative piece to challenge the wisdom of the Green Revolution in actually improving overall human conditions. A brief excerpt here explains why:

> With the possible exception of the domestication of wheat, the green revolution is the worst thing that has ever happened to the planet. For openers, it disrupted long-standing patterns of rural life worldwide, moving a lot of no-longer-needed people off the land and into

the world's most severe poverty. The experience in population control in the developing world is by now clear: It is not that people make more people so much as it is that they make more poor people.[36]

We are entering a period of crisis with the *real* population bomb of our time: urban growth, especially in megacities in fragile places. Even as the UN's Population Division in most recent estimates suggests that global population growth will virtually halt by 2050, our challenge now is how to manage the glide path from where we are today to a time when future population decline will change the global landscape. Managing such a transition will be no simple task.

We repeatedly emphasize in this work that the changes taking place today are a fuse waiting for ignition. We have never been here before in human history—and the dangers of moving too far, too fast loom about the edges of every potential solution or pathway toward improvement. Moreover, twenty-first-century developing states with rapid population shifts and urban concentrations will have far lower per capita incomes than many industrialized states had when they emerged—and their emergence is happening much more quickly. (China may soon have the world's largest economy, but its per capita income pales in comparison to Japan's.) The much touted "youth bulge"—in which young, unemployed males fifteen to twenty-nine years old can further destabilize social and economic infrastructure—is another contributing factor.[37]

In the extreme, these conditions lend themselves to Dickensian poverty and anomic violence in many parts of this emerging world landscape. Governments simply cannot compete with many criminal networks, organized (and even disorganized) armed gangs, and insurgencies. As Goldstone observes, these problems resemble European urbanization in the nineteenth century where insufficient policy, wretched sanitation conditions, and lack of education created widespread labor unrest, violence, and—in 1848—social revolution.

The one additional factor present today but not in nineteenth-century Europe (limited by transport speed, technology, and access) holds the greatest threat as well: sustainable international terrorism. Though we may be oblivious to the advantages of high-speed Internet and digital communications, as well as multiple infrastructure vulnerabilities and high-value urban targets, adversaries most certainly are not. Megacities offer grounds for recruitment, retention, and hiding of terrorist networks. Sprawling urban centers offer the perfect location for "supernests."

This reality becomes even more complex when we realize that much of this growth takes place in the so-called "Muslim world." In 1950 Bangladesh, Indonesia, Egypt, Nigeria, Pakistan, and Türkiye had combined populations of roughly 240 million citizens; by 2010 these six countries had 900 million; by 2050 their combined totals might reach 1.4 billion. Even as the overall population is expected to decline, we will nonetheless see a significant global demographic shift take place. This shift suggests multiple warning signs. First, unless governance makes significant, continual, and improved progress, there are troubles ahead for these states and their respective megacities. (We should be more optimistic about Türkiye but less so about Bangladesh and Pakistan.) Secondly, relations between the developed world—most commonly known as the West—and the Muslim world must improve. Further alienation, distrust, and poor communication will only degrade an already fragile knowledge base in which each side does not sufficiently understand or appreciate the other.

OCCIDENTALISM AND "THE EVIL CITY"

Extremism compounds this complex dynamic. Inherently, what the West values most and extremist adversaries despise stems not so much from a clash of civilizations as from a clash of values. Take a recent *National Security Strategy of the United States* as example:

> The United States believes certain values are universal and will work to promote them worldwide. These include an individual's freedom to speak their mind, assemble without fear, worship as they please, and choose their own leaders; they also include dignity, tolerance, and equality among all people, and the fair and equitable administration of justice.[38]

Such sentiments, unfortunately, are *not* universal. We should address, therefore, the philosophical view of cities as a source of wonder and a source of shame.

It all depends on your "mental map." Many, after all, continue to flock to cities for the opportunities they offer: health care, jobs, education, sense of community, a new beginning. Yet influential observers—from nineteenth-century German natural philosophers to Al Qa'eda—have viewed modernity as evil and the City as evil incarnate. In Western culture, the City has been viewed as both "Parisian whore" and automaton—evidenced in films from Fritz Lang's *Metropolis* to Ridley Scott's *Blade Runner*. Within the City, there is deep-rooted "sinfulness" and disconnectedness; the human spirit becomes distorted in a materialistic, market-driven society, we witness the loss of organic community; bourgeois life dominates all.

There are jarring and irreconcilable differences in how many view the City and its architects of modernity. Islamist jihadist abhorrence of the United States, for example, is only one of a sequence of anti-Western conceptions that stand in vicious opposition to the rise and opportunity of modernity. In their seminal work, *Occidentalism: The West in the Eyes of Its Enemies,* Ian Buruma and Avishai Margalit call these prejudices and antagonistic images of the West conjured by its enemies "Occidentalism," a phenomenon that originated in the West itself in the late eighteenth century. German romantics, reacting to the Enlightenment and the rise of capitalism, coldly rejected rational Europe as a "machine civilization" rife with imperialism, urbanism, and cosmopolitanism. From there, we led eventually—some might claim inevitably—to the rise of National Socialism. The roots of fascism—whether in Italy, Germany, or Hungary—sprang, after all, from the changed expectations of many European lower middle classes. Whereas in 1848 many were sympathetic to revolt and provided recruits for the barricades, after the shock of the First World War and Bolshevik revolution, what most sought was security and progress and to stop from slipping back into the proletariat—providing instead eager recruits for fascism.

Buruma and Margalit suggest a "cluster of images and ideas of the West in the minds of its haters" emerge in Occidentalism: the sinfulness, rootlessness, and "evil" of urban life; the corruption of the human spirit in a materialistic, market-driven society; the loss of organic community and the rise of the rule of law over faith; and the glory of heroic self-sacrifice in overcoming the shallow blankness of bourgeois life. The role of women, needless to say, is subjugated as well.[39] In short, Western liberalism is a threat.

This deep-seated aversion has religious roots as well. Consider these lines from St. John the Divine's writings in Chapter 17 of the Book of Revelation, from the New Testament: "And I saw a woman drunken with the blood of saints, and on her forehead a name was written: 'Mystery, Babylon the Great, Mother of Whores and Abominations of the Earth.' And the woman whom you saw is that great city, which reigns over all the kings of earth."

The residents of the City have become the targets of mistrust over time. Writing during the First World War, the German philosopher and historian Oswald Spengler argues in *The Decline of the West* that "in place of a type-true people, born and grown in the soil, there is a new sort of nomad, cohering unstably in fluid masses, the parasitical city-dweller, traditionless, utterly matter-of-fact, religionless, clever, unfruitful, contemptuous of the countryman."[40]

By contrast, to deny the advantages of modernity—"urban civilization: commerce, mixed populations, artistic freedom, sexual license, scientific pursuits, leisure, personal safety, wealth, and its usual concomitant, power," as Buruma and Margalit phrased it—is to in a sense purify oneself. Whether we speak of Mao or bin Laden, such enemies of the West (or, if one prefers, modernity) aspire to be heroes. In their quest for crusade, thousands and hundreds of thousands can be left in their wake.

We need not overstate our case. Occidentalism and international terrorism that comes with it encompass immense challenges to global security. There are other socioeconomic and inequality issues as well. While it might be far easier to shrug off these enormous challenges and recall Joseph Stalin's notion that "a single death is a tragedy; a million deaths are a statistic," we do so at our peril. We must guard against a backlash of mistrust—of places and peoples whose values, religions, cultures, or traditions differ from ours. As Buruma and Margalit phrase it: "We should not counter Occidentalism with a nasty form of Orientalism. Once we fall for that temptation, the virus has infected us too."

As we address specific locales and explicit hurdles in the following pages, it seems worthwhile in contrast to remember Orwell's adage that "this squalid brawl in a distant city is more important than might appear."

3

CANARY IN THE COAL MINE

Gaza

Perhaps it is our perennial fate to be surprised by the simultaneity of events, by the sheer extension of the world in time and space. That we are here, prosperous, safe, unlikely to go to bed hungry or be blown to pieces this evening, while elsewhere in the world, right now in Grozny, in Najaf, in the Sudan, in the Congo, in Gaza, in the *favelas* of Rio . . .

To be a traveler . . . is to be constantly reminded of the simultaneity of what is going on in the world, your world and the very different world you have visited and from which you have returned home.

—*Susan Sontag*

We are used to thinking of Gaza as a flashpoint in Arab-Israeli relations, a place from which terrorists launch their periodic attacks on Israel and where Israel retaliates with airstrikes, military incursions, and—when deemed necessary—assassinations. One recent example of this tit-for-tat violence occurred in 2008 and 2009 when Israel launched a military attack into Gaza in response to a series of rocket attacks on Israeli communities in the Negev Desert. Hamas provocation and the Israeli response is an indication that

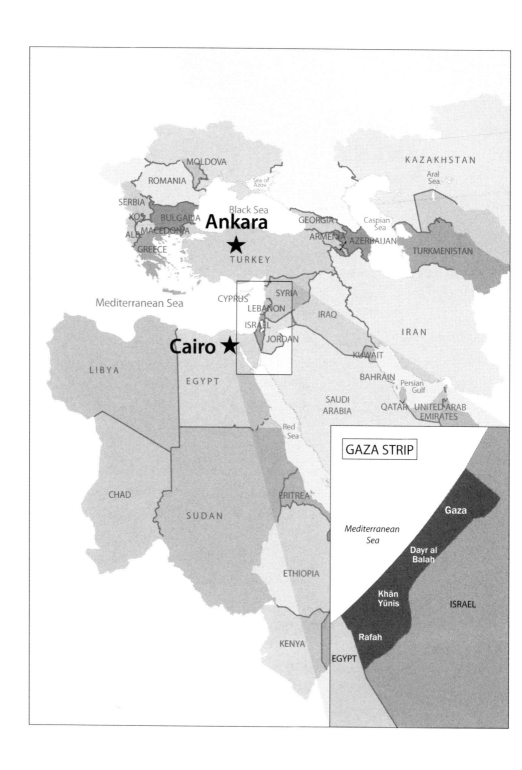

when the next Arab-Israeli war is fought, it will likely start in Gaza or be provoked by events there.

WHERE EVERYTHING DIVIDES

Gaza is the place where the political and religious divisions within the Palestinian and larger Arab community are vividly, garishly, on display. Tensions between moderate, secular Palestinian factions and radical, Islamist factions boil over into violence in the streets of Gaza. The most dramatic outbreak of internecine violence was the so-called Battle of Gaza of June 2007 between Fatah, the dominant component of the umbrella Palestine Liberation Organization and of the Palestinian Authority government, and Hamas, the radical Islamist organization that opposes compromise with Israel. Hamas is an acronym of حركة المقاومة الاسلامية Harakat al-Muqāwamat al-Islāmiyyah, meaning "Islamic Resistance Movement." Founded in 1987 as an offshoot of the Muslim Brotherhood, its main strength lies in Gaza. In January 2006 Hamas won a decisive majority in the Palestinian parliament, defeating the then dominant Fatah party. Fatah is an Arabic acronym for the Movement for the National Liberation of Palestine, founded in the 1960s by Yassir Arafat, and is currently the main political party in the West Bank.

Reasons for the fighting in 2007 are less important than the reality that there have long been tensions between Hamas and Fatah, largely over their policies towards Israel. Fatah once shared Hamas' view that all of the land on which the state of Israel stands should be returned to the Palestinians and into the fold of Islam. Fatah now accepts Israel's right to exist, at least within its 1967 borders. Hamas continues to deny that right. There has also been simmering discontent with Fatah's inability to provide public services effectively to the people of Gaza while it was in power and with the corruption of Fatah leaders notorious, among other things, for building seaside villas while living standards of constituents spiral ever downwards.

One of the "highlights" of the week-long Battle of Gaza was the bombing of Fatah headquarters. The technique was right out of prison escape or bank heist films. Bombers dug a two-hundred-foot tunnel to the base of the headquarters building and placed explosives where they could do the most structural damage.

Tunnels have played an important role in the history of Gaza, and this was not the first time that a tunnel has figured prominently in Gazan violence. For years weapons, explosives, and *fedayeen*—as well as assorted contraband— have been smuggled into Gaza through a network of narrow-gauge tunnels dug under the border with Egypt. Israeli sources estimate there could be as many as three thousand such passageways. (With that many excavations honeycombed under a border, one wonders why the ground does not collapse.) According to some reports, thirty thousand people in Gaza are employed in the business of tunnels, either by digging and maintaining them or using them to smuggle—almost as many as the Gaza government employs.

If using a subterranean tunnel can be said to be low in terms of altitude, other signal events in the battle of Gaza took place at higher elevations. They include a Fatah leader being thrown off the roof of one of Gaza's tallest buildings by Hamas henchmen. Not to be outdone, Fatah strong-arm men promptly responded in kind, tossing a Hamas leader from an equally tall building. Both men were reportedly wearing handcuffs when they hit the ground. By the time the Battle of Gaza had wound down, Fatah had lost control over Gaza, and seven hundred were either dead or injured.

Hamas has now taken over Gaza, and it administers Gaza City and the surrounding territory, as if independent from the Palestinian Authority, which nominally rules both the West Bank and Gaza. Given its ideology, Hamas promptly began imposing Islamic law on residents of Gaza and, less idealistically, settling scores with its political opposition. As a result, Hamas is in the ironic and hypocritical position of dealing with its fellow Gazans with almost as heavy a hand as the Israelis. The 2009 Human Rights Watch World Report, *Under Cover of War: Hamas Political Violence in Gaza*, found that Hamas security forces and "masked gunmen believed to be with Hamas" have murdered almost forty people and wounded many others. Many of the victims were killed in gangland-style executions, shot in the back of the head while kneeling down. From December 2008 to January 2009, Hamas gunmen reportedly shot forty-nine people in the leg—a practice eerily reminiscent of the grisly "kneecapping" by Irish Republican Army terrorists in the 1980s. Kneecapping requires painful, lengthy, and costly reconstructive surgery and recuperation. Even if the victim regains full use of the leg, he and his family have to endure years of pain and suffering—enduring reminders to the victims and their acquaintances of the penalty for offending Hamas. Human Rights Watch also reported numerous beatings and abductions by Hamas and its supporters. This is not to imply that Gaza was Switzerland before Hamas took over. Far from it. Fatah also had a decidedly spotty record in terms of respect for human rights and the rule of law when in charge of Gaza.

There are reports that Fatah operatives who steal into the city perpetrate violence in Hamas-controlled Gaza, not unlike Gaza-based *fedayeen* who slip into Israel to launch terror attacks. Clearly, law and order have suffered under both Hamas and Fatah. But there is an important distinction between what Hamas and Fatah have done.

When Fatah administered Gaza, it did so on behalf of a national government, the Palestinian Authority. Hamas, on the other hand, administers Gaza in defiance of that national government and institutes a legal code much different than the one in force in the rest of the territory of the Palestinian Authority. While this distinction may be cold comfort to residents of Gaza, rights and livelihoods have suffered under both regimes. Our point is not to paint Hamas as being worse than Fatah when it comes to respect for human rights and the rule of law. Rather, we focus on how Hamas-controlled Gaza defies its parent government, uses force against that parent government with impunity, hijacks the government apparatus, and establishes its own legal code.

Hamas-controlled Gaza has also done something that subnational municipalities in the contemporary era are not supposed to be able to do: conduct an independent foreign policy and initiate and fight a war with another state. Results have been destabilizing.

Hamas is virulently opposed to a two-state solution with Israel; that would mean relinquishing the Arab claim to the territory of Israel proper. It would also mean forfeiting the trust or responsibility that Allah placed in Muslims to restore formerly Islamic lands (Israel itself) to Islamic rule. Hamas favors a one-state solution: a single Islamic republic in the territory of Gaza, the West Bank, and Israel. Hamas' opposition to the two-state solution has seen the Gaza government deliberately undermine peace negotiations between its parent, the Palestinian Authority, and Israel. Terror attacks from

Gaza—directly conducted by the party in control of the Gaza government—accelerate whenever there is evidence of progress towards peace. The purpose is two-fold: first, to cause the Israelis to retaliate militarily, which in turn sours Palestinian public opinion towards compromise with Israel, and, second, to cause Israeli people not to trust negotiations with the Palestinian Authority if it cannot control its own territory.

It would be one thing if a rogue, nonstate actor operating from bases in a remote outback launched terror attacks on Israel. This happens in many parts of the world, though few attacks involve rockets being fired across an international border. It is different when a government entity facilitates such attacks. In 2008 the Hamas government of Gaza provoked and fought a war with Israel by firing thousands of rockets into southern Israel during an eight-month period that proved successful in derailing negotiations between Israel and the Palestinian Authority. The Israeli Foreign Ministry estimated that twelve thousand rockets were fired into Israel, although a vast majority were unguided, small rockets that landed "harmlessly" in the desert. Yet when such weapons fail to hit a populated area, they are hardly harmless. When rockets hit nothing but sand, they provoke fear; they deter others from moving or investing there. In short, they achieve Hamas' objective.

While at war with Israel, Hamas continued to conduct violent operations against Fatah and pilloried Fatah and the Palestinian Authority as "fifth columnists." Hamas propaganda described Fatah and the Palestinian Authority as "the very people who committed national adultery in broad daylight by collaborating with the Shin Bet [the Israel Security Agency] and the CIA for the purpose of raping the Palestinian people's will and achieving America's morbid goals in this tortured part of the world."

Hamas' ability to fight this war against Israel was based upon the support it has received over the years from other states, especially Iran and Syria, who have provided military training to members of Hamas' security forces as well as weapons. Hamas maintains headquarters in Damascus to protect its leaders from Israeli attack. North Korea is alleged to have also supplied the Hamas government with weapons. Since Hamas is receiving this aid as it runs Gaza, a disturbing precedent has been set—one likely to be followed in other ungoverned and undergoverned places in the future. Perhaps one equivalent would be Venezuela (with a government that everyone loves to hate) supplying weapons and paramilitary training to the municipal police force of Houston, knowing such weaponry would be used to fight a war with Mexico or to physically resist U.S. federal law enforcement. Unlikely, to be sure, for the United States or most other so-called developed states, though less difficult to envision for a city such as Lagos or Karachi where national governments exert less and less influence.

GAZA'S INDEPENDENCE

There is yet another dimension to the Gaza government's independent foreign policy: foreign aid. The exact proportion of the Gaza budget ($540 million in 2010) funded directly by Iran is unclear. Some estimates put it as high as 90 percent. Hamas' budget is also supplemented by the United Nations Relief and Works Agency, which provides humanitarian assistance and public services such as education to Palestinians in refugee camps—one-third of Gaza's population. Whatever the exact percentage paid by Iran, the critical issue is that the Gaza government has financially disconnected itself from its own government and has connected to a foreign state with very different policy objectives.

The Palestinian Authority is itself dependent upon international aid. Though not technically a state, it is treated as such by the UN and most states globally when it comes to representing the Palestinian people in international negotiations and accepting foreign aid. The Palestinian Authority is a permanent member of the League of Arab States and maintains diplomatic missions throughout most of the world.

It holds observer status at UN headquarters in New York, supports a permanent mission in the UN office in Vienna—where several UN agencies are headquartered—and in September 2011 appealed to the General Assembly directly for recognition as a state. In sum, the Palestinian Authority resembles a state closely enough for the Gaza precedent to be of great concern.

There are thus similarities between what has happened in Gaza and what has begun to happen in megacities across the globe. Megacities in Africa and

Asia are on the path to becoming what Gaza has become: a municipality that the government is unable to control. In Gaza's case, this developed because the national government is both new and weak. Without time to build capable institutions, Gaza's parent government was unable to provide services that Gazans wanted most. Hamas filled the vacuum by sponsoring hospitals, schools, and sports leagues (much as Hezbollah did in southern Lebanon)— paid for by Iran and private donations from Arab states—and thereby substantially eroded public support for the Palestinian Authority.

The Palestinian Authority came into existence in 1993 after the Oslo Peace Accords and is recognized as a state by many parts of the international community. The international community has been generous in terms of financially supporting the Authority and expects it to act as a government in terms of providing public services, enforcing laws, and representing all Palestinian peoples in international negotiations. The Palestinian Authority's ability to live up to these responsibilities has been constricted by its own corruption and ineptitude, perhaps even more so because it has never fully controlled its own territory. As part of the Oslo Accords, Israel has kept a hand in Gazan and West Bank affairs and imposed restrictions on the kind of military and security apparatus that the Palestinian Authority can develop. From an Israeli perspective, restrictions have been a sensible precaution since key figures in the nascent Palestinian government have histories of promoting violence against Israel, and there has been the fear that a strong Palestinian security force might eventually be used against Israel. Whether the Palestinian Authority has had as fair a shot at governing and providing public services as other national governments is ultimately irrelevant. From our perspective, what is important is that it has failed and has suffered the consequences: a disaffected population and a city that is independent.

None of the megacities we address in subsequent chapters are quite the same with respect to the immaturity of their governments as Gaza. All are similar in that their established national and municipal governments have, despite their relative maturity, failed in exactly the way the Palestinian Authority has failed: they have not provided enough in the way of public services to the populations of their largest cities nor created conditions either conducive to economic growth and increased prosperity or favorable for law and order. Just like the Palestinian Authority, they allow—sometimes even encourage—divided loyalties to form and create voids in public services inevitably filled, in one way or the other, by criminal organizations, radical groups, or ethnic militias.

Major cities in other states are in situations analogous or parallel to Gaza in the years before Hamas takeover. These cities are becoming ungovernable for the same reason Gaza became ungovernable: inability or refusal of government to grow institutions of governance to keep pace with urban population growth. Though the reasons why these governments failed to provide essential services vary, in all instances a key factor was sudden and sustained rise in population. Put simply, populations of megacities have surged—much as adolescent youths outgrow their clothes overnight—while parent governments are unable to keep pace.

WHAT GAZA MEANS

Gaza is more than a place where Palestinians and Israelis occasionally exchange gunfire and where Arab factions brutalize each other's members in the name of political ideology and religion. Naturally, it is hard not to concentrate on these realities, because Arab-Israeli tensions in Gaza affect the Greater Middle East. The outcome of the Hamas-Fatah struggle will determine the regional balance of power between moderate, secular Islam and militant Islamists.[1] When we too closely focus on these things, however, we run the risk of overlooking something far more basic: important insight about the world in which we are going to be living ten and twenty years from today, where there emerge evolving relationships between ungovernable cities and parent national governments.

Gaza is a place where one can glimpse the future. Gaza is an omen. It is the proverbial canary in the coal mine. More precisely, it is a dead canary in the coal mine. The future that Gaza forecasts is one in which important municipalities become so powerful that they are able to defy weak, inept national governments and chart their own courses, much as Hamas has done.

Roughly twice the size of the District of Columbia, Gaza includes Gaza

City and a number of small cities and villages. The total population is one and a half million, making it about 50 percent more densely populated than Washington. As with other cities we consider, its population has grown significantly in recent decades, though nowhere as dramatically as in cities such as Lagos, Karachi, Kinshasa, and Dhaka. One unique feature of Gaza's demographics is that two-thirds of its population are refugees. This matters.

First, most refugees in Gaza receive public services from a UN agency rather than from the Gaza or Palestinian Authority government—formally institutionalizing a "dependency syndrome" whereby populations look to international agencies rather than their own governments for support. This ought to make the process of providing public services more manageable for the Gaza government than population statistics suggest. Even so, the Fatah government was unable to meet the need for public services, with the result that the Palestinian Authority was discredited and eventually forced out of Gaza.

Second, several of the most critical megacities have what amount to virtual refugee populations—large groups of people who migrated to the city to avoid violence or grinding poverty and who have effectively been isolated from the larger city because so few public services have been made available to them. As internally displaced persons rather than formal refugees that have crossed an international border, these virtual refugees have no UN agency dedicated to caring for their needs. This is not to say that the UNRWA (the UN Relief and Works Agency for Palestine Refugees in the Near East) fully cares for the needs of those in Gaza—it does not. Poverty and unemployment are widespread, and there is a dire shortfall in educational and medical resources available to the population. (Hamas does not make the medical shortage any better by kneecapping doctors.) Even as wretched as the situation is for the people of Gaza, it is even worse for those in Lagos, Karachi, Kinshasa, or Dhaka. In these places, government is as hopeless as the Palestinian Authority at delivering public services, *and* there is little outside help—at least in comparison to the contribution the UNRWA makes to Gaza.

DEMOGRAPHIC DISASTER

The demographic profile of Gaza is similar to the profiles we see in other fast-

growing metropolises in Asia and Africa. A high proportion of the population is young. The Palestinian Central Bureau of Statistics reports that half
of Gaza's population is fourteen or younger. Sixty percent is under than twenty, and three-quarters of the population is under thirty. The unemployment
rate in Gaza is high—officially about 40 percent—though a recent Harvard
study indicates the effective rate is higher, the result of women being discour-
aged to join the workforce under Hamas' conservative Islamic social policies.
Most Gazans have incomes below the poverty line. The Harvard study claims
that as the population ages and continues to grow, there will be increased
demand for medical care and education services—something that the Fatah
government did nothing to plan for and that the Hamas government has
done little to address. Hamas has only made the shortfall worse. What foreign
educators or medical personnel would actually want to work there?[2]

Hamas and European states blame the Israelis for many of the current
problems in education and public health in Gaza—both because of Israel's
economic blockade along the Gaza-Israel border and because of the deaths
and destruction caused by periodic military incursions into Gaza. Israel
launched military incursions and air strikes in 2004, 2006, and 2008. These
attacks were in retaliation for terrorism by groups based in Gaza (including
Hamas both before and after it took over). The Israeli attacks did cause considerable damage to a Gaza infrastructure that was shoddy to begin with. One
could argue that if Hamas and the other radical groups really cared about the
quality of the Gaza infrastructure and its negative effects on the people, they
would not have poked the Israeli cobra, but that is another matter. Our aim
here is to illustrate that public services available were deficient and that the
deficiency has grown worse over time. The Israeli blockade is also a retaliation
against Hamas violence and its efforts to run guns into Gaza and bombs into
Israel. Egypt has also imposed a blockade along its border with Gaza; these
blockades have made tunneling such a popular occupation among Gazans.

An incident in 2007 in Gaza, for example, demonstrates governmental
failure at multiple levels. An earthen dam collapsed, spilling tens of thousands
of gallons of untreated sewage and filth into the town of Umm Nasser. Five
people drowned in floodwaters, and homes and shops were fouled. Hamas

blamed the situation on the West, claiming that the dam would have been better maintained if the United States and others had not stopped sending foreign aid to the Palestinian Authority.

Looking to secure propaganda points and glossing over failures as party in power, Hamas overlooked larger, more telling points: that an antiquated and unsanitary method of handling sewage had been used for too many years and that an important piece of local infrastructure had obviously not been maintained despite the evident health and safety risk to the residents of Umm Nasser. This small vignette speaks volumes, less about the Hamas-led government elected in 2006 than about the quality of governance in Gaza over the long term.

Whether or not Hamas will ultimately lose popular favor (as Fatah did) because of its shortcomings as a provider of services in Gaza remains to be seen. Even if it does, it may well not relinquish power. Hamas is a more determined and capable organization than Fatah was. Hamas has the tangible support of Iran and Syria. It would be in Hamas' interest to retain power even if the population turns against it.

Another condition that Gaza shares with the emerging megacities such as Lagos is rampant corruption. While Fatah was in power, government ministers in Gaza ran their agencies as if they were family monopolies whose primary purpose was to line the pockets of their owners. Licensing requirements presented formidable barriers to entry for would-be competitors, and the citizens had nowhere else to turn except eventually to Hamas, which promised higher ethical standards and to run a cleaner shop than Fatah.

Gaza is less well connected to the outer world than the megacities we address in subsequent chapters. It exports virtually nothing to nowhere, other than to Israel and Egypt, and both Israel and Egypt seem intent on keeping their commercial interactions with Gaza at a minimum. Both countries have erected barriers along their borders with Gaza to limit the cross-border flow of Gazans. U.S. and European economic sanctions applied against Gaza because of Hamas' role in terrorism are also a factor but a slight one, since Gaza had exported little outside its immediate neighborhood even before sanctions were applied. The consequence is that the economic ripple effects of

Hamas' takeover and Gaza's breakaway from its national government have been slight. This will not be true for a megacity such as Lagos or Karachi—far more integrated within the global economy.

The Hamas government in Gaza is an anomaly and a precedent. Gaza is administered as if independent of its parent government, yet it has not declared independence, and the national government has (due to its own weakness) chosen not to contest the situation. If the Palestinian Authority were to vigorously contest Gaza's autonomous "independence," the result would be a civil war that would spill over into neighboring states and invite intervention by Iran and Israel, at a minimum. That is presumably why neither Hamas nor the Palestinian Authority has pushed the issue of Gaza's political status to its logical extreme.

Despite its small size and relative economic insignificance, Gaza has done some things that few cities or provinces in the modern world have been able to do so far: destabilize a region, provoke interstate war, and maintain an independent foreign policy. As we will see in the following pages, there are other, more important cities in the world where national governments have failed in the same ways the Palestinian Authority failed, though not for the same reasons. As social problems in these cities continue to fester as populations surge, residents will do what residents of Gaza did. They will withdraw support and begin to rely on other organizations for personal security and other social services. Eventually, national governments may lose control of their largest cities and choose to do nothing, since the costs of asserting and maintaining control would be too high. If these cities then take the kinds of steps that the Hamas government took in Gaza, effects on international security will be severe.

4

TRIUMPHANT FAILURE

Cairo

What are we going to do? Where is the way out?
—*Essam Muhammad Hussein, Cairo*

Al-Qahira, the Arabic name of the Egyptian capital (and indeed the capital of the Arab world), is variously translated as "city victorious," "triumphant," or "the vanquisher." The name was appropriate centuries ago when Cairo was one of the leading cities of the civilized world, one of the cradles of civilization, and center of a vibrant, powerful empire. Today the sobriquet seems more than ironic given the social problems the city has failed to master. The crowds that flooded central Cairo's squares in January and February 2011 did more than force the regime to change; they brought the state to a halt and in so doing forced the world to recognize the severity of unemployment, poverty, and overcrowding that have plagued the city for decades. While the long-term consequences of Cairo's latest round of civil disorder remain to be seen, managing the city in a way that satisfies its population will likely prove too great a challenge for even the most talented and committed reformers. Yes, miracles do happen. But with the departure of President Hosni Mubarak from office on February 11, 2011, the real work has just begun.

In effect, Cairo deserves to be labeled triumphant about as much as the Egyptian military deserves the praise that the government's propaganda machine lavished on it for its "outstanding" victories during the first days of 1967's Six-Day War against Israel—a war where Egyptian forces were humiliated from the start.

THE CITY WHERE YOU CAN'T HEAR YOURSELF SCREAM

To experience Cairo is to know an assault on the senses, both positive and negative—sometimes simultaneously. Although removed by several decades, journalist and author Tony Horowitz portrays the city in *Baghdad without a Map* in imagery similar to today:

> Between myself and Tut's tomb lay a dense moat of flesh and combustion, swirling dizzily through the gloom.
>
> There were trucks, taxis, trolleys, buggies and buses, the latter so overloaded that bodies draped from the doors, limbs stuck out of windows and a few brave passengers even clung to the rooftops, their turbans unraveling in the wind.
>
> There were men on bicycles, men on oversized tricycles, men on motorbikes—whole families on motorbikes, children crammed in the drivers' laps, sometimes two in a lap, clutching the handlebars. There were donkeys and burros and even a camel: toting firewood, toting fruit, toting garbage, toting ashes. There were two-legged men in wooden wheelchairs, one-legged men with crutches shaped like tree limbs, and a no-legged man on a wooden skateboard, propelling himself with rapid pawing motions across the ground.
>
> There were pedestrians, erupting out of the earth and swarming into the traffic from a newly built subway. Men in white robes and sandals, black Sudanese in foot-high turbans, men in frayed business suits, women in full-face veils, women in what looked like bathrobes, Africans with rings through their noses and tribal markings burned on their cheeks. And at the eye of the maelstrom, an old man selling melon seeds and stalks of sugar cane spread on a scrap of cardboard that served as his open-air shop.[1]

With noise pollution levels that rank it among the world's worst, Cairo assaults residents with daily averages of 85 decibels—the equivalent of standing fifteen feet away from a speeding freight train—all day, every day. (In Tahrir Square and Ramses Square, residents are subjected to daily levels approaching 95 decibels—the equivalent of standing next to a jackhammer.) Such impacts, while perhaps not inducing violence, do grind away at human lives. With the cacophony of banging, screaming, honking, there is no privacy, no place to be quiet—no place to keep sane.

Beyond its chaos and failures, Cairo is quite different in some important respects from other cities we examine. For one thing, migration from the countryside no longer primarily fuels the city's growth. Twenty years ago, there were two migrants for every birth in the city; now migration is a trickle—perhaps because word of the appalling overcrowding and abysmal job prospects in the city has begun to circulate in rural areas. Unemployment in Cairo is twice as high as in the rest of the state, and half the city is classified as poor, so economic incentive for young men to migrate from the countryside is reduced. Even so, Cairo will grow thanks to a high birth rate—despite years of government investment in family planning programs. One-third of inhabitants is under fifteen and three-fifths are under thirty; its population in 2025 will number over 22 million residents—30 percent larger than today. The results of these trends were evident in the protests of 2011.

A second difference between Cairo and most of the other megacities we address is that the Egyptian government has not washed its hands of the megacity's problems. Quite the opposite. Unlike Nigeria and Pakistan, which have more or less acted as if their unruly megacities were located in some other state, Egypt has not moved its capital to a city less densely populated and more easily governed. Instead, Egypt has assumed direct responsibility for managing its capital and largest city. The president of Egypt appoints a governor to administer municipal affairs, and Cairo's annual budgets are set by the national government. The national government decides how much Cairo authorities can spend on capital costs (infrastructure improvements) and the operating costs of the city's agencies and social programs. This is one reason why demonstrators in 2011 directed their ire at the national government and President Mubarak, rather than municipal figureheads.

GOVERNMENT AS "PUPPET MASTER"

National authorities really have no choice other than to stay directly involved in managing Cairo given the city's centrality in Egyptian culture. Many Egyptians refer to Cairo as *Masr*, which is also the Arabic name for the entire country. The government realizes from past experience that if it were to lose control of Cairo, it could lose its control of the entire state. Historically the streets of Cairo have been volatile, and disorder in Cairo has in the past led to political change at the national level. The year 2011 was not the first time that disorder in Cairo roiled the country. Riots in Cairo during 1952 set the stage for the coup that toppled the Egyptian monarchy and again in 1954 led to the resignation of the country's first president and prime minster. Fear of riots also compelled Gamal Abdel Nasser Hussein—known universally simply as "Nasser"—to rescind his resignation after the disastrous 1967 war with Israel, although surely he did not need his arm twisted to stay in office. Riots in 1977 caused the Anwar Sadat government to reimpose price controls on food products after a too-brief attempt to liberalize the retail economy. Since then, there have been riots over a wide range of issues: food prices, the supply of bread, soccer scores, the construction of a suburban Christian church, cartoons in a Danish newspaper that lampooned the Prophet, and the national government's occasional foreign policy decision.

Egyptian authorities have always recognized the threat that disorder in Cairo poses to the regime, evidenced in often heavy-handed approaches against protest marches and demonstrations. Human Rights Watch and other civil rights organizations, including Egyptian organizations, routinely criticize the government for unlawful arrests and other abuses. A recent example occurred in April 2010 when police were accused of arresting and beating protesters who were peacefully calling for the revocation of Egypt's Emergency Law. The existence of the Emergency Law is itself a clear indication of the authorities' concern about keeping a lid on public outbursts of protest and violence. The law allows the authorities to ban public demonstrations, search individuals and properties without court authorization, restrict where citizens are allowed to travel or even live, and detain people without trial. Egyptian authorities claim that the law, which was renewed in 2010, is necessary to deal with terrorism and drug-related crime. But the law has been continuously in force for thirty years and has become standard operating procedure for maintaining stability in Cairo and across the country.

While national control over events in Cairo may have contributed to the dismissive opinion most Cairenes have towards municipal government, many residents of the city basically regard municipal government as either remote and indifferent or hostile. For good reason. Virtually no public services are provided in many of the city's poorest neighborhoods, and city officials are widely regarded as corrupt. In much of the city, private sector organizations have stepped in to attempt to fill at least some of the vacuum in public services. Authorities' harsh approach to law enforcement also contributes to residents' resentment.

FILLING THE VOID

Prominent among the organizations that have tried to fill the vacuum is the Muslim Brotherhood, which earned enduring popular support by its ongoing programs but also for its noteworthy response to a 1992 earthquake in Cairo. The Brotherhood built shelters for, and distributed cash to, thousands of people left homeless. It also distributed large quantities of food and other emergency supplies. By comparison, the government's response was sluggish. A journalist quoted in the *Harvard International Review* described the public's reaction to the earthquake response this way: "When the Muslim Brothers are asked, they open the drawer and they give you something. When you ask government officials, they open the drawer and then ask you to give something."[2]

The Muslim Brotherhood has been implicated in numerous acts of violence and terrorism, including attacks against government targets and Western tourists in the 1990s, the assassination of President Sadat in 1981, and several attempted assassinations of President Nasser in the 1950s and 1960s. Consequently, the Brotherhood has been technically outlawed since 1954. It has nevertheless grown in popularity and, despite its legal status, actually controls about one-sixth of the seats in the national parliament. Brotherhood members ran for office as independents under a tacit understanding with the government that was made possible by the organization's renunciation of violence and commitment to work for reform within the system.

Whether the Muslim Brotherhood remains committed to peaceful reform is an open question, but for our purposes the main point is that government failure to effectively administer Cairo (and the rest of the country) created a niche in which a powerful, violent organization was allowed to prosper. Further, that organization has demonstrated the ability to proliferate internationally. It is not simply an Egyptian phenomenon. It is an international phenomenon with offshoots in many other Muslim countries and adherents in many Western countries.

While we cannot specify which ideology might capture groups in other megacities, it is clear from developments in Cairo and Gaza that government failure to attend to the needs of its people creates conditions under which violent, destabilizing organizations can gain political and paramilitary power. Whether these organizations are morally better or worse than the governments they oppose is, of course, important, but we also need to look at how their rise affects international relations and regional stability.

To be fair, Cairo authorities have in recent years launched attempts to alleviate the poverty, unemployment, illiteracy, and overcrowding for which the city is justifiably notorious. In this respect, Cairo is more similar to Rio de Janeiro than other megacities we examine. Rio has, of course, benefited from Brazil's heady economic growth in recent years, and, once it was selected as host city for the 2016 Olympic Games, the country and the city have had common cause to improve urban infrastructure and upgrade the quality of public services (notably public safety and law enforcement)—though Brazil's results to date remain questionable. These are advantages that Cairo has not had, but more has been done to address social problems in Cairo than in cities such as Karachi and Lagos.

Each of the megacities we focus on in detail in this book has periodically announced master plans of one sort or another for urban renewal, economic development, poverty reduction, a crackdown on corruption, or reform of abusive practices by law enforcement agencies. Often announcements have been accompanied with great fanfare and pledges that "this time" authorities really intend to implement plans effectively. Too often, though, these plans consist of empty words intended more to create the illusion of resolve for the benefit of government's domestic critics and international organizations, such as various humanitarian and economic agencies in the UN system. Or the plans are simply unrealistic in the first place, given the mismatch between resources available and the extent of social issues they purported to address.

CITY OF THE DEAD

Of all Cairo's daunting problems, overcrowding may be the most pressing. Descriptions of Cairo by scholars, municipal authorities, and travelers often note how many residents are forced to live in shacks built on rooftops and in cemeteries. An estimated five hundred thousand infamously live in Cairo's most famous four-mile-long cemetery known as the City of the Dead. Many others inhabit cemeteries in and around the city. Tombs in Egypt are often designed with a room or two that relatives of the deceased can use for visits. People also inhabit these rooms. City services are not provided, so the conditions are not sanitary, but residents have illegally tapped into the electric grid, much as they have in shantytowns in other cities. In 2001, according to the Asian Coalition for Housing Rights, 1.5 million Cairenes lived in the capital's "second city"—on rooftops, where conditions may be cooler than inside tenements but exposure to desert sand and pollution from traffic and industrial plants is pervasive. Today, these second city residents may be upwards of two million.[3]

    We find further evidence of overcrowding in so-called "informal settlements"—the Egyptian equivalent of Rio's *favelas* and the shantytowns that make up half of Karachi and Lagos—established in less desirable areas in and around the city. Often these informal, ramshackle settlements are in areas prone to rockslides and other hazards. A 2008 rockslide in one, killed over a hundred people. Despite numerous complaints to the authorities by residents over the years about falling rocks, nothing was done to shore up hillsides, and only after deaths did authorities take action. Then authorities resorted to a typically heavy-handed approach, forcefully evicting settlers from land they had illegally occupied for decades.

Forceful eviction is neither an enlightened nor practical solution to the problem of informal settlements. Over half of the population in greater Cairo resides in informal settlements; evicting millions of people and throwing them onto an already deficient housing market is a recipe for civil disorder. As is the case in Karachi and elsewhere, authorities are to a considerable extent complicit in the formation of illegal communities. Many are actually on state land, and, even so, authorities looked the other way when settlers first moved in and the settlement's population was small—when the time would have been right for regulating how the land was used. Since 2005 Cairo has also allowed some settlements to legally tap into the electric grid.

Air pollution is another serious problem. Cairo has some of the foulest air on the planet and consequently a high incidence of lung disease and other medical problems. The city's air is more than ten times worse than the standards set by the World Health Organization (WHO). The air is acidic enough to accelerate the erosion of Egypt's signature monuments, the pyramids. A 2006 study comparing air quality in the world's major cities found that Cairo's was second worst in the world. Only New Delhi was worse. New York and Los Angeles, American cities with the most pressing air pollution problems, had one-sixth as many particles per cubic meter of air as Cairo.

None of these problems can be solved soon. Since the megacity continues to mushroom like the Red Queen in *Alice in Wonderland*, Egyptian authorities will have to pedal their public service bicycle faster just to maintain status quo.

THE MEGACONFERENCE ON MEGACITIES

Ironically, in 1994 Cairo was the site where the UN and the international community first officially acknowledged the extent of social, environmental, and international security issues that fast-growing megacities in less-developed states could witness. Cairo was already in the spotlight when the megacity issue was first seriously discussed. The occasion was the UN International Conference on Population and Development. The conference report concluded that: "The alarming consequences of urbanization visible in many countries are related to its rapid pace, to which Governments have been unable to respond with their current management capacities and practices." Plainly, "current" practices in the Cairo of 1994 were not up to the task then, and not enough has been done since to build more useful and effective "capabilities and practices." Even less has been done in other megacities.

The conference did suggest that what were then "emerging" megacities threatened to jeopardize the national economies and environments of numerous states by collecting too many poor, discontented people and too many unregulated activities. Problems with poverty, crime, disorder, and pollution that were already stressing developing countries in 1994 would only grow worse—a lot worse—as the largest cities continued to expand. The prognostication was correct. Urban Leviathans have created zones of instability and humanitarian suffering on scales never seen before. But what about the conference's recommendations to fix the problems?

Unfortunately, the conference's recommendations are like many UN products: long on high-principled generalities; short on practical and realistic steps. Many recommendations fall squarely into the "easy to say, hard to do" category. Even so, recommendations on cities such as Cairo are worth reviewing because they reflect prescience on basic themes that need to be addressed to avoid the instability and suffering that the conferees foresaw and we foresee now. The recommendations are to

> increase the capacity and competence of city and municipal authorities to manage urban development, to safeguard the environment, to respond to the needs of all citizens, including urban squatters, for personal safety, basic infrastructure and services, to eliminate health and social problems, including problems of drugs and criminality, and problems resulting from overcrowding and disasters, and to provide people with alternatives to living in areas prone to natural and man-made disasters.[2]

This recommendation amounts to little more than a restatement of what was already obvious in 1994 and has becoming painfully obvious now: governmental entities responsible for providing public services to urban populations ought to gear up and get their acts together because demand for services is growing at least as fast as megacity populations. The real question is how cash-strapped and overwhelmed governments are supposed to acquire time and resources to upgrade capacities. Given the size of the problem that ineffective megacity governments face, this recommendation is akin to telling a fisherman with a fly rod to catch a swordfish. The last phrase in the recommendation amounts to little more than an obligatory tip of the hat to another UN program—the International Decade for Natural Disaster Reduction:

> Improve the plight of the urban poor [and] promote the integration of migrants from rural areas into urban areas and to develop and improve their income-earning capability by facilitating their access to employment, credit, production, marketing opportunities, basic education, health services, vocational training and transportation, with special attention to the situation of women workers and women heads of households. Child-care centres should be established, and special protection and rehabilitation programmes should be established for street children.

Again, an exceedingly wide-ranging set of recommendations. Unemployment and poverty were problems in Cairo when the conference was held and are even larger now. Creating better opportunities in Cairo and other megacities would be desirable—and there have been improvements in public education, job training, and public transportation in Cairo. Improvements, however, have not kept pace with increasing demands of a growing population and rising expectations of residents familiar with higher living standards in many other countries, thanks to the media, the Internet, and perhaps even the 1994 conference and succeeding conferences and publications that the UN and nongovernmental organizations have sponsored.

> In order to finance the needed infrastructure and services in a balanced manner, taking into account the interests of the poor segments of society, local and national government agencies should consider

introducing equitable cost-recovery schemes and increasing revenues by appropriate measures.

Financing and infrastructure are two areas where Egypt seems to have taken conference recommendations at least partially to heart. Strong efforts at encouraging foreign investment have been made, and important infrastructure projects have been completed or are planned for the Cairo metropolitan area. A third leg of the Cairo subway system, for example, is under way, and the construction of the Cairo Ring Road, which circles the city and diverts some traffic from city streets, was completed in 2009. Infrastructure for many municipal services (schools, clinics, fire stations, police stations, wastewater treatment facilities, and water mains), however, requires substantial and costly expansion. Financial innovations have been skewed toward attracting foreign direct investment in private sector enterprises. While good for job promotion, these actions only indirectly and incrementally affect municipal infrastructure.

In 1997—three years after the UN conference—Egypt passed an Investment Incentives Law designed to lure foreign investors with promises of reductions in customs tariffs and tax holidays, rights of repatriation of capital, guarantees against arbitrary nationalization of investor property, and relaxed regulatory and licensing requirements. One of the law's stated objectives was to decentralize industry away from overcrowded Greater Cairo and the shores of the Nile. In 2004 a Ministry of Investment was established to oversee and promote the privatization of selected inefficient state-owned industries. The net effect of these innovations has been a sharp increase in foreign investment. Foreign investment in Egypt was valued at $2 billion in 2002 and more than a still-too-modest $13 billion in 2008. Unfortunately, the 2011 protests and the consequent uncertainty about future government policies have likely undermined the confidence that foreign investors and employers have in Cairo and Egypt as a whole and set back desperately needed job promotion.

Business-oriented reforms, though, were not exactly what the conference had in mind as they only indirectly help the poor and do little to enhance the provision of public services in Cairo:

Strengthen the capacity for land management, including urban planning at all levels, in order to take into account demographic trends
and encourage the search for innovative approaches to address the
challenges facing cities, with special attention to the pressures and
needs resulting from the growth of their populations.

If this recommendation were made today, it might seem like the rancher slam-
ming the barn door shut after the horses have escaped. Growth in Cairo and
other megacities has already taken place. But if acted upon in 1994, megacity
problems would likely not be as difficult as they now are.

Much of that population growth in Cairo and other megacities was unplanned and unmanaged. Megacity authorities have made little or no serious effort to enforce building codes or to regulate where people actually set
down roots. As we know, especially from studies of informal settlements by
economist Hernando de Soto and others, shantytowns typically form when
small numbers of squatters erect ramshackle buildings on vacant land. If they
are not immediately evicted, other squatters join them, and soon a community forms. Often squatters' land is privately owned agricultural acreage not
actively farmed. Other times, a government authority owns the land and remains either blissfully inattentive or negligent about the uses to which land is
being put. Once the squatter community is formed, "land management" can
only mean one of three things: recognizing the community and providing it
public services; denying it recognition and services but leaving it in place; or
closing it by evicting squatters and bulldozing their makeshift houses. Most of
the time, cities such as Cairo, Karachi, Kinshasa, and Lagos chose the second
or third options. Wholesale evictions seem a particularly shortsighted policy
in that throwing large numbers of people onto an already overburdened housing market means only that existing informal settlements will become even
more densely packed or that new squatter communities will sprout elsewhere
in the metropolitan area.

Since megacities continue to grow, pressing need for effective land management and building regulation remains. The problem today is the same as
in 1994: inadequate governance. Municipal authorities lack the capacity to
implement urban plans effectively. As the UN conference noted, this is largely

a consequence of rapid population growth that megacities have witnessed. What the conference did not suggest was what Cairo and the Egyptian government should do to improve their land management and urban planning capacities:

> Promote the development and implementation of effective environmental management strategies for urban agglomerations, giving special attention to water, waste and air management, as well as to environmentally sound energy and transport systems.

Environmental concerns are typically thought of as a secondary priority in comparison to issues that more directly and immediately affect people and their livelihoods. As we know, in megacities such as Cairo even the most direct and immediate issues have not been effectively addressed for the majority of the population. Moreover, environmentally sound energy and transportation systems have yet to be installed in many more economically advanced cities and countries.

Collectively these recommendations are important for their depiction of pressing social needs in megacities such as Cairo. They are equally important for what they don't say. Perhaps reflecting a political bias or a more naïve approach to the problems of emerging megacities, the conference chose not to highlight one of the most basic requirements: the need for public safety and the rule of law.

The conference also chose not to answer the most basic question of all: Why haven't the capacities and management practices of megacities kept pace with mushrooming populations? The answer to that question is also the answer to the question of why more has not been done in Cairo and elsewhere since 1994 to address the issues the conference identified. As they are presently constituted, many cities are incapable of tackling these issues. The Cairo government was overwhelmed in 1994 and is still overwhelmed today. It will be even more overwhelmed tomorrow. Megacities such as Cairo need help from the international community, but the international community is still not "seized with" (to use a phrase common to UN resolutions) the megacity issue.

Bluntly, we need new approaches to urban challenges. The UN conference recognized the need for new approaches but did not actually recommend any. It recommended instead that municipal authorities do more—a lot more—even though they were already failing to meet demand in 1994.

To some extent, the conference contributed to the international community's lack of "seizure" in addressing a wide number of issues quite controversial in the West and even in the Middle East and Africa, where some of the most problematic megacities are located. These other recommendations drew the focus away from what was arguably the conference's most important contribution: the recognition of serious problems that poorly governed megacities would have not merely for their host countries, but for the world at large. Among the other high-visibility problems that the conference identified and provided recommendations for were the spread of Acquired Immune Deficiency Syndrome (AIDS), child exploitation, poor health care for women and children, inadequate support systems for the elderly and disabled, and the need to promote reproductive rights of women, including abortion.

THE CRITICAL CITY

We view Cairo as critical for several reasons. First, perhaps foremost, it is the capital of a state that—despite its history of autocratic government, corruption, and half-measures toward democracy—remains crucial to the United States in the Middle East. Second, Cairo is a city in which national governance heavily invests. The Egyptian government recognizes that disorder in Cairo threatens the stability of the entire state and, for that matter, the entire region. Other national governments should have as clear an appreciation of the strategic consequences of events in their megacities, but they do not. This is a lesson that Pakistan, Nigeria, the Democratic Republic of the Congo, and Bangladesh could well learn from Egypt.

Yet Egypt's approach to maintaining control in Cairo has been shortsighted. It addresses the symptoms (disorder) rather than the disease (overcrowding, poverty, unemployment, pollution, and ineffective governance). Egypt is the city's "puppet master," attempting to prevent events in Cairo from spinning out of control, while failing to invest in the public and private infrastructures necessary to provide essential public services to city residents. At the same time, Egypt's focus on maintaining control over Cairo has led to in-adequate attention to less populated sections of the state. The result has been resentment and disaffection in both urban and rural areas. Residents of Sinai, for example, have long felt ignored by the Egyptian government. As one re-sult, antigovernment violence and domestic terrorism on the peninsula have increased in recent years. In Egypt—as with so many majority world states with Leviathan cities—if it's not one thing, it's another.

5

THE MOST DANGEROUS PLACE
Karachi, Lahore, and Rural Areas

U.S. intelligence officials say Pakistan is the likeliest source of terrorist attacks on the United States. It's the most dangerous place on earth: nuclear-armed, menaced by terrorists, economically in crisis and mired in political turmoil.

—*Mort Kondracke, American journalist*

Yes, there are extremists here. But they are a small minority. Most of us want nothing to do with violence.

—*Mohsin Hamid, Pakistani novelist*

I would say that half of the country has some sense of central government control. . . . The other half is a mix of tribal/provincial/ethnic groups and interests. If this is what makes a rogue state . . . then Pakistan is definitely a rogue state.

—*Nadeem F. Paracha, Pakistani journalist*

You believe violence and cruelty to women are part of the path to higher knowledge—and faith. In the madrassa *where you study, you are taught that Muslims speak Arabic, that non-Muslims should be killed, and women who go to market should be beaten. This is the only education you have known. Your enemy is your own government—an American puppet regime, an infidel imposition that stands in the way of a true Islamic state. Their savaging of the Lal Masjid—the Red Mosque—and the martyring of the jihadists inside show that no one can be trusted, no one spared, who does not follow a path leading Pakistan towards its one true future.*

Pakistan today is known for many things—none particularly good: periodic military coups; unruly and uncontrolled border regions; persistent, pervasive government corruption; oversized armed forces; documented complicity in spreading nuclear weapons technology to rogue regimes; and mixed performance in the "long war" against violent extremism. While Pakistan has helped the United States pursue Al Qa'eda and the Taliban, it has also, until recently, turned a blind eye towards terrorist havens in the western borderlands.

By actively conniving through what is a rogue military intelligence agency (the infamous Directorate for Inter-Services Intelligence, or "ISI"), Pakistan has long assisted terrorist groups along its western and eastern borders. Pakistan has also been a base for terrorist attacks in neighboring India and the disputed region of Kashmir. Pakistan's tensions with India and the nuclear weapons programs in both countries have been the most defining features of the geostrategic terrain of the Asian continent. While it may be an extreme truism, some observers offer the caustic insight that "most states have a military, but in Pakistan the military has a state."

MASSIVE CITIES—AND GROWING POPULATIONS

In the world of tomorrow, Pakistan will be one of the world's most populous states, with two of the world's largest cities located inside its borders. By 2009 Pakistan was already the sixth-most-populous state, with a population of 170 million people. By 2015 it will be the fifth-largest state in terms of population, with more than 200 million people, and in 2025 Pakistan will be home to 250 million people. Only China, India, the United States, and Indonesia will have greater populations.

By 2025 half of Pakistani people will live in cities, with Karachi and Lahore the two most-populous urban centers. Karachi and Lahore already have huge populations, and both remain on rapid growth trajectories. Lahore's population is estimated at around 7 million today, and by 2025 it will be more than 10 million. Karachi currently holds 12 million people, and its residents will number almost 20 million in 2025. In 2015, it will have attained status as the fifth-biggest city in the world. (Today New York City is in fifth place.) By then Lahore will also have joined Karachi on the list of the twenty-five most-populous cities on the planet. Many aspects of rapid urbanization of Pakistan, and especially the particularly sharp rise in the populations of Karachi and Lahore, are alarming and should receive attention.

KARACHI AND LAHORE: DISTINGUISHING FEATURES

The cities themselves are quite different. While Karachi is a relatively new city, Lahore is ancient—the capital of an eleventh-century empire that encompassed what is now northern Pakistan. It remains to this day the country's cultural center. Karachi, on the other hand was a small, obscure fishing village as recently as the early nineteenth century. It did not begin to grow until after it was occupied by the British in the 1840s. Its early growth resulted from a British decision to use it as a port for exporting agricultural produce from interior provinces. Post–World War II era witnessed another spurt when Muslim immigrants from India relocated to the city after India and Pakistan gained independence. Millions of immigrants—derisively called *mojahirs*, or refugees—were not integrated into the social or political fabric of the city. Consequently, *mojahirs* gradually built their own political structure in Karachi—including a militia to resist attacks by other ethnic groups and, for that matter, the Pakistan government. During the 1990s, the violence in Karachi between *mojahirs* and other ethnic factions was so extreme the military was sent in to restore order. The army occupied the city for two and a half years and then withdrew without having quelled communal violence.

Karachi is now the industrial capital of Pakistan and the state's major hub for international commerce. Perhaps because it did not receive a wave of immigrants from other countries, Lahore experiences less urban rioting and crime than Karachi and has, therefore, attracted its own share of foreign investment. But its infrastructure is not adequate and will soon be overwhelmed. One telling sign of inadequate infrastructure is that Lahore has only a hundred traffic lights—not remotely enough for a city of 7 million. Manhattan, by comparison, has twelve *thousand*.

CITY CHALLENGES

Despite important differences, the problems that these two cities will pose for the Pakistani government and the international community are similar and should concern us most about events there. Problems stem from the inability or simple failure of municipal and national governments to manage staggering growth. While there are poorly governed and underserved cities across the globe, few are as strategically important as Karachi or Lahore. Few are as tightly integrated into the global economy. The United States, the United Kingdom, and Germany are among Pakistan's largest trading partners in terms of exports and imports, and criminals and terrorists are known to follow routes where commerce has established.

Environmentally, Pakistan's cities in general, but Karachi and Lahore in particular, are disasters. In 2006 Pakistan's own Space and Upper Atmosphere Research Commission found that air pollution in Karachi posed a serious threat to the health of those living in and around the city. The commission called for an immediate end to "addition of automobiles to the existing fleet." Since then, the number of cars on city streets has only grown. That same year, the commission estimated that air quality in both Karachi and Lahore was twenty-two times worse than what the WHO regarded as safe.[1]

Only 1 percent of the wastewater in the entire country is treated, and less than half of the solid waste in its cities is even picked up off the streets and fields. Industrial waste is untreated and channeled into rivers that run to the Arabian Sea. Authorities in Karachi do nothing to prevent bilge dumping and oil spills in the busy port. The results are that the flora and fauna in both the river and the coastal sea are fouled. The WHO, again, estimates that much of the groundwater reserves in and around Lahore are already contaminated.[2] Since Pakistan has yet to establish effective environmental protection and remediation programs, conditions will only deteriorate as Karachi and Lahore grow. Given the number of higher-priority issues facing the country—not the least of which is widespread poverty and violence in these cities—it seems unlikely that environmental problems will be tackled soon.

While the UN attempts to help, there is only so much it can do without genuine commitment by national and municipal governments—one that goes beyond platitudes about good intentions and actually puts muscle into regulations and inspections at the local level. From the perspective of Pakistan's largest cities, it is ironic that one of the outcomes of the 2009 UN climate change conference in Copenhagen was a plea by the UN Human Settlements Programme for national governments to give municipal governments the freedom to address environmental issues independently. While such advice is sound, it also assumes that overly tight reins on municipal regulators and inspectors are the real problem in Karachi and Lahore.

The Karachi municipal government has been unable to perform the most basic of government functions, one essential to effective environmental control: regulating land use. Fully half of the city's residents live in illegally built residences. One consequence of this haphazard growth is that in much of Karachi there is not even a street-address system. If conditions remain as they are, 10 million people will be living in illegal settlements erected without deference to or consideration for master plans on the books for Karachi's long-term development. According to the head of the UN-HABITAT program, "the mayors have shown leadership and must now get a conducive atmosphere to operate."[3] This may be true for elected officials in cities such as Berlin, Shanghai, Buenos Aires, and even Mexico City, but it simply does not apply to either Karachi or Lahore.

SOCIETAL AND HUMAN CHALLENGES

Sociologically in Pakistan, the situation is extreme and heading south. Poverty is rampant throughout the country, life expectancies are low, and services such as education, law enforcement, and medical care are already scarce for most urban residents. According to an Asian Development Bank report, in 2009 about 30 percent of the national population lived below the poverty line, and more than 20 percent lived on less than $1.25 daily.[4] While comprehensive or current statistics about poverty in cities do not exist, most estimates reflect high and growing levels of urban poverty. According to one report, the number of urban residents living below the poverty line has grown by

40 percent since 1993. Arif Hasan of the Asian Coalition for Housing Rights notes that the population living in Karachi's sprawling, unregulated neighborhoods known as *katchi abadis* doubles every decade.[5] Even those who are so-called "better off" slum dwellers bear the brunt of living conditions where land is unfairly distributed—or never developed at all. The Karachi government limits the number of land plots an individual can own; the use of family proxies soon becomes a convenient workaround. Capital and tax laws favorable to investors (who acquire land they never intend to occupy) further compound the problem: nearly 40 percent of land the Karachi Development Authority secured in the 1970s was held for investment and lay dormant a decade later. As one result, *dalals* (which translates variously as "middlemen" or "pimps") have emerged as malevolent figures for the poor, akin to the ruthless property managers and absentee landlords of Irish history before and during the potato famine. Akhtar Hameed Khan, founder of the Orangi Pilot Project, describes "entrepreneurs who learned the art of collaborating with and manipulating our greedy politicians and bureaucrats. With their costly patronage, the *dalals* secure possession of tracts of land, buy protection against eviction, and obtain water and transport facilities." Pirate subdivisions such as Orangi make up the *katchi abadi* landscape, where half of Karachi's population lives. By 2025 more than 7 million Karachi residents will be living in a state of abject poverty—a combustible situation, to be sure.

WHAT COULD BE DONE?

From a humanitarian (and urban planning) perspective, reducing poverty is a matter of importance and urgency. The issue, nonetheless, must have far greater urgency than efforts to clean up Pakistan's urban air and streams.

For two reasons, we will not argue here that reducing poverty is crucial to international efforts to suppress terrorism. On the one hand, there is abundant evidence that poverty does not *directly* cause terrorism. Too many well-off people and too few poor people have become terrorists for poverty to be the cause of terrorism. On the other hand, reducing poverty in cities as large as Karachi and Lahore is a daunting task that takes decades of intense focus and hard work. Counterterrorism programs cannot and will not be put on hold until such time that unemployment is a problem for only 5 or 10 percent of the Pakistani people or when a majority of Pakistani city dwellers have incomes above the poverty line.

Poverty, nevertheless, can be a destabilizing factor under certain conditions, especially when heavily concentrated in densely packed cities such as Karachi and Lahore. Extreme poverty contributes to popular dissatisfaction with the status quo and helps create conditions in which unemployed or at least underpaid individuals are more susceptible to the siren songs of religious or ethnic militancy and the lure of criminal organizations.

UN statistics claim that Pakistani children can expect only seven years of schooling, far less than even Yemen and Ethiopia—even as an astonishing 99.4 percent of Ethiopian urban residents are slum dwellers. (By contrast, the equivalent number for most advanced countries is fifteen years or more of schooling.) These statistics must be treated with care, of course; it is unwise to assume that a year of schooling has the same value in one country as another and that consequently Yemeni and Ethiopian children are better educated than Pakistanis. The number of years of schooling, nevertheless, is a reasonable proxy for the quantity or volume of educational services that government provides. Pakistan has not done enough. There are simply too few public schools.

Deficiencies in Pakistan's educational system have created not just niches, but chasms that have been filled by privately funded religious schools, or *madrassas*, of which twenty thousand exist. These schools have an infamous reputation in the West. Many teach an intolerant, jihadist brand of Islam, and many graduates have been implicated in terrorism plots or in the Taliban insurgency in Afghanistan—and now in the provinces of Pakistan that border Afghanistan. *Madrassa* graduates created the Taliban in the first place.

Even though most *madrassas* teach a mainstream brand of Islam (the Pakistan government claims that 90 percent have no ties to radicalism) and provide useful services such as keeping young, unemployed men off the streets and providing them food and shelter, all focus on religion to the detriment of technical and secular areas of study that the economy requires. Many *madrassa* students are foreigners. As one sign of Pakistan's fundamental dysfunction, religious schools have been providing social and educational services to students from neighboring countries even as Pakistani children are denied the opportunity for an education.

In the mid-2000s, then-president Pervez Musharraf recognized problems that radical *madrassas* were creating and attempted to place them under the supervision of the Ministry of Education. He also aimed to introduce secular subjects to curricula. As with almost all of Pakistan's fitful attempts at reform, this one secured little progress. As often happens, incompetence and corruption, as well as competing vested interests in Pakistani society, stymied government efforts. Liberal critics opposed Musharraf's reforms on the grounds that they would legitimize *madrassas*, arguing that government funds used to pay *madrassas* to develop secular courses could be better spent on improving or expanding public schools. Defenders of *madrassas* argued that government had demonstrated inability to run public education and that no purpose could be served by placing religious schools under the aegis of the Ministry of Education. All these positions were correct: *madrassas* do need reform, public schools do need more funding, and government can improve neither public nor religious school systems.

IN BUT NOT OF: CITIES OF REFUGEES

The population surge in Karachi and Lahore will continue to be a story of unregulated and undergoverned slums. When a new shantytown forms or an existing one expands, the size of the greater metropolitan population grows. Because growth largely takes place here, the preponderance of poor, new residents are in dire need of public services. Not only are there more mouths to feed—there is more physical territory over which the feeding must take place. Karachi has grown in terms of territory as well as population, as shantytowns closed by the military and moved miles outside the city are now enfolded within the city. As long as such growth remains unplanned, unregulated, and so rapid, financially strapped and slow-moving municipal bureaucracies will perpetually struggle (and fail) to catch up with evolving needs. As Karachi and Lahore grow, there will be ever more broad geographic and demographic expanses over which public services are *not* provided. Over time, these under-served expanses become the functional equivalent of refugee camps.

Palestinian camps in the West Bank and Lebanon were established more than a half century ago, and during the ensuing years nearby villages grew into cities, and eventually cities surrounded refugee camps with densely populated neighborhoods. From the air, the cities and refugee camps are indistinguishable. Refugee camps are nevertheless *in* but not *of* the cities. They are separate political entities, and social services inside them are not provided by the nearby municipalities or parent national government, but by the UN and by foreign governments that fund the UN agency that services the camps. (Now in its sixth decade of operation, the UN Relief and Works Agency still provides service to 4.6 million refugees in the Palestinian camps.)

The slums that proliferate in and around Karachi and Lahore are also physically in but not of their respective cities with their corporate headquarters and international airports. Just as the Palestinian refugee camps draw little in the way of basic public services and economic opportunity from the Lebanese and West Bank communities that surround them, so, too, the shantytowns in Karachi and Lahore. Basic public services we take for granted in the West are simply not provided in anywhere near the required volume. There is no UN agency to take care of feeding, educating, and providing medical care for the residents of these virtual refugee camps. Building infrastructure for supplying basic services (schools, police stations, clinics, transfer stations for trash, wastewater treatment facilities) has so far proven too great a task for the Pakistani government. As the number of residents continues to grow faster than public service infrastructure, pressure on the government from dissatisfied and discontented citizens will continue to mount. Discontent is high.

THE WORLD'S MOST DANGEROUS CITY

Karachi is the most dangerous city in the world. A professor at the National Institute of Urban Infrastructure in Peshawar, Pakistan, describes the dismal state of Pakistani cities and Karachi here: "Streets are littered with waste, drains are overflowing with sewage, low-lying communities are inundated after rainfall, traffic congestion is ubiquitous, and the violent crime in urban centres is on the rise."[6]

Karachi witnesses considerable urban violence and all-too-frequent civil disturbances; Lahore is better off for now because its infrastructure and over-crowding problems have not quite reached crisis stage, yet. (Even so, violence can suddenly erupt in Lahore. There were riots in 2005 after city fathers an-nounced a plan for a marathon in which women would be allowed to run in shorts and in shirts that did not fully cover their upper bodies.) In Karachi, not only is crime widespread, there are terrorist bombings of parks, religious celebrations, government buildings, and Western businesses. Protest march-es and demonstrations occur frequently and often turn violent. (Ironically, Karachi's too-few street lights are apparently favorite targets of vandalism during such demonstrations. As with much street violence, it degrades the infrastructure that needs expansion.) Protests so frequently result in violence that the U.S. embassy advises giving wide berth to any demonstrations visi-tors encounter.

As in all cities, there is organized crime in neighborhoods where gangs exert control. In Karachi, there is a sinister twist with important internation-al consequences. The *New York Times* has reported that the Pakistani Tal-iban has been using Karachi as a base where fighters go to get away from the fighting—for what GIs in Vietnam used to call "R&R" (rest and recreation leave).[7] Further recent reporting confirms Karachi as home port for terrorists. As such, the city represents the urban frontline in Pakistan's struggle against violent extremists. The identifying and screening of potential recruits, the advantage of safe houses in hidden havens, and the blooming of brutal ide-ology find home here. Faisal Shahzad, the Pakistani American convicted of planting a car bomb in New York's Times Square in 2010, set out from Karachi to the tribal area of North Waziristan, where he received training from the Taliban. He was a resident of Karachi in the 1990s as well and—though specu-lation—could well have found connections with the Pakistani Taliban during this period.

Karachi is also an R&R spot for the Afghan Taliban. Mullah Abdul Ghani Baradar, a senior Afghan commander, was arrested on the outskirts of the city in 2010. Despite this, some claim that senior Afghan Taliban commanders still remain in wealthy areas under control of the Defense Housing Authority and have free passage in and out of the city. As many Taliban fighters are seasonal, they often stay in Karachi during the winter and take low-paying jobs, disappearing in the urban landscape. One Taliban fighter who lived in Karachi for six months was quite direct: "We are well organized here."

As Karachi is a vital economic and shipping hub—Pakistan's equivalent of New York City, Chicago, or Los Angeles—extremists find work in the vital trucking industry, which carries weapons, food, fuel, water, and other logistical supplies to NATO-led International Security and Assistance Force (ISAF) in Afghanistan. Funds generated in the trucking industry flow back through Pashtun businessmen, who dominate the industry, as well as to politicians, and in cruel irony, to the Taliban itself. Militants are paid not to attack these convoys.

Amid the chaos that is Karachi, the Taliban also raises funds. Much fundraising is through cooperative ventures with local criminal gangs involved in activities such as bank robberies, kidnappings, and extortion of legitimate businesses. What this means is that the Pakistani Taliban has a source of income that will be difficult to eradicate given the corruption and limited capabilities of law enforcement systems in the city. That slums in which half of the population resides (10 million in the near future) are not effectively policed at all means insurgents will be able to rest, recharge their batteries, and raise funds right in the heart of urban Pakistan. At some point they will bring their fight against the government to the cities and are already finding pools of recruits among legions of discontented, unemployed, and impoverished young men.

According to recent studies, a majority of Taliban foot soldiers in Afghanistan are motivated less by Islamist ideology than by need for money, desire for camaraderie, anti-Americanism, and mutual disgust for the status quo. Whether motives are "pure" or not, they can be effective fighters. Since unemployment in Karachi's poor neighborhoods is unofficially estimated at 20 percent, and most who do work are in the "informal sector" (such as day laborers without strong ties to a regular employer), the city is fertile recruiting ground for the Pakistani Taliban and other insurgent, extremist, and criminal groups.

We also know that the source of terrorist attacks that killed 173 (and wounded 308) in Mumbai in 2008 originated in a specific location: Karachi. According to evidence compiled by the Indian government (including undisclosed transcripts of telephone conversations) and shared with Pakistan, ten gunmen boarded a small vessel in Karachi at 8 a.m. on November 22, before boarding a larger ship believed owned by *Lashkar-e-Taiba* (an Islamic terrorist group dedicated to an independent, Islamist Kashmir). Shortly thereafter, the gunmen commandeered an Indian fishing trawler and sailed 550 nautical miles along India's Arabian Sea coastline. The trawler reached Mumbai on the twenty-sixth. What followed was a three-day takeover of key buildings in the city and the mass murder of innocent people. The terrorists targeted Westerners and symbols of Western business. Victims were killed at hotels, a hospital, a college, and in the harbor area.

Though *Lashkar-e-Taiba* was banned in 2002, its headquarters is near Lahore, and the group has been implicated in numerous attacks in India, including the 2001 attack on the parliament, a 2002 attack on Indian border guards, and the 2005 bombing of a market in Delhi. The 2001 attack on the parliament included bombings of the building itself and an extended exchange of gunfire with Indian security personnel. Nine guards, one parliament employee, and all five of the terrorists were killed. In response to the attack, India mobilized its military along the Pakistan border, Pakistan ordered a countermobilization, and the United States had to step in to mediate the crisis in order to prevent another Indo-Pakistani war from breaking out—this time, with the potential for the first use of nuclear weapons since World War II.

After the 2008 Mumbai attacks, India quickly determined that the terrorists were Pakistanis. Despite the horror of this atrocity and evidence trailing back to Karachi, India and Pakistan did not go to the brink of war—presumably because they were chastened by the close call in 2001, because the United States was already deeply involved with both countries in fighting terrorism and was counseling restraint on both sides, and because both recognized that once the genie of war got out of the bottle there was no telling what the consequences would be.

Terrorists in Pakistan, as we know, do not always stay there and do not always attack India or Kashmir. Travel to Europe and North America from

Pakistan by air or ship is relatively inexpensive, and there have already been instances of "insecurity exports" from that country. As a result Karachi and to a lesser extent Lahore may turn out to be bases for future terrorist attacks against the West, as well as ISAF forces in Afghanistan.

CRITICAL MOMENT, WRONG INVESTMENT:
PAKISTAN'S URBAN AND RURAL PROBLEMS

Karachi and Lahore are not experiencing what we might consider growing pains. Their governments and civil organizations are long-standing political entities and not adolescents awkwardly and uncomfortably being shaped into more elegant adult bodies. Both are mature cities seriously overburdened while even greater burdens loom ahead.

Signs of trouble have been evident for some time, though more so in Karachi than Lahore. That the Pakistani government has been unable to rouse itself to address the problems is a sign that things will not improve without effective international community action. Whatever its motives, the Pakistani government has not done enough to improve urban governance, dramatically upgrade urban infrastructure, and build effective service delivery systems as populations soar. Still, much of the population will be left with little choice but to change course and attempt to correct underlying problems. Challenges will soon become insurmountable for any government, not to mention one with Pakistan's corruption and spotty record of achievement. The more likely course will see Pakistan invest instead in military and police tools to suppress antigovernment agitation and urban violence.

WHERE STRATEGIC INVESTMENT WENT ASTRAY

Historically, instead of investing in its cities, Pakistan chose to invest heavily in military capabilities. The general approach of the national government has been to concentrate on national security and keeping violence and civil disorder from toppling the status quo, rather than addressing factors that contributed to violence and disorder in the first place. Emphasis on defense is understandable, given Pakistan's obsession with the security threat coming from the giant next door—India—and the existence of separatist movements inside the state, particularly in Baluchistan. (The province itself accounts for 40 percent of Pakistan's land mass but has less than 5 percent of the population. The government attributes much of the terrorism inside Pakistan to Baluch separatists.) India and Pakistan have fought several wars in the decades since partition in 1947, one of which forced the loss in 1971 of what was then East Pakistan and now is Bangladesh. During the 1990s and again in 2001, there were crises in which both sides mobilized their militaries in response to a provocation by one side or the other. Further, there is always the possibility that Islamic terrorists not under Pakistani control could create an incident that would spark a military mobilization by India and countermobilization by Pakistan, leading to war. This is not mere speculation; it almost happened in the 2008 Mumbai attacks.

India proceeded cautiously after that attack, but that does not mean that it will be so temperate in the future. As terrorist attacks spark outrage among the public, the next time or the time after that the Indian government may feel it has no choice but to accede to public demands for a forceful response against the state where the terrorists live: Pakistan.

SPLIT PERSONALITIES

Another reason why the state's domestic agenda has not been more progressive is that factionalism among tribes, sects, classes, and political parties has made reform of governance politically difficult to sustain.

The issue that should concern us is not whether the government should have made a different choice about where it spent its money in the past. Nor is it that greater priority should have been given to building urban infrastructure, fielding capable and conscientious municipal agencies, and promoting civil sector organizations in addition to *madrassas* that can supplement services that government offered. Instead, the issue is whether steps will be initiated soon enough to mitigate oncoming effects of rapid urban growth and to improve municipal infrastructures, particularly in the state's two megacities. Given the country's track record, however, there is no reason to assume that it will spend enough or spend wisely enough to dramatically reduce poverty, improve education, and provide reliable law enforcement and responsive medical care in Karachi or Lahore. Instead, what is likely to happen is that government will make halfhearted efforts at reform that will absorb needed budgetary resources without fixing the problem and continue to emphasize national defense and suppression of insurgency.

Apart from the objective requirements for defense spending, the military's extreme influence assures that it continues to receive the lion's share of national budgets. The armed forces actually ran the Pakistan government during the 1960s and 1970s, and from 2001 to 2008 General Musharraf was the country's president. For most of his time in office, he was also army chief of staff.

The focus on national defense and on keeping the lid on the events in Karachi, Lahore, and other cities may compel Pakistan to resume a general policy that has produced adverse effects on the state itself, its neighbors, and the world at large: the benign neglect of the Federally Administered Tribal Areas (FATA), four extremely rugged and underpopulated provinces along Pakistan's border with Afghanistan. The FATA itself is a semiautonomous tribal region in the northwest, situated between the province of Khyber Pakhtunkhwa, Baluchistan, and neighboring Afghanistan. The FATA comprises seven tribal districts and six frontier regions, almost exclusively inhabited by Pashtun, Sunni Muslim tribes. Protected by their mountainous terrain, this territory has been notorious for centuries for fierce resistance to control by outsiders. In terms of how the people live, they are part of Pakistan in name only.

Rather than expend resources that would be required to tame and control them, Pakistan followed the lead of the British Raj, which allowed leading families in the provinces to run things, provided they did not interfere in the affairs of the rest of the state. As a practical matter, this approach made considerable sense, since the provinces had no important economic resources and were so sparsely populated. Only about 2 percent of the Pakistani people live in the FATA, and almost all of them live in tiny villages and isolated farms.

Pakistan and the world have learned that such a hands-off policy towards the FATA region no longer makes sense, but a Pakistan trying desperately to tame the tigers of Lahore and Karachi and fearful of the supposed military threat posed by India will not have the resources or incentives to firmly assert and maintain control over these provinces. While the provinces are worthless economically, they have assumed strategic importance in the struggle against violent extremism because they harbor Al Qa'eda and other extremist organizations.

Groups in these provinces have become part of a domestic insurgency seeking to topple the Pakistani government that, for all its faults, is at least secular and democratic, and replace it with an Islamic republic. It is unlikely that the military would allow an Islamic republic in Pakistan, but if one were established, the ripple effects would be intense. Tensions with India would jump; Islamic terrorists in Kashmir, India, and Central Asian states would be emboldened; and the West would be at a major disadvantage in the fight against insurgency in Afghanistan.

Terrorist groups and Islamic insurgents have take advantage of the provinces' autonomy and weak internal structures by setting up bases of operation and havens from which they have launched attacks into Pakistan proper and neighboring Afghanistan. Al Qa'eda relocated its bases in Afghanistan to the FATA and has continued from there to plot attacks against the West. Within Afghanistan, the deadly influence of Pakistani spillover effect—though "contagion" is the more appropriate term—is evident. Militants scrawl graffiti messages on boulders in mountain valleys posting cellphone numbers in Pakistan to call for recruitment training, weapons, and support. Sebastian Junger in his masterpiece of journalism, *War,* describes how American soldiers fighting in the Korengal Valley—the aptly named "Valley of Death," where a fifth of the combat that 70,000 NATO troops engaged in was fought by the 150 men of Battle Company that he lived with and 70 percent of the bombs dropped in Afghanistan were dropped in and around the valley in northeast Afghanistan across from the FATA—saw Pakistan:

> The men know Pakistan is the root of the entire war, and that is just about the only topic they get political about. They don't much care what happens in Afghanistan—they barely even care what happens on the Pech—but day after day they hear intel about fresh fighters coming in from Pakistan and wounded ones going out. Supposedly

there's a medical clinic in Pakistan entirely devoted to treating insurgents. Somewhere in the valley there's a jihadist graffiti, but it's in Arabic instead of Pashto because locals aren't as enthused about the war as outsiders. You don't have to be in the Army to notice that Pakistan was effectively waging war against America, but the administration back home was refusing to even acknowledge it, much less take any action. Now an American colonel is bombing Pakistani troops inside their own country and the feeling at Restrepo is, *Finally. . . .* [8]

The Afghan Taliban is also active in the provinces and has spawned a domestic offshoot, the Pakistani Taliban, which has been conducting terror operations inside Pakistan and guerrilla warfare against the government since 2007.

DIRECT ENGAGEMENT

Pakistan has had to temporarily abandon its hands-off policy due to the Taliban's guerrilla warfare operations outside the FATA provinces. Some of the most troubling fighting has occurred in the Swat Valley, which is close to the national capital, Islamabad. To counter the insurgency, the military fought back in Swat and launched attacks into the FATA where extremists were based. From the beginning it was clear that the army had neither the strength nor desire to completely eradicate insurgents and extremists in the FATA. Traditionally, Pakistan has chosen half-measures when addressing domestic insurgents—preferring compromise to an all-out fight to the finish in remote provinces where it has no interest other than maintaining the façade of sovereignty. In 2009, for example, Pakistan announced it would cease operations in the FATA, supposedly to consolidate its gains, and since then it has been reluctant to resume operations. The army had good reason for its reluctance. Pakistan was hit with devastating flooding during the summer of 2010, and the army, neck-deep in relief operations, claimed it was stretched too thin to reopen the FATA front.

The fighting in Swat in 2009 was, however, a different matter. Swat is not part of the autonomous areas, yet even there the government initially opted for half-measures. It was willing to split the difference with the insurgents by allowing the imposition of *Sharia* law in a 2009 ceasefire. (The ceasefire fell apart, and the military eventually drove the insurgents out of the area. Whether they stay out remains to be seen.)

That the government is even willing to consider compromise with the insurgents in Swat is a sign that it will not pursue a complete victory in the FATA and consequently the region will continue to be a source of instability and violence. As long as extremists in these regions avoid directly confronting government forces in areas that have not traditionally been autonomous, the government will succumb to compromise and reversion to the status quo ante in which areas functioned as ungoverned wildernesses open to exploitation by terrorists, other extremists, and criminal organizations.

On Christmas Eve 2010, in a large, precisely coordinated strike, 150 Taliban attacked Pakistani outposts manned by government paramilitary forces. Engaged in hand-to-hand combat with insurgents, eleven members of the Pakistan Frontier Corps died in a total of five separate attacks—two direct assaults on outposts in Mohmand Agency and three strikes from afar with machine guns and rockets. Insurgents had been driven into a minute mountainous area of Mohmand that adjoins the Bajaur tribal area in Pakistan and Kunar Province in eastern Afghanistan. From there, they periodically attacked Pakistani forces as well as singled out civilians allied with the government. "All the bad guys are now there," Amjad Ali Khan, the administrator of the Mohmand region, declared. "Kunar's border region has gone to the dogs due to the absence of international forces there. These guys go there and come back to launch attacks on our forward positions."[9]

Ultimately, Pakistan cannot afford to administer the territories effectively. To do so would draw desperately needed resources away from central challenges: keeping a lid on its two megacities and maintaining a military capable of defending the state against outsiders and against insurgents in the main, more populated parts of the country.

Pakistan has both a megacity problem and a rural problem. Both present security risks in addition to humanitarian concerns. Attempting to solve one will prevent any serious effort to solve the other. City hazards will demand ever more attention—that is, after all, where most voters live—and draw resources away from remote rural zones of the FATA. When the army withdraws from the FATA, as it must, autonomy and benign neglect will return, the status quo ante will be restored, and terrorists and insurgents will rely once again on provinces as havens and bases for attack.

All this begs the larger question, one U.S. policy makers have neither been blunt nor honest enough to admit: Is the real war we have been fighting—the war we will inevitably have to fight—with Pakistan?

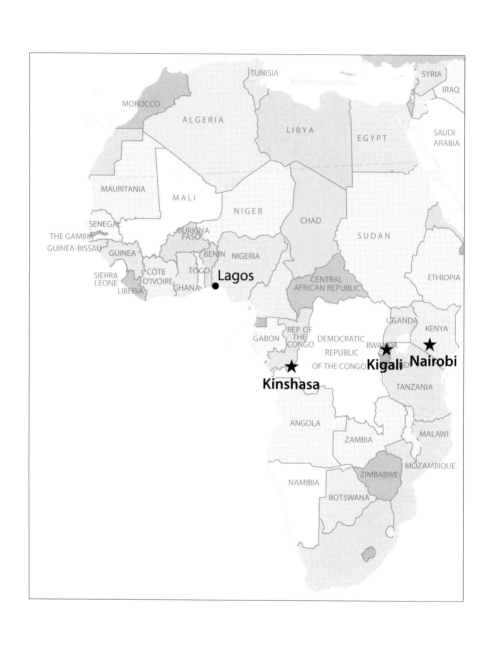

6

OIL, GUNS, AND CORPSES
Lagos and Kinshasa

Some cities are littered with garbage. Lagos is littered with corpses.
—*Harry Goldstein, "How Not to Make a Megacity"*

Kinshasa is a dead city. It is not a city of the dead.
—*Thierry Mayamba Nlandu*

Your parents named you Wole, after Africa's greatest playwright who, like you, has roots in an Egba family of the Yoruba nation. You never learned to read; you have never received an inoculation; you know no one your age who has been to school. By the time you were five, you suffered permanent "stunting" from malnutrition. You live in a city that was not among the world's thirty largest in 1990 but will be the third largest on the planet by 2014. The filth and menace of Lagos confront you every day. If a crime takes place, you must provide transportation for investigators. Police never respond or enter your "neighborhood." Raw sewage empties in the river that flows past your tin-roofed home, the same river where you fish every day for the only income you can manage. Mile after mile after mile, there's human struggle and a blighted landscape, in a country filthy rich with oil revenues.

To the extent that Lagos in Nigeria or Kinshasa in the Democratic Republic of the Congo (DRC) has ever figured prominently in any scholarly or policy discussions about major cities of the world, it is not because either has done much right. The only remarkable thing about both is the immensity of problems they face and the dire living conditions their largely uncounted residents are compelled to endure. Given their wealth of natural resources (petroleum in Nigeria and precious minerals and agricultural products in the DRC) yet virtual impoverishment for the vast majority of their citizens, three words form a brutal metaphor for their present condition: oil, guns, and corpses.

DISTINGUISHING DIFFERENCE

There are important differences between these cities, but they have much in common. Although Lagos (because of its strategic and economic importance in the most populous state in Africa) looms large, we consider here the hazards both cities face and close with observations about implications of the all-too-likely failure of Nigeria and the DRC to manage incredible population spikes in their major cities.

Perhaps the most important differences between Lagos and Kinshasa are also the most obvious. One is a major port on the Atlantic, and the other an inland metropolis. The port city, Lagos, is well connected to global markets by virtue of Nigeria's booming oil exports and the investment of foreign oil companies in and around the city. The U.S. State Department reported that in 2009, Nigeria exported more than $65 billion annually and imported $30 billion. These trade volumes are ten times amounts for the DRC.[1] Located upriver in a state that exports relatively little to the rest of the world, Kinshasa lacks fundamental economic advantages that Lagos has frittered away. The city lies a hundred miles inland on the Congo River, and the stretch between it and the Atlantic is not navigable by large ships. Goods traveling inland come by rail from the coast or by air from the exporting country.

Lagos is the largest city and economic nerve center in a state that is economically and strategically important to the world and in particular to Africa.[2] With its relatively large economy, Nigeria looms large in West Africa;

what happens in Lagos can have critical international impact. Kinshasa is the largest city in a state that ought to be important—if only because of the high value of its abundant natural resources—but isn't. At least for now.

Lagos and Nigeria are relatively stable, but the same cannot be said for the DRC. It has been torn apart by civil war and interstate conflict for much of its life as an independent state, so it is difficult to say that instability in Kinshasa will have the same strategic or economic effects as instability in Lagos. Some of these effects are already being felt thanks to persistent civil war in the country's easternmost provinces, which has been continuous since the mid-1990s.[3] UN peacekeepers have attempted to restore order in the region since 1999. The peacekeeping force itself is the single largest peacekeeping mission in the world, numbering nineteen thousand troops. The only larger peacekeeping presence is in Sudan where there are two separate missions.

Nigeria has also had separatist movements, and it is currently struggling with insurgents in the oil-rich Niger Delta region, but it has not experienced foreign intervention in the same way that the DRC has. From 1996 through 2003, military forces from Uganda, Rwanda, and Burundi operated inside DRC borders, fighting alongside indigenous client militias and creating militias where none existed. While in country, Ugandan, Rwandan, and Burundi forces helped topple the national government and at the same time smuggled important natural resources out of the country for private gain. A UN panel evaluated the extent of the mineral smuggling and found that not only was there "mass scale looting" of mineral stockpiles, but that Ugandan and Rwandan forces actually conducted their own mining and logging operations inside the DRC.[4] Among resources that were mined, logged, or looted were gold, lumber, copper, diamonds, and coltan (a metallic ore used in cell phones and other consumer electronics).[5] This is a critical issue as the economies of emerging giants such as China, India, and Brazil surge ahead and the economies of North America and Europe rebound, global demand for the DRC's natural resources unquestionably increase. As long as the state is unable to police its borders and regulate economic activity in its hinterlands, temptation for future interventions can prove irresistible and involve powers far more dangerous than Uganda and Rwanda.

DIVERSE DYNAMICS

Nigeria and the DRC and their two major cities are also similar in other respects. Both have remarkably diverse populations. Numerous ethnic groups, religions, languages, and European-drawn borders that did not reflect the realities (or desires) of those who actually lived there have all compromised efforts to form a national identity in both states. Then, too, both are relative newcomers to the club of independent states. Both states secured independence in 1960 and were, almost immediately, forced to confront separatist conflicts and political turmoil. Nigeria fought the Biafran War (also called the Nigerian Civil War) with separatists in the southeastern part of the country from 1967 to 1970 and endured numerous military coups throughout the 1960s and 1970s. The DRC (then called the Republic of the Congo) had its own civil wars and military coups in the 1960s, and in 1965 the government was taken over by a corrupt dictator who ruled the state for thirty-two years. The state's new leader, Joseph-Désiré Mobutu, led a regime that was patently corrupt—and continuing corruption is common to both the DRC and Nigeria.

Mobutu also led a campaign to bring the DRC back to what he perceived as its African roots and eliminate vestiges of colonial influences. This campaign took peculiar turns. Families were instructed to adopt African names, and Mobutu led by absurd example, adopting as his moniker Mobutu Sese Seko Nkuku Ngbendu wa Za Banga, which translates as "the All-Powerful Warrior Who, Because of His Endurance and Inflexible Will to Win, Goes from Conquest to Conquest, Leaving Fire in His Wake." More simply, he just called himself "the Supreme Guide." Mobutu changed the name of the state to Zaire, a name that stuck until 1997. While Nigeria was spared the indignity of such misguided flamboyance, it has endured decades of military coups and countercoups, running through each change of government to see only continued corruption and mismanagement.

As with other states we have considered, Nigeria and the DRC faced serious challenges while taking first steps as independent nations. Most pressing were the threats separatist movements posed to national unity; understandably, emerging states treated these threats as their most pressing concerns. Efforts to hold the country physically together drew at least a decade's worth of attention away from other work that might have been accomplished, such as building domestic infrastructure and institutions of governance necessary for the needs of the people. Other challenges included cultures of corruption and divided loyalties among population groups with very different perspectives about governance, particularly when it came to *another* group dominating government and making decisions about distribution of resources.

Nigeria and the DRC should not be excused for their failures at building needed institutions and infrastructure, yet we should understand the pressures that governments of these (and other) newly independent states faced. The roots of many problems in Lagos and Kinshasa stem from decisions made in the 1960s. The conditions of these states' first decade(s) helped establish patterns of governance that led to decades of underinvestment in the kinds of social programs that might have prevented Lagos and Kinshasa from becoming virtually ungoverned—a status both cities are on the verge of achieving.

CHOKING TO DEATH

Surrounded by vast amounts of valuable natural resources, both cities have become sweltering swamps of grinding poverty, deprivation, crime, and violence. Events in these cities will do more than shake the windows of their national governments and rattle the walls of the sub-Saharan region. Since Nigeria is more strategically important from the perspective of the global economy and international security (with the continent's largest population, its third largest economy, one of Africa's biggest militaries, and straddling one of the fault lines between the Muslim and non-Muslim world), we will focus primarily on Lagos and then conclude with observations of Kinshasa.

From the perspective of a satellite hovering over the coast of West Africa at an altitude of two hundred miles, Lagos appears as a brown triangle wedged into seas of inland green and coastal blue. From ground level, however, much less benign images are impossible to ignore. Famous for its air, water, and noise pollution, the city assaults the senses—all of them. Vast amounts of solid waste are burned in unregulated pits, and the streets are choked with millions of old cars without emission controls. *National Geographic* described Lagos' traffic jams as "staggering," and not surprisingly: air pollution is so wretched that there has been a ten-fold increase in the number of citizens who visit hospitals due for respiratory complaints. The actual increase is undoubtedly higher, as many residents are too poor to afford the trip, are too far from the nearest facility, or simply prefer folk remedies.

The quality of Lagos' water is no better than its air. The city lies on land low enough to be frequently flooded by saltwater from ocean storms—Lagos is situated at the head of an outlet to the Atlantic Ocean—and by overflow from the lagoon that borders much of the city. The Lagos Lagoon is a shallow, thirty-mile-long lake of brackish water fed by the Niger River, whose currents flow south through the city harbor into the Atlantic. (The name of the city is from the Portuguese word for "lakes.") The lagoon itself is badly polluted thanks to years of dumping untreated human waste and is unsuitable for drinking or fishing. Yet fishing is one of the main occupations of city residents. During the rainy season, the lagoon floods and polluted saltwater spreads onto the land, fouling fields and crops. Moreover, the lagoon overflows and seawater from storms has been gradually seeping into the groundwater that is the source of the city's drinking water.

As serious as environmental issues are, they were not the primary reason that in 2009 *BusinessWeek* magazine rated Lagos as the "hardest hardship place" in the world where an expatriate can work: "Lagos not only has a severe crime problem and extremely poor infrastructure, the city has inadequate housing, sanitation, and medical facilities. . . . The risk of being caught up in sectarian violence is another concern."[6]

One telling example of infrastructure failings, from the perspective of someone who does not have to live there, is the occasional reports of business travelers experiencing multiple blackouts at the airport while waiting at baggage claim and then having to be driven to the city with armed escorts, past burnt-out hulks of abandoned cars lining the road like bleached skulls in Death Valley—and miles of depressing slums.

Jeffrey Taylor in the *Atlantic Monthly* describes Lagos as "de-developing" in the sense that its infrastructure is collapsing beneath the weight of neglect and corruption:

> A drive across Lagos . . . reveals unmitigated chaos. The government
> has left roads to decay indefinitely. Thugs clear away the broken as-

phalt and then extract payments from drivers, using chunks of rubble to enforce their demands. Residents dig up the pavement to lay cables that tap illegally into state power lines. Armed robbers emerge from the slums to pillage cars stuck in gridlocks (aptly named "hold-ups" in regional slang) so impenetrable that the fourteen-mile trip from the airport to the city center can take four hours.[7]

HOW MANY PEOPLE ARE THERE?

As is often the case for a city that has grown too fast for its parent government, no one knows exactly how many people live in Lagos. The Nigerian government has attempted to collect census data but has been heavily criticized for shorting the count in what everyone knows is Nigeria's largest city by far. Some of the reasons for undercounting may be political. Lagos is not administered by a single government. The city instead is divided into five separate administrations independent of each other—much as New York City's boroughs but without an overarching mayor and city council to oversee the city. The national government may not actually want to know how many Nigerians live in Lagos. If true figures were known, there could be even greater political pressure upon the Nigerian government to pay closer attention to Lagos' chaotic and squalid conditions. After all, one of the reasons that the Nigerian capital was switched from Lagos to the new city of Abuja in 1991 was to put some distance between the national government and the city it was unable to manage.

Official UN population data estimates that the city contains about 11 million people today; other estimates place the number beyond 17 million. The differences are related not only to the practical complexity and expense of counting heads in a megacity. (The United States spent about $15 billion for its 2010 decennial census and still could not guarantee a completely accurate population count.) Some estimates address the city proper, others the wider metropolitan area. For our purposes, the latter is the more important since our focus is on the challenges that massive urban population centers are causing and will cause in the future until better governed and provided with essential public services. Kinshasa's current population is estimated at 10 million, and there has not been a census there for more than two decades—the two decades in which the city's growth has been dramatic.

Lagos' population is not only huge and densely packed—it is projected to continue growing at a rapid pace. By 2025 it will grow to 25 million in the city itself and metropolitan area. By some estimates, Kinshasa proper will be slightly larger, although Kinshasa's metropolitan area is more rural than Lagos'. If this occurs and if both cities' populations continue to be underserved and undergoverned—as will be the case barring effective action soon—direct effects will be powerful and indirect effects on West Africa and the rest of the world will be substantial.

There are only three cities in the world with higher population densities than Lagos: Mumbai, Kolkata, and Karachi. (Kinshasa includes a large amount of rural land, so citywide density is lower.) Conditions in Mumbai and Kolkata are by no means perfect, but the Indian government has demonstrated the ability to promote vigorous economic growth and keep a lid on disorder and crime that plague Lagos and, as we have considered, Karachi. Density statistics are as questionable scientifically as overall population data—for basically the same reasons. They do, nevertheless, give at least a rough order of magnitude to compare cities and social pressures they face. The population density of Lagos is estimated to be two or three times higher than the most crowded cities of Western Europe and the United States. Madrid and London rank forty-second and forty-third among the world's most densely populated metropolises, compared to Lagos' fourth. New York City ranks one hundred and fourteenth. Moreover, New York City's population density has been decreasing ever since the heyday of European immigration in the nineteenth century, whereas Lagos continues to not only grow but become more crowded due primarily to migration from rural areas.

ANOMIE AND ANARCHY

One might think of crowding as contributing to and being a consequence of urban bustle: commuters going to work, people being drawn to the shops, restaurants, and cultural centers, and their collective presence creating service jobs for local residents. This image does not apply to Lagos, although there are commuters and shoppers. In Lagos bustle is the jostling of disgruntled and resentful citizens. Lagos swarms with violence, crime, and civil disturbance.

Street gangs, ethnic and religious militias, and criminals have virtual free rein in much of the city. Guns are everywhere. The only thing of value distributed evenly across social classes is weapons. A study that the United Kingdom's Department for International Development and Bradford University's Center for International Cooperation and Security funded in 2005 found that small arms and light weapons were freely available throughout the city. It also found that the various armed gangs in Lagos were engaged in what amounts to an arms race among themselves, and between themselves and the police, to acquire more lethal weapons. According to reports, gangs have done well in the municipal arms race: their members tote AK-47 assault rifles and sport bulletproof vests. Presumably this is one reason why police rarely enter slums and rely instead upon periodic heavy-handed action in other parts of the city. In the early 2000s, for example, crime was so rampant police adopted a shoot-to-kill policy. Later claims suggested that this brought surging crime rates under control, but the effect was largely temporary, since conditions that bred the crime wave were never corrected.

Residents of Lagos' pervasive slums know they cannot rely on police to enforce the law. Even in better neighborhoods, residents have had to pay transportation costs for detectives to come to the scene to investigate a crime, in effect making victims pay twice for the privilege of having been robbed. No wonder then that neighborhoods occasionally experience outbreaks of vigilantism. A particularly grisly form of instant justice (as in Nairobi) is "necklacing," in which a tire is flung around the neck of a miscreant, doused with gasoline, and then set on fire. Fighting between ethnic and religious groups is also common in the city and in the countryside as well, notably in the northern provinces on the Muslim side of the Muslim-Christian fault line.

Pervasive crime and civil disorder are serious matters. They impose high costs on the population; the longer they continue, the more they corrode public confidence and trust in government agencies. Once lost, confidence and trust are difficult to restore. Crime and disorder deter potential investors and entrepreneurs who might otherwise establish factories or open businesses that could soak up Lagos' countless unemployed. Thus, when crime and dis-order become widespread, huge opportunity costs (lost jobs, lost incomes) are created as investors and entrepreneurs move to safer, more stable locations.

SOCIOECONOMIC DEPRIVATION

Law enforcement is hardly the only public service in short supply in Lagos, and poverty is rampant. It is difficult to disaggregate statistics on the city from national statistics (themselves imprecise) on the extent of poverty and illiter-acy. One would expect the literacy rate to be better in cities than in the coun-try as a whole given the requirements of modern commerce and the types of jobs that people hold, or at least aspire to. Yet the poverty rate is perhaps even worse in the city since rural communities can live off the land, which resi-dents of a city with polluted lakes and rivers simply cannot do.

UN statistics on the social conditions in Nigeria paint a grim picture. The UN has ranked 169 countries according to its "Human Development Index," which factors in the overall population's life expectancy, standard of living, and level of education. By this standard, Nigeria ranks among the worst, 144 out of 169. (The DRC ranks even worse, 168 out of 169.) This ranking stands as testament to the Nigerian government's failure to invest in public health, medical care, and education, and to create conditions that encourage eco-nomic growth and employment such as better crime control, tighter restric-tions on corruption, and public sector infrastructure for roads and intracity bus networks. In 2009 UN reports claimed 60 percent of Nigerians had in-comes of less than $1.25 a day, despite the state's wealth in natural resources, which has been riding the boom in oil prices since the late 1990s.[8] The U.S. State Department estimates that real per capita income of Nigerians is actu-ally lower today than it was in the 1970s. To put this in perspective, incomes in most parts of the world have risen sharply over the same time period. In the United States, incomes have tripled since the 1970s.

At birth the average Nigerian has a 60 percent chance of living to age forty.[9] The average life expectancy is, of course, also low: forty-seven years. This is 30 percent worse than the world average—among the lowest life ex-pectancies in the world. Only thirteen countries have life expectancy statistics lower than oil-rich Nigeria. (UN estimates claim that the average for the DRC, with its civil wars in which millions have been violently killed or starved, is similar to Nigeria. While U.S. government estimates suggest that the average for the DRC is about eight years higher than in Nigeria, the DRC's remains substantially below the global average.)

Malnutrition rates for children are another useful measure of a state's quality of life. By such standards, Nigeria fares poorly. Thirty-eight percent of children under five are "stunted," having not developed physically at a normal rate. Twenty-nine percent are underweight. Infant mortality rates per thousand births are 10 percent higher than the average for all sub-Saharan countries and 50 percent higher than the average for all middle-income countries. While statistics for the DRC are comparable, they are more understandable than Nigeria's statistics. War is a great disrupter of agriculture and other economic enterprises. War brings death and disease. People flee their homes, garden plots, and support systems and, in so doing, sow seeds of future poverty and deprivation. Brutal conflict, which has engulfed the eastern parts of the DRC from the late 1990s—and continues in various forms of disruption even today—has contributed to high infant mortality and malnutrition rates and low life expectancies. The DRC's dismal statistics can be partially explained as a consequence of war; Nigeria's cannot.

UN estimates claim the Nigerian government spends only $15 per capita on health and the DRC slightly less than that. This is less than many nearby African states spend and far less than what developed nations spend. Health expenditures account for 5 percent of Nigeria's government budget (4 percent of the DRC's budget)—less than half what most African governments, and a small fraction of what developed state governments, spend. The UN has not reported on Nigeria's investment in education, presumably because Nigeria could not compile necessary data. One could speculate that public education has not kept pace with the population growth, since almost 40 percent of the adult population in Nigeria is illiterate.[10] (The rate is worse for the DRC.) With respect to health care and education, two primary public services, Nigeria is getting what it pays for, to the detriment of the economy and the living standards of the people.

PLAGUES OF WAR AND OPEN THEFT

Nigeria has been forced to play catch-up with the challenge of providing services to the burgeoning mass of humanity in Lagos. There are three broad
reasons for this. All three apply to both Lagos and Kinshasa.

First, Nigeria's and the DRC's initial primary domestic priority after independence was building institutions of governance at the national level. While
there are reasons to question the extent to which their efforts actually yielded
effective national institutions, the initial focus on establishing a national government made sense given that both countries had so many different ethnic
and language groups and their borders were drawn by colonialists inattentive to the wishes of the people and ignorant of natural frontiers between
different ethnic groups. After both states had been independent for only a
short while, nascent national governments were confronted with secessionist
rebellions. While minorities in the Katanga and Kasai provinces attempted to
break away from the DRC, the more serious threat was in Nigeria. The Biafran
War lasted more than two and a half years, and rebels received aid and even
diplomatic recognition from several African states before the Nigerian military was able to suppress the rebellion. The rebels were based in southeastern
Nigeria, the same part of the nation that today is roiled with dissatisfaction
with the status quo and that witnesses periodic bursts of antigovernment violence. This is also where the state's most precious economic resources, its oil
fields, are located.

The war ended in 1970, and the immediate postwar priority was building
national—not municipal—institutions such as the army, which increasingly
dominated Nigerian politics for the next three decades. Numerous military
coups took place, and consequences included disastrous economic and social
policies, extensive corruption, and overinvestment in the symbols of national
government—principally the military and a temporarily glittering new capital, Abuja. Another glaring example of Nigeria's economic mismanagement
and misguided priorities was the construction of a $300 million soccer sta-
dium in 2001. The tab exceeded the combined national budgets for education
and health for that year. Military coups took place in the DRC as well, but in

the mid-1960s Mobutu took over and maintained power for decades, managing through corruption, patronage, and heavy-handed repression to incompetently guide his country on a steady glide path to wretched living standards.

Until recently, the Nigerian economy did not generate enough revenue for the government to seriously address social issues such as the lack of health care and an inadequate educational system. According to the World Bank, in 1960 the Nigerian GDP was $4 billion, and grew sluggishly through the 1990s, apart from a short spike in 1980 when oil prices skyrocketed. Nigeria's GDP did not consistently exceed $50 billion until 2002, but since then has continued to climb as oil prices have soared and remained high.

Even as Nigeria's oil revenues have surged to unparalleled heights, the per capita incomes of Nigerians have fallen—by as much as 60 percent—as corruption and government misspending siphoned off profits into the hands of a tiny sliver of the population or into misguided development schemes. Thus, despite substantial inflow in oil revenues, the state has consistently been a "bottom feeder" on the UN's Human Development Index. Per capita incomes in DRC have taken roughly the same distressing trajectory—and for the same reasons: corruption and inept economic decision making. In 1990 the per capita income in DRC was $250; today it is less than a third of that.

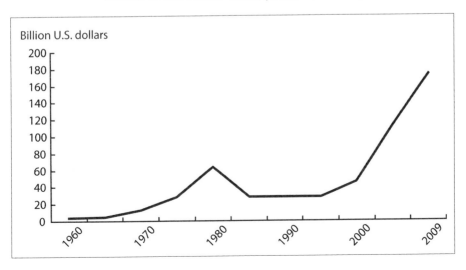

NIGERIA'S GDP: 1960–2010 (World Bank data)

LAGOS' POPULATION: 1960–2010 (World Bank data)

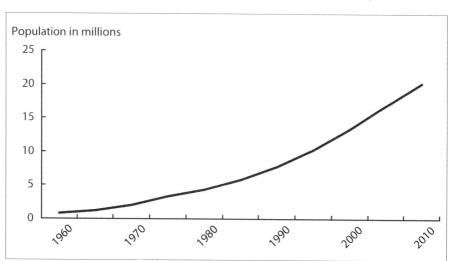

There is striking resemblance between the slope of the growth for Nigeria's GDP as shown here and the upslope of population growth in the Lagos metropolitan area.

In both examples, we see that growth spurts occurred simultaneously, at the end of the twentieth century. This suggests that the state's economy began to generate substantial revenues at the same time as Lagos' population began to soar. These two trends are related. People were more likely to migrate from the countryside to the city when the economy was growing and the prospects for jobs and other economic opportunities seemed relatively bright. The exceedingly rapid surge in Lagos' population occurred just as Nigeria was beginning to adjust to increased economic growth and revenue sparked by rising demand for oil and attendant rising prices. Since urban population and government revenues grew roughly simultaneously, revenue was not available ahead of time for government to prepare the city for managing itself. While likely that urban conditions would have been improved had revenues been invested in infrastructure and institutions of governance, it seems unlikely that investments would actually have been made in Lagos for a variety of reasons, one of which must have been reasonable uncertainty about long-term trends in energy prices. The spike in oil prices in 1979 and

1980 did not, after all, last, and the state's GDP fell off its early 1980s peak and did not rebound until the late 1990s.

WHERE EVERYTHING CAN BE BOUGHT AND EVERYTHING IS FOR SALE

Kinshasa's greatest growth has been recent as well. By 2025 the city's population will swell to 17 million and the effects of overpopulation on the region's environment will be amplified by the presence of another 3 million people in the cross-river twin city, Brazzaville, the capital of the Republic of the Congo—sometimes known as Congo-Brazzaville.

UN estimates suggest that in 1950, Kinshasa's population was less than two hundred thousand and lower than 2 million as recently as 1975.[11] This means that the city's population grew by fifty times over the course of only sixty years. If Newark, New Jersey, which had a population of less than 450,000 in 1950, had grown at the same rate, its equivalent population would today be 22 million, two and a half times the population of the entire state and 10 percent larger than the entire population of New York state. As we know, Newark's population has being shrinking steadily since 1950, and even so the city has not been up to the task of providing the kind of public services its population merits despite strong governing institutions at the state and national government levels—advantages that did not accrue to Kinshasa. Although the DRC is rich in natural resources, there was no equivalent to an oil boom in its export commodities during the time when Kinshasa's population was doubling, tripling, then doubling again and again. Overly rapid population growth in any city would strain even an established, more effective governmental structure. But there can be no doubt that the Nigerian and DRC governments' inadequate response has not only allowed the conditions to worsen—it has created a culture of dissatisfaction with the government itself and distrust of its motives. In Kinshasa under "Zaireanization," little was done to bridge the chasm between La Ville kleptocracy of the *blancs* and La Cité of the *noirs*.[12] As former dictator Mobutu once declared, "[This a place] where everything is for sale and everything can be bought."

Distrust reflects in widespread allegations, for example, of electoral fraud that invariably follow every Nigerian election and in recent opinion polls. In

2000, 84 percent of respondents reported being satisfied with their government. (The poll was taken at a time of great optimism shortly after the military relinquished power in 1999.) By 2006 public opinion had flip-flopped: 75 percent of respondents expressed dissatisfaction. Public opinion polling in the 2000 to 2008 timeframe indicates that dissatisfaction existed at the local government level as well. In 2000, 60 percent of the public expressed confidence in local governments—theoretically the level of government closest to and most accountable to the population. From 2004 to 2008, the number has hovered near the 18-to-28 percent range. Substantial majorities report that their local governments had done "fairly badly" or "very badly" at providing basic public functions such as trash collection and maintaining roads. Sixty-eight percent believed that local governments did fairly or very badly at "guaranteeing that local government revenues are used for public services and not private gain." In other words, the public was convinced that decades of concern about corruption and international pressure for reform had made no difference.

Another poll found that 60 percent of the population believed that "most" or "all" local government officials were involved in corruption. Corruption in Nigeria is widely regarded as an inevitable and ubiquitous feature of the landscape. As one observer puts it, corruption is pandemic, affecting every level of society and every geographic region. In 2007, governors of thirty-one of Nigeria's thirty-six states were under federal investigation for corruption, visible examples of the geographic breadth of the problem. U.S. Secretary of State Hillary Clinton observed that Nigerian corruption was "unbelievable," and she recounted an incident that occurred when speaking at a public meeting in the Nigeria capital in 2009. Attendees in the town hall–type meeting "were literally standing and shouting about what it was like to live in a country where the elite was so dominant, where the corruption was so rampant and the criminality was so pervasive."[13]

Distrust of government can also be seen in criticism leveled at the census for deliberately undercounting residents of Lagos and in the street battles that erupted during April 2007 elections. Forty people were killed in fighting between groups concerned that that outcome would unfairly favor other groups. Tellingly, the police inspector-general opined that the forty deaths was actually a lower total than he expected.

Distrust is perhaps even more a factor in the DRC where for decades the government was renowned for its corruption, cronyism, human rights abuses, and incompetence. For much of the history of the DRC's independence, national authorities in Kinshasa proved competent at only one thing: looting government coffers and the state's natural resources. By the 1990s the Mobutu regime began to fail even at that as a rebellion in the east eventually ousted the president, and his successor, Laurent-Désiré Kabila, was assassinated four years later in an attempted coup in 2001. As one result, the national government lost control not only over large swathes of the countryside but even over its own army. (In September 1991, for example, Kinshasan slum dwellers engaged in widespread, massive, and celebratory pillaging of warehouses, factories, and stores—with full army collusion. Under the pressures of runaway hyperinflation and a bankrupt labor market, many resorted to anomie with vigorous enthusiasm.) The DRC military, in parts of the country, functions more or less as a private militia, serving its own bureaucratic goals and the selfish interests of some of its senior commanders. Too often these goals have been served at the expense of the rights of the civilian population. The population in the DRC views the military as predatory and abusive, much as it would an invading army or rebel militias that terrorize villagers.

Consequences of this distrust and of the rampant corruption and violence will only make problems in Nigeria and Lagos and the DRC and Kinshasa virtually insurmountable and ever more complex to resolve. The yawning gap between the fast-growing needs of the people and the slow or often declining capacity of municipal and national governments will only worsen.

Consider the truth. Described by its inhabitants as *cadavre* or *épave* ("cadaver," "wreck"), Kinshasa is called *Kin-la-poubelle*—"Kinshasa, the garbage can," where less than 5 percent earn a regular salary.[14] The so-called parallel economy is the actual one, where its people—*les Kinois*—survive by haggling, tending minuscule vegetable plots, buying whatever they can, selling whatever they've got, and living by their endless wits. Anthropologist Filip De Boeck observes in "Kinshasa: Tales of the 'Invisible City' and the Second World" in the edited work *Under Siege*:

Why continue the social convenience of referring to a banknote as "money" when one is confronted daily with the fact that it is just a worthless slip of paper? What is the use of distinguishing between formal and informal or parallel economies when the informal has become the common and the formal has almost disappeared?[15]

Congo specialist Theodore Trefon, who directs the contemporary history section at the Royal Museum for Central Africa, writes "the population [in Kinshasa] refers to basic public services as 'memories.'"[16] Two-thirds of residents earn less per day than necessary for basic nutrition. In 2003 average income had fallen below $100 annually, most residents were malnourished, the middle class was extinct, and one in five was HIV-positive. Situated on the banks of the world's second greatest river, the poor paid 600 percent more for vendor water than they would for piped-in water. The cost is so exorbitant that, as one observer notes, "water in Kinshasa is as rare as it is in the Sahara."[17] *Se débrouiller* is the unofficial city slogan: "To cope in spite of all."

Coming to seek their economy of fortune, many who migrated to or resided in Kinshasa found themselves caught up in a desperate fury of diversion: horse betting, bottle-cap games from soft-drink companies, and lotteries from breweries. Ultimately—as happened with economic collapse in Albania in 1997—a pyramid money scheme, which the military secretly controlled, brought gifts and loot to initial investors and inevitable catastrophe to the much more numerous late entrants.

In the abyss of absence that is Kinshasa, *Kinois* must negotiate their own paths. In a wondrous turn, poet Thierry Mayamba Nlandu writes, "The shanties, too, sing Kinshasa" while also asking, "How do these millions survive the incoherent, miserable life of Kinshasa?"[18] With no functioning city to inhabit, residents have formed their own smaller communities, similar to those in the thousands of villages many have migrated from. Anthropologist René Devisch, who has worked with Filip De Boeck, argues that ordinary *Kinois* seek to escape *yimbeefu kya mboongu*—the fatal illness of money. Outcomes can take bizarre twists, such as the rise of shamanism and Pentecostal sects that encompass (or, rather, assimilate) elements of tribal, cultural, and traditional rituals. In absence of any social structure, *Kinois* are creating their own forms of order, organization, and purpose.

Mike Davis details in *Planet of Slums* the attraction of faith healing and gospels of prosperity, which offer alternatives to nonexistent, or at least non-functioning, social structures, as well as hold out the promise of the "world to come," one that strips away poverty and inequality. Drawing on Devisch's lectures and papers, Davis illustrates how such "mother-centered communities" provide *Kinois* a moral center, worth, nesting, and a sense of home. Such practices assimilate the appeal of animism while holding out the promise of Christian reward.[19]

Inevitably, there is a darker side as well. With the erosion of social order and the inability of *Kinois* to provide basic or sustainable care for themselves and their families, Pentecostals portray their faith as a kind of angelic armor against witchcraft. Perversely, belief in the fictional character Harry Potter—and his world of sorcerers and witchcraft—has turned literal in Kinshasa. Thousands of children, some of them infants, became victims of mass-hysteria accusations that they were witches. In the Ndjili slum, residents claimed that flocks of children flew about at night on broomsticks. Children also fed into this frenzy. In a piece written for *The Courier* (the official magazine of African, Caribbean, Pacific, and European Union cooperation and relations) titled "Growing up on the Streets of Kinshasa," Vincent Beeckman describes one boy's hallucinatory beliefs:

> I've eaten 800 men. I make them have accidents, in planes or cars. I even went to Belgium thanks to a mermaid who took me all the way to the port of Antwerp. Sometimes I travel by broomstick, other times on an avocado skin. At night, I'm 30 and I have 100 children. My father lost his job as an engineer because of me—then I killed him with the mermaid. I also killed my brother and sister. I buried them alive. I also killed all of my mother's unborn children.[20]

WHAT RESOURCE WEALTH DOES AND DOESN'T DO

It's been said that "as Nigeria goes, so goes West Africa." (No one says that about the DRC in relation to Central Africa, of course, since the state has been a basket case for decades.) While there is much to this observation, it does not fully convey the importance of the country and its largest city. Nigeria is the most populous state in Africa, and it has the third highest GDP on the continent, after South Africa and Egypt. Plainly, collapse or serious disorder in Nigeria will have dramatic ripple effects on its neighbors and African trading partners. Moreover, the Nigerian economy is well connected to the West in general and the United States in particular. Despite the harsh conditions for expatriates working in country, many important American, European, and Asian corporations conduct operations there. Many, such as the oil companies Shell and ExxonMobil, develop oil fields and refine petroleum products for export to the West. Others, such as Cisco Systems, sell telecommunications and computer equipment and expertise to a government flush with oil revenues and in desperate need of infrastructure improvement. They are drawn to Nigeria for the same reason that Nigeria is well connected to Western economies: oil and the profits from the oil trade.

Nigeria is a major supplier of petroleum products to the United States. According to U.S. Department of Energy statistics, more than half (52 percent) of Nigeria's oil exports are sold to the United States; only Canada, Mexico, Saudi Arabia, and Venezuela export more oil to the United States than Nigeria. Over 90 percent of Nigeria's export earnings and 40 percent of government revenue derives from levies on the oil industry.[21] When exports and prices boom, as they have in recent years, government revenues soar. Nigeria has thus done well in terms of economic policy by reducing foreign debt to low levels. Reducing debt, however, does little for the living standards of ordinary people—although it could help create the conditions for improvements in the future *if* the infrastructure were upgraded substantially; violence, crime, and corruption were curtailed; and other progrowth economic policies were adopted. The DRC lacks the reliability of revenue from high oil reserves, but has abundant natural resources that could promote a balanced economy. The problem is that neither Nigeria nor the DRC have demonstrated genuine commitment to improving governance and infrastructure overall, in particular in their most important cities.

Because growth has taken place and was not attended to, both Lagos and Kinshasa have requirements their respective governments cannot satisfy. Over the next two decades, shortfalls in hospitals, clinics, sewage facilities, police stations, schools, and trained personnel to man them will only grow—even assuming national governments are committed to "doing the right thing." Tragically, this assumption, history suggests, remains unwarranted.

WHY AFRICA MATTERS

While acknowledging the intense investment, involvement, and attention the People's Republic of China has shown Africa, global strategic focus on the continent will, and ought to, only grow. While West Africa is a region that has historically been a strategic afterthought for the economically advanced states of Europe and North America—even during the era of the slave trade when slaving stations dotted the coastline and in the nineteenth century when the European colonial powers "scrambled" with each other for control over hunks of African territory—the region has received little attention in terms of applied foreign policy. Once Britain, France, and Germany established their slave trading stations or colonies, attention quickly reverted back to Europe where larger foreign policies issues were always found. Robert Kaplan, in his seminal article "The Coming Anarchy," depicts West Africa as a wasteland of irrational violence and unmanageable chaos; the region, nonetheless, has stabilized and at the same time assumed considerably new importance.

Stabilization occurred for a number of reasons. Two are the continued march toward economic globalization and economic growth in major sectors such as China and India, which have created markets for the region's products, particularly natural resources. Another reason is intervention by peacekeepers and mediators from the UN and the Economic Community of West African States (more commonly referred to as ECOWAS), the most experienced and capable regional peacekeeping organization in Africa. Peacekeeping missions by the UN and ECOWAS contributed to the termination of civil wars in Sierra Leone, Liberia, Côte d'Ivoire, and the DRC. West Africa's heightened strategic importance is in particular the result of the discovery of major oil reserves in the Gulf of Guinea.

While Nigeria is already a major supplier of oil, the Gulf of Guinea has been estimated to contain the world's largest deepwater reserves. Though not as large as reserves in Saudi Arabia, they are unquestionably large enough to make a major difference in world oil markets. This is of particular importance to the United States because West African oil is closer than Persian Gulf oil.

West African oil is also of higher quality and can be refined more inexpensively. As a result, American oil companies are investing heavily in the development of Gulf of Guinea reserves and will continue to do so for many years. Naturally, as reserves are more fully exploited, Nigeria and its neighbors will become even more critical sources of energy for world markets. The Gulf of Guinea itself will be home to high-value and environmentally sensitive drilling platforms, oil tankers, deepwater-drilling service and supply vessels.

These assets need to be protected—something currently beyond the capability or capacity of local navies and maritime patrols. Piracy is already an issue along the coast of West Africa. There has been a three-fold increase in recent piracy in Nigerian waters—troubling but not nearly as serious an issue—yet—as off the Somali coast. Oil tankers and drilling platforms could become targets for terrorists and antigovernment insurgents.

Nigeria, by virtue of its leadership role, size, and dominant economy, will have to play a central role in ensuring the safety of the oil-drilling, refining, and export operations in the Gulf of Guinea. It is not prepared to play this role; none of the countries in the region are. That is why the United States and some of its NATO allies have established the African Partnership Station (APS) program. Under APS, West African navies and maritime forces, are offered training and military exercises with each other and the naval forces of the United States and NATO. The objective is to promote regional stability. The program's existence signifies that West African oil reserves matter.

Training sailors in navies with little or no offshore capabilities, however, will not be enough to keep the oil flowing smoothly out of the Gulf of Guinea. Countries in the region will need to invest more heavily in military tools they need to protect growing offshore oil industries. Given the competing priorities that the Nigerian government will face in the future, it's hard to see where resources will come from for Nigeria to professionalize and upgrade its maritime forces. The most pressing social problems will continue to be separatism and the social ills afflicting Lagos.

The primary instrument that the Nigerian government uses to prevent separatism and to contain ethnic fighting is the army, and there is no reason to suppose this will change any time soon. One thing that may change is Nigeria's commitment to international peacekeeping missions. In 2009 Nigeria contributed troops to eight different UN peacekeeping missions—its largest troop contingents going to Liberia and the Darfur region of Sudan. Nigeria has also been the main troop contributor to ECOWAS peacekeeping missions. The time is coming, nonetheless, when the state will no longer be able to afford the "luxury" of peacekeeping and will instead have to focus military energies on domestic stability and even reduce military spending to free up resources for social programs, improvements in urban infrastructure, and the construction of effective governance structure for Lagos. This will be an unfortunate, but necessary, consequence of the domestic pressures that are building on the Nigerian government.

While Nigeria's peacekeeping forces have been criticized for human rights abuses and playing favorites in the ECOWAS mission to Sierra Leone, overall the state has played a constructive role in building African peacekeeping capabilities. They are critical players in the peacekeeping game, since the UN has repeatedly demonstrated inability or unwillingness to respond effectively to humanitarian emergencies in Africa. The capabilities of the African Union and especially ECOWAS help fill the gap between UN intentions and actions.

CHALLENGES AHEAD

This is not to say that the Nigerian military has been remarkably effective at maintaining domestic tranquility since civilian authorities assumed control a decade or so ago. There have been repeated insurgencies in the oil-rich Niger Delta, and the military has not been able to pacify the area. In practice this has meant that existing oil facilities are frequently attacked and oil workers kidnapped; soldiers, too, have been taken hostage. The army's counterinsurgency efforts too often have amounted to attacks on villages that do little more than inflame antigovernment feelings among affected peoples. Criticism of the military for human rights abuses in the delta is widespread. A Nigerian human rights organization recently filed a petition calling for the International Criminal Court (ICC) to investigate whether Nigerian leaders should be charged with crimes against humanity. (A sitting vice president of the DRC is already on trial at the ICC due to actions of the militia associated with his political party.)

Nigeria is the linchpin to regional efforts to enhance stability and security in West Africa. If Nigeria were to implode—and turmoil in Lagos is as likely a cause as any—the consequences could be severe. The net effect of the turmoil in Lagos could be dramatic. In combination with separatist fighting in the oil-rich delta region or in the Muslim provinces of northern Nigeria, instability in Lagos has the potential to cripple one of Africa's most important countries and *the* most important in West Africa. Sustained turmoil in and around Lagos could also trigger a serious interruption in oil exports, as well as a wave of refugees—the border with Benin being less than a day's walk from Lagos—in a region already beset by weak governments, poor economies, and intrastate tensions. The most likely alternative scenario is almost as bad. The Nigerian government could recognize that a restive, unruly, and supersized metropolis is indeed its most pressing challenge and might respond with a crash effort to contain and suppress its violence and disorder—tightening the cover on the Lagos pressure cooker. Such an effort would address symptoms, not causes, and therefore only postpone the explosion.

Events in the DRC are important for different reasons than in Nigeria. Whereas Nigeria projects power in the region and instability there would create a dangerous power vacuum, the DRC is a sucking chest wound to which states in the region are drawn by the lure of easy slaughter. This disaster will only desperately devolve over time, thanks to growing global demand for natural resources and pressure on the DRC government to do more for Kinshasa. As the government struggles to maintain order—not to mention actually improve deplorable living conditions—in an ever-more-overpopulated Kinshasa, efforts to assert control over resource-rich provinces will founder. The consequence will be ungoverned provinces, similar to the tribal areas of Pakistan, that could become havens for terrorists. Even more likely, they could again become what they have been in the past: free-fire zones where militias and invading armies loot the state's resources. In the past, Congolese militias received funding and support from other countries, notably Rwanda and Uganda. This is likely to happen again, though next time the puppet masters might be based in Paris or Beijing instead of Kigali and Kampala.

The debility of the DRC government has been a precipitating factor in wars fought over the country's abundant resources. The DRC government, perennially weak, can only grow weaker as its undergoverned and unattended capital city hurtles towards becoming the most populous city in Africa.

In the end, though, the similarities between Nigeria and the DRC—and for many megacities in the majority world—are closer than the differences: the grinding inequities, government failure to provide social support, the anomie and violence. We can choose to look away, pretending to have seen nothing. Or we could choose to look again, with perhaps a jaded, jaundiced eye, as Harry Goldstein sees Lagos—images we could see from the window of our crawling vehicle in any of the megacities we consider in this work:

> Despite Nigeria's enormous oil wealth, tens of billions of dollars have gone missing over the years in this country—one of the world's most corrupt—and few investments have been made in infrastructure. The streets of Lagos turn into lakes as fat drops of rain mercilessly pound down on the traffic. When the downpours abate, the massive puddles become breeding grounds for mosquitoes and malaria. . . . So, when traveling in Lagos, sit back and relax. Feast your eyes on the mounds of garbage lining the roads; on the market stands where freshly slaughtered goat carcasses steam in the sun, obscured by clouds of flies gorging on warm blood; or on the endless slums whose rusty corrugated metal roofs shelter the vast majority of citizens, many of whom subsist on less than US $1 per day and who have no access to clean water or sanitation, let alone health care or education.[22]

7

CITIES OF GOD
Death and Desperation in Rio

President Luiz Inácio Lula da Silva has pledged that Rio de Janeiro will be a different city in 2016—with living conditions in the dilapidated and depressed shantytowns transformed by increased investment in modern infrastructure.
—*October 19, 2009, Security Management: Security's Web Connection*[1]

We are living in a civil war.
—*Former Rio mayor César Maia*

You call yourself Caralho, *crude Brazilian for "Dick"—forceful obscenity that peppers almost every crude, and rare, utterance you make. You are thirteen years old. Since you were ten, the best friend, the only friend, you've ever had is the handgun that never leaves you. To you, every person is a thing, framed by a barrel narrowing its sights. A lifelong resident of a Rio favela, you roam the streets and alleys in a pack of others just like you. You don't belong to an organized criminal group; instead, those who roam with you are family. Mostly, you don't think. You know you'll never see the end of your teenage years. . . .*

October 2009. The *cidade maravilhosa* (marvelous city) of Rio de Janeiro—one of the most densely populated locales on earth—is named the site of the 2016 Summer Olympic Games. Bypassing stunned contenders such as Chicago, Madrid, and Tokyo, Rio emerged as the first city in South America to host an Olympic event and asserted its position as a major player on the world urbanization–globalization stage.

All, however, was not well. Within days violence had broken out across the city. Though perhaps not directly related to the upcoming Olympics, its significance and its symbolic impact suggested that the games (and the 2014 World Cup finals) could be placed in jeopardy. In the end, thirty-three people were left dead in the space of a few days and the unbridled optimism of the Olympic "win," which had left President Luiz Inácio Lula da Silva sobbing with happiness at its announcement, was shattered. Members of the dominant criminal gang in Rio, the Comando Vermelho (Red Command), had attacked a rival gang in the Morro dos Macacos ("Hill of Monkeys"). From the moments shots were first fired, everything—literally and figuratively—went downhill.

The eruption took place during a predawn Saturday invasion after the lead *traficante* ordered the members of the Comando Vermelho—known simply as "CV"—from Morro São João to challenge the Amigos dos Amigos (Friends of Friends, or ADA) gang in Morro dos Macacos. By the following Wednesday, police had arrested Rodrigo Mello, a CV commander, said to have ordered the invasion of the neighboring "hill" (as the slum communities of Rio are known), which was not under his gang's control. In the interim, at least twelve police stations in different parts of the city were attacked with grenades and rockets, ten public buses were torched, bus service was suspended to numerous communities, both CV and ADA *traficantes* were killed by police, and a number of innocent residents were caught in the vicious crossfire.[2] "It was a night of chaos. . . . We are still really scared," said seventeen-year-old slum resident Cristina Soares.

Six police officers were flying overhead the pitched battles of Morro dos Macacos when their pilot was hit by gunfire. Despite being wounded, the pilot managed to set his helicopter down in the middle of a football pitch, and the aircraft exploded in flames. Two officers were burned to death; four others were wounded, one of them seriously. In a cruel twist, the helicopter was shot down only one mile from Estádio do Maracanã—where the opening and closing Olympic ceremonies are set to take place and the World Cup final will be played.

Nominally the attack was about control of drug trafficking—who controls what, who gets the profit, who's in charge. In reality, and as the governments of Rio and Brazil have been slow to adjust to, the struggle is over turf. Increasingly sophisticated in organization and increasingly aggressive in their approaches to power, leaders of criminal networks use violence as means to secure territory and to eliminate competitors. This is no longer about the sale of drugs. The stakes are far higher now—and anyone who gets in the way dies.

Rio, among South American megacities, is not unique. In São Paulo, for example, Primeiro Comando da Capital ("First Capital Command") exercises similar authority, able to shut down the city for days at a time with drive-by shooting waves and public bus immolations. The incident in Morro dos Macacos was not exceptional, either—though its timing so close to the Olympic announcement certainly brought unwelcome international scrutiny. In truth, over the past decades Rio (and São Paulo) has experienced extraordinary levels of violence. In 2008 there were 4,631 homicides in the Rio metropolitan area; New York City proper, by contrast, saw 523. Those sensitive to these statistics either contrast these numbers with the 5,143 Rio murders that took place in 2006—or they simply shrug away the significance as of no real consequence. Referring to cases of school violence in a nonchalant way, Ricardo Teixeira, head of the Brazilian Soccer Federation, declared, "There was a natural reaction, the same way we turn the TV on and see the attacks of crazy kids in the United States killing and shooting everyone."

But violence in Rio, both in its cruelty and its randomness, does have consequence. Writing in the *Georgetown Journal of World Affairs*, scholar Bryan McCann details that in the vicious, explosive year of 2006, lurid news accounts left an impressionistic image of anarchy and chance. Rodrigo Netto, lead singer of the rock band Detonautas, was killed by teenage carjackers who seemed to believe he was too slow in pulling his car to the side of the road. André Costa Bordalo, a nineteen-year-old Portuguese tourist, was fatally stabbed at 8:30 on a sunny morning because he resisted handing his backpack over to a thief. Ana Christina Johanpeter, the wife of a wealthy businessman, was killed at a stoplight in the affluent neighborhood of Leblon (which commands the highest land prices in Latin America). Apparently, while seeing an armed thief approach her vehicle, she attempted to remove her wristwatch and her car rolled forward. The teenager shot her in the head and fled on bicycle.

One of the most horrific incidents took place in early 2007 when carjackers forced a vehicle to the side of the road in a working-class neighborhood. The thieves motioned for the mother and her two children to exit the vehicle and move to the sidewalk. One of the children, a six-year-old boy, could not unlatch his seatbelt. The thieves took off—with the boy still hanging from the driver's-side rear door. He was dragged for four miles across the city, even as the driver violently swerved the car from side to side to shake his limp body loose. Eventually, they abandoned the car. The boy's corpse was still hanging from the seatbelt.

Cariocas, as Rio residents call themselves, refer to these episodes as *fatalidades*, meaning "fatalities" but also suggesting that such events were simply preordained. But there are underlying causes—and ominous implications. And although Rio de Janeiro, of all the megacities considered in this book, is geographically isolated from Cairo or Kinshasa, the emblematic and very real significance of what forms this city's mosaic suggests that patterns can replicate in other locales and affect not only cities but the larger world as well. Even as then-President "Lula" promised additional federal funds and forces to improve security and declared, "I need to clean the filth that drug traffickers impose on Brazil," there are deeper meanings and root causes that reside in the communities where this violence was born.

WHEN THE "HILLS" TAKE OVER THE "ASPHALT"

With a population nearing 14 million, Rio is considered the cultural heart of Brazil. With roots deep in the heart of many *favelas*, Rio has seen a spike in violent—and organized—crime. Gangs have regularly attacked tourist sites, police stations, and buses, and acted with impunity. Violence continues indiscriminate and unchecked. As one resident of a *favela* confided to Liotta about the fate of most young men growing up in these ramshackle communities, "They start young . . . usually around eleven years old . . . and they die young."

Derived from the Brazilian equivalent for "shantytown," *favelas* (with inhabitants known as *favelados*) are common in the megacities of Rio de Janeiro and São Paulo. Characteristically *favelas* are both in the middle of cities and on the periphery. Lacking formal electricity or plumbing for sewers and drinking water, they are constructed from materials ranging from bricks to boards to garbage. *Favelas* are cramped and overcrowded—each a malignant culture rife with unrest and disorder, violence and insecurity—plagued by fetid sewage and rampant crime.

Favelas of Rio dominate the city's landscape. They rise just inland from the famous beaches of Copacabana and Ipanema. Two major *favelas* are located in tourist attractions: on the slopes of Corcovado, its enormous statue of the Christ figure with arms outspread high above the city, and on Pão de Açúcar (Sugarloaf Mountain). Robert Neuwirth, who lived in Rocinha and who remains optimistic about its vitality and potential, writes that the first *favelas* came into existence in the late 1890s when a freed group of slaves was drafted into the Brazilian army. After quashing a rebellion in the north, they returned to Rio expecting to be provided for, including being given quarters. Instead, they were given nothing. As a result, they built ramshackle homes out of mud and scrap wood on Morro da Providência, near both army headquarters and the city's mercantile district. They named their "neighborhood" *Morro da Favela*, partly to honor a weed that thrived in the rough landscape of the north where they had crushed the rebellion. A decade later, there were over fifteen hundred homes there.

To wealthier Brazilians, of course, *favelas* are looked on as a disgrace and an embarrassment. Rio's middle- and upper-class residents sometimes see their nightmare becoming reality: The "hills"—as *favelas* are known as—taking over the "asphalt"—the developed parts of the city. Yet, with over six hundred *favelas* in Rio alone (with many of them bordering neighborhoods of the wealthiest residents), these communities have become a permanent feature of the Brazilian megacity landscape.

Nestled between two of Brazil's wealthiest neighborhoods, São Conrado and Gávea, Rocinha, for example, began as a outcropping of shacks during the global economic depression of the 1920s. Rocinha—pronounced "Ho-see-nya," Portuguese for "little ranch"—may have a population as high as 400,000 residents. It has a developed infrastructure and businesses such as banks, pharmacies, bus lines, two cable television stations, and even a McDonald's franchise. At the same time, the community is subject to frequent landslides during rainy seasons and gun-toting *traficantes* who patrol the streets. And, as Fernando Meirelles, director of the 2002 Oscar-nominated film *City of God* (which depicts life, crime, and drug wars in an infamous *favela*), has suggested, a functional autonomy and dysfunctional social contract have always existed: Tolerance of *favelas* suggests a local "peace" where crime is not committed against neighbor and one remains fiercely loyal to the *favela*. As one resident told Liotta, "If you marry outside your *favela* and move, you can never come back."

Two illustrations of this sometimes perverse social contract became evident during a recent visit. In one instance, a local bank branch had opened in a smaller Rio *favela* and within its first weeks of operation was held up at gunpoint by masked thieves. The local drug lord, nominally both mayor and chief enforcement officer at the same time, used his network to track down the thieves, who were in actuality not members of the community at all. Rather, the four thieves were undercover policemen (which illustrates corruption and criminality within police forces themselves).

The second incident suggests that even wealthier residents actually find attractions in living in *favelas*. Because these communities are squatter areas, residents pay no taxes and appropriate electricity and water from city sources without incurring costs. (As with numerous squatter communities—whether Dharavi in Mumbai or Mathare in Nairobi—*favela* residents have no title deeds, since they have no property right to the land they inhabit.) Nominally, as long as there is some agreement with *traficantes*, a level of security exists. As Liotta learned, one resident received assurance from a local gang leader that he and his family should have no fear of robbery while living in his *favela*. Unfortunately, the residents' apartment was robbed shortly after they moved in. After approaching the gang lord about the incident, the residents saw their entire property returned to their apartment, with an additional "souvenir" left on their coffee table: a human hand.

The *favela* of Cidade de Deus ("City of God") in Jacarepaguá, in the west-ern zone of the city of Rio, was planned and executed by the state govern-ment of Guanabara as part of the policy to systematically remove *favelas* from the center of Rio. Many displacements came from Rocinha in a failed effort to reduce and ultimately remove the "eyesore" of the first well-established *favela*. Founded in 1960, and shockingly portrayed in Meirelles's film, CDD (as it is commonly known to its residents) was intended to settle inhabitants in suburbs. Ironically, the city of Rio has now enveloped CDD and reached far beyond its boundaries; the City of God has, in effect, "returned" to the heart of Rio. The *favelas* of Rio are now themselves *cities* of God.

In their own contribution to urban sprawl, the *favelas* represent Norman Myers's "termite queen" phenomenon, discussed in our introduction. Urban environments, acting as a kind of supernest, attract resources and residents—both positive *and* negative—from rural centers, including human capital and skills, food, water, and raw materials. By now, almost a century after the *favela* of Rocinha began, Rio's six hundred *favela* communities form the city inside the city, permanent features on the human landscape. Generations have grown there, and the "hills" now have conquered the "asphalt."

CRIME AND PUNISHMENT

While there is much to admire in the ingenuity and resilience of *favelados*, we should recognize, nonetheless, that parallel power structures control these communities, superseding any external authority.[3] Premier among these control agents are the criminal gangs resident in *favelas*. The most promi-nent group, Comando Vermelho, was founded in 1979 in the prison Cândido Mendes, on Ilha Grande. As a collection of ordinary convicts and left-wing po-litical prisoners who were members of the Falange Vermelha (Red Phalanx), which fought the military dictatorship during the gang's formative years, the CV morphed and transitioned into larger areas of interest and involvement. In the 1990s CV was the strongest criminal element in Rio, though now its principal leaders have either been arrested or are dead, and the organization lacks the controlling authority it once had. Such loss of power can make an entity more dangerous than ever.

Today the Comando Vermelho still controls parts of Rio. It is not uncommon to see streets tagged with "CV" in many *favelas*. CV often posts populist graffiti on neighborhood walls with the initials "PJL," which represents "Paz, Justiça e Liberdade" (Peace, Justice, and Liberty). This is a bit difficult to swallow for an organization that, among its various criminal activities, runs a lucrative kidnapping ring. The principal rival gangs of the Comando Vermelho are the Terceiro Comando Puro (TCP, Pure Third Command) and the ADA. The TCP emerged out of a power struggle amongst the leaders of the CV during the mid-1980s. Notably, in late June 2007, Rio police launched a large-scale assault on CV areas, where as many as twenty-four people were killed. According to a study by Rio de Janeiro University's Violence Research Center, in 2008 the group controlled almost 40 percent of the city's most violent areas, down from 53 percent two years previously.

One of the distinctive features of criminal Rio gangs is both recruitment and control. Incarcerated *favela* youth ages twelve to eighteen are sent to juvenile cells where criminal gangs have become legendary. The *Washington Post*, in an extensive series on gang culture in Brazilian prisons, reported that leaders have succeeded "in turning the cells into petri dishes where renegade social orders multiply with viral efficiency. Torn between gangs and the government, while in prison most turn to the gang system of drug trafficking, arms dealing, and kidnapping."[4] Part of this dynamic was a strategic choice by gang leaders. Whereas conditions in prisons were deplorable, with little or no government services, in the late 1960s the CV helped give prisoners a voice, leading social organization movements for prisoners to take charge of their prison conditions, demand improved services, and even garner respect. (In São Paulo, the dominant PCC gang even created a system of laws for gang members and delivered resources for both prisoners and their families on the outside.)

Typically when youths arrive in juvenile cells, they are assigned blocks according to which gang controls their respective *favela*. And while wretched prison conditions may have created fertile initial recruiting grounds, criminal networks now proliferate and rule the prison system. The CV command structure, which directs car thefts, bank robberies, kidnappings, hold-ups, and drug trafficking, now controls virtually every aspect of prisons. The government has been both slow and ineffective in reacting. Laughable concerns about blocking cell phone transmissions by utility companies were never taken seriously, because prisoners knew their cell phones would not be taken away. Some prisons provide "open regimes," even for those arrested multiple times, in which prisoners are allowed to leave during the day and return to prison at night.[5]

With most residents living in extreme poverty, and with limited opportunities beyond what ingenuity can provide for, in neighborhoods where police most often refuse to patrol, the parallel power structures of *favelas* encompass highly organized, ferocious, and armed gangs that operate in lieu of normal government institutions. It may seem like chaos, but there is precision and control—and a power struggle going on—everywhere.

"THE BIG DEATH"

Given the turmoil, no solution to the challenges of *favela* gangs and their security impact seems to exist. Action inside *favelas* by government agencies, especially by military forces, is hugely unpopular. Liotta interviewed a senior military officer who had operated inside several *favelas*. Ordered to lead a Marine helicopter raid into one of the most notorious communities, the officer related that he had little or no direction on how to conduct the raid other than to apprehend a specific list of individuals. When asked what the rules of engagement were for others not specifically targeted for arrest, he received vague advice. "What should I do," he asked, for example, "if a ten-year-old boy is holding a Kalasnikov in our face as we land?" "That decision," he was told, "will have to be yours."

Fortunately, that decision never had to be made. But the officer confessed he had made up his mind prior to the mission: he was set on killing anyone, including a child, who stood in his way. Although the raid was conducted as planned—basically landing on a high hilltop of garbage and shanties and working down through the landscape of ramshackle homes and seizing targets as they presented themselves—there were also high levels of frustration. Within a week, all the apprehended suspects were back, free, inside the feral city. That same week, intelligence intercepts tracked what appeared to be the sale by *favela* overlords of Stinger antiaircraft missiles to drug traffickers, possibly FARC guerrillas of Colombia. "The answer to this problem," the officer confessed, "is not a military one. We're not cops. And even the cops can't solve this."

Specially trained police units often operate against drug gangs in *favelas* with tank-like armored vehicles, known as *caveirãoes*, which translates as "big skulls." Partially named for the symbol painted on the side of many of these vehicles—a skull pierced by a dagger with two crossed assault rifles in the background—the *caveirão* also represents the powerful symbolic failure of public security policy. As Amnesty International details in numerous reports, the symbolism is not lost on *favelados*. As one resident described it in agonizing frustration, "Imagine an official armored vehicle, emblazoned with a skull and a sword, with police who come in shooting—first at the streetlights, then at the neighborhood's residents. . . this is the *caveirão*. An 11-year-old boy had his head torn off his body by shots which came from the *caveirão*—and we, the residents, still have to prove that it was the police."[6]

While all armored vehicles are known as *caveirãoes*, Rio police actually make a distinction between three types of vehicles: the *caveirão* is used by the *Batalhão de Operações Policiais Especiais* (BOPE), the "paladino" (Gladiator) by the *Batalhão de Choque,* and the "pacificador" (Pacifier) polices the Complexo da Maré in central Rio.[7] Collectively these vehicles have spread terror and intimidation whenever they enter a *favela*. With their introduction, however—intended to control the escalation of violence among criminal groups—the level of armed response from gangs has only intensified. Each *caveirão* is impressively armored as a result: able to carry 12 heavily armed officers, able to reach speeds of 72 mph, equipped with a 360-degree rotating turret with rows of firing positions running along each side of the vehicle, protected by dual armor layers with glutinous tire coatings to prevent punctures, and with two escape hatches in case of emergencies.

When *caveirãoes* enter a *favela*, residents expect intimidation, not protection. While loudspeaker pronouncements vary from "Residents, we are here to defend your community. Please don't go out of your homes. It is dangerous," to "There is going to be a shootout," to "We have come to take your souls," all realize that nothing good comes from their presence. Perhaps the most notorious example occurred in 2005 in the *favela* of Acari when BOPE mounted a blitzkrieg on the community. According to local residents' reports, seventeen-year-old Michel Lima da Silva was shot in the head, and his body then hoisted onto a hook on the *caveirão*, which then paraded through the community demanding money for his corpse's return.

In a word, police are not "welcome" in *favelas*. Residents—unless forced by circumstance to "snitch"—tend to not cooperate. With good reason: in 2008, police killed an average of three people for every twenty-three they arrested. With rival gangs exercising nearly total control (as well as providing resources such as natural gas and the basic trappings of security), the government has no control. Thus far, only twelve of Rio's six hundred *favelas* are secured. When government forces move in, *traficantes* slip out. The violence continues unabated. George Howell, manager of the Rio office of the International Council on Security and Development, tells Brett Forrest in the *Atlantic Monthly*: "The favelas have a different law, a different economy, and their own defense forces. The only way police can go in is with megaoperations involving hundreds of men. These are incursions into foreign territory."[8] Thus, as with any occupying force, police routinely savage the law: cops take bribes; cops sell drugs—and guns (many of which are already illegal for police use)—to *traficantes*; cops arrest *traficantes* and sell them to rival gangs for their torture and inevitable deaths.

Yet, in contrast to storming neighborhoods only when violence erupts, there have been attempts to bring "softer" community policing efforts to communities. None has proven particularly effective. To the contrary, the *Christian Science Monitor* reports that most met with embarrassing results. In one experimental area, "seventy percent of the participating officers were accused of wrongdoing and removed. . . . The project eventually fell apart and violence returned."[9]

One effort touted as success as Rio marches toward its modest goal of securing forty *favelas*—out of six hundred—by the Summer Olympics is the *Unidade de Polícia Pacificadora* (UPP), or, more simply, the Peace Police. The goal is simple: to instill trust, even respect, for police where none previously existed and to transfer assurance security from gangs to good governance. The UPP official website proclaims its goals as:

The Pacifier Police Unit (UPP) is a new model of Public Security and policing that intends to bring police and population closer together, as well as to strengthen social policies inside communities. By re-establishing control over areas that for decades were occupied by traffic and, recently, also by militias, the UPPs bring peace to communities like Morro Santa Marta (Botafogo South-zone); Cidade de Deus (Jacarepaguá West-zone); Jardim Batam (Realengo West-zone); Morro da Babilônia e Chapéu Mangueira (Leme South-zone); Tabajaras and Cabritos (Copacabana South-zone) and Pavão-Pavãozinho/Cantagalo (Ipanema/Copacabana South-zone).

Today, the Government and the Security Department (SESG/RJ) can rely on the UPPs as an important "weapon" to help them regain control over territories long lost to traffic, and also to reintegrate these economically challenged communities into society.

Created by the current administration of Rio's Security Department, the UPPs work with the principle of the Communitarian Police. Communitarian Police is a concept and a strategy based on the partnership between the population and public security institutions. Rio's government is investing R$ 15 million (US$ 8 million) in the qualification of the Police Academy, so that by 2016 the contingent will have been enlarged by 60 thousand officers. Until 2010, 3.5 thousand new officers will be sent to the Pacifier Divisions.[10]

While the methods may seem mild, the means should be welcomed as an alternative to vicious cycles of occupation, force, fear, and desperation that have defined this struggle.

Granted, police forces have an impossible task attempting to control gangs in *favelas*. But there are too many examples of police corruption, excessive use of force, and general effectiveness to claim that their actions are somehow admirable. Levels of stress imposed on these forces are extreme. As one officer relates the struggle, "I always used to come home from a mission and tell my father, 'Oh, today we killed two people,' or 'Today we killed four.' He used to congratulate me and say 'Good job!' But eventually he no longer wanted to hear these stories of death and killing. He said, 'Every day you come home and tell me how many people you killed. But what difference does it make? I still can't walk outside. I still can't feel secure.'"

"POORISM" AND PROMISE

Despite such bleak assessments and stark realities, there are positive examples that rise out of the urban complexities that characterize Rio today. Robert Neuwirth, who has overlooked the negative and violent aspects of *favela* life, offers a positive portrait of the ingenuity, resilience, and even optimism of the human spirit in *Shadow Cities*:

> This is how a squatter community develops. This is how a city develops: organically.
>
> So I say: Thank God for mass production. Praise be to the plastic pipe. All honor the prefab window. Bow down to sheets of old plywood, stock-model sinks, mass-produced tile. Three cheers for cement and cinderblock. Exalt the lowly rebar. Let's hear it for quick-drying concrete. Hooray for easy plastic wiring, easy plug outlets, and modular telephone service.
>
> With these products, a mud or cardboard hut gives way to wood, and wood gives way to brick, and brick to reinforced concrete. Suddenly a community goes from small huts and barracks to stylish apartment blocks but without developers or builders. All built by the squatters themselves.

None of these assessments are incorrect. Though a *favela* may look horrific from the "outside," there is an organic coherence in each community. Usually, the greatest activity for business and community activity is at the bottom of each hill; the higher one climbs, the less intense the activity and the more its residents are both physically and perhaps even somehow spiritually removed from the *favela*'s daily life. Yet with banks allowing customers to open savings accounts and obtain modest credit card limits (though building loans are out of the question), and with the Rio power company viewing *favela* residents as potential customers, there is a determined process in which each community is separate from yet somehow integrated into the larger life of Rio. A nonprofit effort to provide "legal" electricity in the huge *favela* of Rocinha is ongoing. This is a remarkable opportunity; over the first three years of its operations, the nonprofit saved 210 gigawatts, enough to power 100,000 houses for a year. In essence, and even though each *favela* resident is squatting on land he or she does not own, this is an example of achieving some form of legality: by agreeing to a meter installation, the resident becomes a legal utility account holder. By owning a credit card and establishing savings, each resident se-cures creditworthiness.

In Rocinha, there is a phrase—loaded with certain irony—for this process happening in the community: *asfaltização* (asphaltization). Whereas *favelas* in the past had reached out to surround the city, the city's commercial busi-nesses are now invading communities settled on illegal land. Equally, given limited space in these communities, we see a Manhattanization of the *favela*. As Suzana Taschner describes Rio's squatter settlements and slums, "We can see side by side with the peripheralization of Rio's *favelas*, a verticalization of the oldest ones, where buildings with four to six stories appear often for rent."[11]

Aside from actually residing in a *favela*, it is possible to see these com-munities up close and to interact with residents. Although on earlier visits to Brazil, Liotta, honestly, was repulsed by the concept of "poorism"—a kind of ecotourism freak show—he reversed course on later visits. Just as one can visit the massive squatter settlement of Dharavi in Mumbai or witness the wretch-ed conditions alongside thriving small businesses in Kibera in Nairobi, a visit to a Rio *favela* is well worth time and effort. While some may view poorism tourist options as exploitation (and indeed they are), such exploration helps uncover the stark reality of human resilience in the face of daunting odds—a "resilience phenomenon" we consider in our final chapter. Simply witness-ing the progress of life in a *favela*, surrounded by the roar of mototaxis that rumble up and down the hillsides, or standing slightly awestruck at the sight of hundreds of massive Gordian knots where residents run wires to tap into the electrical grid, or walking through endless narrow corridors of streets in smaller neighborhoods with exotic names such as Trampolim (Trampoline), Valão (Sewer), Roupa Suja (Dirty Clothes), or Vila Verde (Green Villa), one not only senses but immediately sees enormous vitality.

Such are the contradictions of modern Rio. Even as Rio and São Paulo face enormous challenges from ever-expanding, and ever-more-accomplished, criminal networks, *favela* residents—caught in the crossfire between governments and gangs—manage to hang on, sometimes even prosper. While government must develop a more coherent strategy to confront more sophisticated crime, problems will continue to evolve and mutate. The solution is not found in placing forty thousand security personnel on the street during times of turmoil. Nor is the problem securing the city for international esteem during the World Cup finals or the Olympic Games. The real challenge for the state is human security. If the state cannot provide for the safety and security of its citizens, then meltdown slowly begins. Ever since Hobbes's *Leviathan,* this has been the basic expectation about what a state can guarantee for its citizens. Sadly, in Rio, the Leviathan state—providing basic security for citizens—does not exist for many residents.

Brazil's entry on the global stage as a major actor has been—and there is no other word for it—miraculous. In 1998 account deficits and a currency crisis had flattened the economy. In 2011, Brazil eclipsed Britain and France to become the world's fifth largest economy. Rio—the spiritual, cultural, and political heart of Brazil—is a prime example of an international city in a state that is a major twenty-first-century power. Both the city and the state suffer and enjoy the benefits of urbanization and globalization. In almost every way, we have never been here before in human history. And it remains unclear how we, and residents of critical megacities around the globe, will emerge from the process.

8

THE MOST VULNERABLE MEGACITY

Drowning in Dhaka

We are eating our country, we are eating our earth,
we are eating our children.

—*Thich Nhat Hanh*

There is no nationbuilding for the damned.

—*Anna Simons*

Bangladesh—a nation-state roughly the size of Iowa with a population half
that of the United States—always appears to lurch at the edge of an abyss.
First known as "East Pakistan" when citizens rose up against India and Britain
in 1947, the nation transformed itself once again in 1971 in a war of liberation
against Pakistan, the Muslim-dominated state on India's western border, to
become Bangladesh—"the Land of the Bengals." This was a violent and trau-
matic break. Pakistani forces committed widespread rape and executions in
the capital city of Dhaka. The military, unsuccessfully in the end, was hell-
bent on imposing the Urdu language on resistant Bengalis. Their methods
were brutal and cruel, and those who doubt these claims can watch videos
today on YouTube of Pakistani soldiers massacring students, professors, and
workers at the University of Dhaka on March 26, 1971.[1] Other videos, easily
found through Internet sources, show further atrocities.

There is good news and bad news about Bangladesh's future. The good news is that despite enduring famines, natural disasters, and widespread poverty, as well as political turmoil and recurring military coups, progress continues. (The military, nonetheless, remains a "guardian" of the state, last stepping aside from its caretaker position in 2008.) As the world's seventh most populous state, Bangladesh ranks among the globe's most densely populated countries with extremely high poverty rates. At the same time, per capita gross domestic product has more than doubled since 1975, and poverty rates have fallen 20 percent since the 1990s. Even more positively, Goldman Sachs listed Bangladesh in 2005 among the "Next Eleven," or N-11, economies: those states who were candidates to follow Brazil, Russia, India, and China as major twenty-first-century economic forces.[2] (This study did not incorporate major demographic hurdles that many of these states, and megacities within them, face.) Despite its challenges, Bangladesh is promising for investment and future growth. The engine of this growth is found in urban centers: Dhaka, the capital city, and other major cities in the state.

The bad news is simply stated. Limited infrastructure capacity, poor and mostly ineffective governance, explosive population growth, topographic factors, and extreme environmental impacts are all short-fuse detonators that could lead to long-term disaster.

The example of well-intentioned but often fragile governance is much in evidence in Bangladesh. Arrested in 2007 on charges of extortion (later dismissed), Prime Minister Sheikh Hasina Wazed (daughter of the founding father and first president of Pakistan, Sheikh Mujibur Rahman) faced a crisis only two months after taking office in 2009, in the form of a brutal uprising by border guards named the Bangladesh Rifles. In its wake, the mutiny, which left seventy-four dead (and all commanding officers of the unit), exposed high anxiety among Bangladeshis and left a widening gap between her administration and military forces. In a video put up on YouTube, army officers openly confronted Hasina after not allowing them to intervene more quickly in quelling the uprising, in a screaming match that shocked many. Tensions have always been palpable, and personal: in 1975, Hasina's father and eighteen members of her family were assassinated by army officers.

The prime minister came to power on promises to root out Islamist guerrillas, continue to improve relations with India, prevent Bangladesh from becoming a haven for extremists staging cross-border attacks against its dominant western neighbor, and bring to justice those suspected of having conspired against Bangladesh's independence from Pakistan in 1971. But the prime minister's most immediate challenge seemed clear: keeping the army in check.

Dhaka's sheer presence looms large as magnet for internal migration, as Bangladesh increasingly succumbs to hazards imposed on its citizens and on the land itself. Thus, we briefly recount here patterns of change, growth, and disruption that have characterized Bangladesh since independence and offer reasons for Dhaka's rapid growth and population density. The citizens of this megacity, if they remain, will face ever-escalating dangers. The potential for catastrophe suggests that Dhaka in general and Bangladesh in particular may represent the first environmental refugee crisis of the century, as peoples are forced to migrate to lands far from origins and roots.

DEMOGRAPHIC DYNAMITE

Known variously as the "City of Mosques" and the "Rickshaw Capital of the World," Dhaka is the world's fastest growing megacity. Although exact forecasts are imprecise, we repeat the astonishing projections we offered earlier for Dhaka: in 1950 the city's population was 400,000; by some estimates, its population in 2015 could approach 23 million—representing a 5,700 percent increase. If New York City were to have grown as rapidly, its population in 2015 would be 684 million—roughly two and a quarter times the current United States population.

Why has this happened? Explanations vary, but the basic answers for why cities act as urban magnets remain uniform in the cases we consider in this work. Given Bangladesh's relatively small geographic size in relation to its immense and densely concentrated population, the capital is both place of opportunity and place of last resort for many. The impact of climate change and rising sea levels—leading to periods of devastating floods as well as periodic droughts—has driven many to the city as well. The root causes of such migration go further back: to the ethnoreligious seismic shocks following

India and Pakistan's partition in 1947, to the Indo-Pakistani War of 1964, and to the creation of the People's Republic of Bangladesh following its violent separation from Pakistan. All these events brought the deluge of refugees to the city.

Modern Dhaka is the center of political, cultural, and economic life for Bangladesh. Although its infrastructure is the state's most developed, Dhaka suffers from pollution, congestion, and lack of adequate basic services. A persistent pattern of government inability to provide services compounds these problems. (As one example, at the turn of the century Dhaka had piped water connections serving only sixty-seven thousand households and a sewage system with only eighty-five hundred connections.) Experiencing an increasing influx of people from across the nation, contributing to what amounts to demographic dynamite, Dhaka is spinning out of control.

Migration from rural areas to Dhaka accounted for 60 percent of the city's growth during the 1960s and 1970s. In the 1980s city boundaries expanded, adding more than a million to the city's population. Yet there persists gross disparity in Dhaka's demographic distribution. Seventy percent of the city's population occupies only 20 percent of the land. There is an intentional pattern of preventing this disparity from radically shifting. As Gita Verma suggested in *Slumming India: A Chronicle of Slums and Their Saviors,* "the root cause of urban poverty seems to lie not in urban poverty but in urban wealth." Land dominance by the more powerful repeats itself throughout the 10/40 Window and much of sub-Saharan Africa.

In Dhaka pressures to survive have created harsh conditions. In her work *Poverty and Vulnerability in Dhaka Slums*, Jane Pryer documents that almost 50 percent of youths ages ten to fourteen are directly engaged in income generation and only 7 percent of youths five to sixteen attended school.[3] With over a million child laborers, Dhaka ranks as Asia's starkest example of what Mike Davis paints as a "living museum of human exploitation." Forced evictions and demolitions, sometimes with less than a day's notice, have become systematic—not only in Dhaka, but in the port city of Chittagong and rural village areas. Perhaps the most pointed incident took place in 1999, when government authorities used the gang murder of a policeman to declare slums "criminal havens" and bulldozed nineteen different communities, making fifty thousand people suddenly homeless. Slum dwellers took to the streets in violent protests. Within days, the government had declared a temporary ban on the slum clearance program. But evictions themselves continue to this day.

GOVERNANCE AND CORRUPTION

Many Bangladeshis will admit the state has the appearance of strong legal frameworks on paper, yet implementation lags far behind. As one business-man lamented to Robert Kaplan in an article for the *Atlantic Monthly*, "We have the best constitution, the best laws, but no one obeys them. . . . The best form of government for a country like ours is a military regime in its first year of power. After that, the military fails, too." The 2010 *Global Integrity Report*, which independently reports on worldwide governance and corrup-tion, ranked Bangladesh seventieth out of one hundred ranked states, with "very weak" overall rankings in civil society organizations and civil service regulations, access to information, and political financing, as well as execu-tive, legislative, and judicial accountability.[4] Transparency International's *2011 Global Corruption Perceptions Index* was even harsher, ranking Bangla-desh 120 out of 182 states.

The report further notes how Bangladesh's private sector, while rapidly becoming the nation's key source of economic growth and employment gen-eration, is rampant (as is almost every other sector) with corruption. Describ-ing one incident in which a Chinese company engaged in collusive bidding to secure a coal mining contract through politically powerful individuals, the report points to significant net loss in funds by the public exchequer.

One might argue, nonetheless, that progress is being made: in 2001 Transparency International named "Bangladesh the most corrupt country in the world" out of its ranking of 91 countries.[5]

RECRUITING GROUND

One result of the inability and unwillingness to provide greater opportunity and improvement for the mass of Dhaka's population has now become evi-dent: the move toward extremism. Although the country itself is linked linguistically, rather than by democracy or a perceived common national identity, there are evident shifts from a moderate Islam to a more assertive Wahhabist strain. As Kaplan observes, Bangladesh and Dhaka seem ripe for Al Qa'eda–type affiliates in a state where the politically powerful cannot say no to money, even as the state sinks before their eyes: "Islamist orphanages, *madrassas*, and cyclone shelters are mushrooming throughout the country, thanks in part to donations from Saudi Arabia, as well as from Bangladeshi workers returning home from the oil-rich Arabian Peninsula." The surprise to date, nonetheless, is how moderate Bangladeshis remain. But the allure is there.

None of this ought to be surprising. In a city such as Dhaka, where the male head of a family is perhaps an auto rickshaw driver competing with a million others in the insane congestion and pollution—traveling sixty kilometers a day for a dollar in wages—and where his wife earns perhaps slightly less breaking rocks or bricks into road-paving material, and where his children are employed in menial labor for the most marginal of wages, how could radical Islam's appeal (which, as Kaplan emphasizes, offers "answers and spiritual rewards for suffering") not be palpable?

RESOURCE STARVATION

The most significant—and blatantly obvious—example of corruption takes place with water resource planning, the broad framework of which took place under flood control, drainage, and irrigation programs in the 1960s. Although government data suggests that 74 percent of the population has access to water from improved drinking sources, most citizens suffer from water scarcity. Phenomenally rapid growth in population and poorly planned urbanization expansion, as well as industrialization and simple ignorance in the use of water, strained relations with India over water, and the influence of climate change on the hydrological cycle, have all contributed to an expanding and ever-more-serious problem.

According to Muhammad Zamir, vice president of the Bangladesh Water Partnership, "Corruption in the water sector in Bangladesh has usually manifested itself in the following areas: (1) in matters of delivery both to households as well as in irrigation, (2) in improper billing of water supplied and consumed, (3) during civil construction work undertaken for water storage and maintenance and (4) lack of strict monitoring of sewerage facilities and effluent discharge by industrial units."[6] The top three forms of corruption in the water sector are negligence of duty, asset-stripping, and abuse of power. Although Bangladesh attracts massive aid in the form of loans from the World Bank and the Asian Development Bank—including investment of around $670 million annually for the efficient operation of the water delivery system in Dhaka alone—the sector itself is a perennial soft target for corruption, with the result that 50 percent of designated funds "go elsewhere." The government established an Anti-Corruption Commission (ACC) in 2004, extant today, which examines a broad variety of corruption allegations (including in 2010 allegations of corruption at the Dhaka Zoo). After significant revamping of its structural integrity and mission mandate, the ACC recently claimed that the Ministry of Water Resources may have diverted as much as $1.5 billion USD during the period 2001 to 2006.

CLIMATE CHANGE CATASTROPHE

Given the critical nature of water resources in Bangladesh, the need to move quickly beyond resource issues and the need to face crucial shortages in the face of impending climate challenges seems evident. What remains unclear is whether or not the government has the will, capacity, or initiative to deal with these looming challenges. As Kaplan perhaps crudely, but accurately, illustrates, Bangladesh "is the world's biggest flush toilet. Once a year over the space of four months, God yanks the handle. First comes the snowmelt in the Himalayas, swelling the three great rivers [the Ganges, Brahmaputra, and Meghna]. Then, in June, comes the monsoon from the south, up from the Bay of Bengal."[7] With the concomitant misery and assault of climate change, the arguments for justice, dignity, and the simple rights of survival stand as prominent as ever.

As further evidence of the looming environmental catastrophes that may well undo the capital city (and the state itself), in 2009 most of Dhaka's more than fifty effluent canals were fully or partially choked, with the rest under serious threat due to unabated encroachment. Efforts by the Dhaka Water Supply and Sewerage Authority to prevent further damage proved fruitless.

DHAKA DEATH SQUADS

In what is a painful echo of genocidal acts by West Pakistani forces against Bangladeshis during their war for liberation, evidence has emerged that death squads in Dhaka have returned—but this time with government sanction. The Rapid Action Battalion—or RAB—formed in 2004 as a quasiparamilitary extension of Bangladeshi police forces, was established nominally as an organization to fight terrorism as well as corruption. The RAB soon acquired what now appears to be its own reputation for terror and for the brutalization and torture of those Bangladeshis it takes into custody. Within a year of its creation, almost two hundred people had died in RAB custody or operations (the latter becoming known as "death by crossfire"). Their all-black uniforms and ruthless tactics have created fear among citizens.

Established by Bangladesh's then minister of law, Moudud Ahmed, the RAB has been swift to respond to the propaganda war, establishing its own Facebook page, touting its achievements and anticriminal activities. At the same time, its activities have touched raw nerves in the state. In March 2010, for example, the photographer, writer, and activist Shahidul Alam staged a provocative photographic exhibition of images suggesting what "victims" of the RAB last saw before they died. Conspicuously devoid of images of violence—while ominously suggesting police actions that were soon to take place—the gallery exhibit proved too explosive to occur. Bangladeshi police closed it hours before its opening. Images from Alam's exhibit were made available on the *New York Times* website—and ominous tension was palpable. "R.A.B. is seen as the force that can take out a lot of violent criminals," said Brad Adams, Asia director of Human Rights Watch. "In a place that has become lawless and corrupt, people want something—anything—to happen."

Alam's exhibit, notably, was titled "Crossfire."

ECOLOGICAL HAZARDS

Nestled between two of the mightiest rivers on earth, the Ganges and the Brahmaputra, the citizens of Bangladesh have become increasingly vulnerable to periods of declining availability of drinkable water and times of uncontrollable flooding. Given the likelihood of significant sea-level rise in the twenty-first century, saltwater will contaminate what is the world's largest delta, drowning out freshwater resources and destroying crops, fisheries, and large swathes of forests. The potential for rising sea levels, the disappearance of large delta agricultural areas, and rapid snowmelt from Himalayan peaks all present immense challenges.

The environmental vulnerability of Bangladesh is impossible to sensationalize. As the Senior Military Advisory Board (comprising eleven retired U.S. admirals and generals) of the Center for Naval Analyses noted in its report *National Security and the Threat of Climate Change,* Bangladesh is vulnerable on numerous fronts:

> The large migration from Bangladesh to India in the second half of the last century was due largely to loss of arable land, among other environmental factors. This affected the economy and political situation in the regions of India that absorbed most of this population shift and resulted in violence between natives and migrants. . . . The location and topography of Bangladesh make it one of the most vulnerable countries in the world to a rise in sea level. Situated at the northeastern region of South Asia on the Bay of Bengal, it is about the size of Iowa with a population of almost 150 million. It is very flat and low lying, except in the northeast and southeast regions, and has a coastline exceeding 300 miles. About 10 percent of Bangladesh is within three feet of mean sea level. Over the next century, population rise, land scarcity, and frequent flooding coupled with increased storm surge and sea level rise could cause millions of people to cross the border into India. Migration across the border with India is already such a concern that India [built] a fence to keep Bangladeshis out.[8]

Although its situation is extreme, Dhaka is not the only large city vulnerable to the forces of nature: New Orleans obviously was (and is) as well, as are Cairo, Lagos, and Karachi.

Environmental stress could result in further mass-migration from Bangladesh in the coming decades. Since the 1950s as many as 17 million Bangladeshis have migrated to India, due in part to natural disasters and food scarcity. Since half of Bangladesh lies just above sea level and critical sectors of the country are flooded during the rainy season, Bangladesh faces the future loss of large areas of coastline due to flooding and sea-level rise. A cruel irony is that the delta itself is sinking more from agricultural overuse than from the rising sea. Pressure on natural resources is extraordinarily high: two-thirds of land area is under crops, the highest proportion in South Asia, and its dwindling forest cover is the second lowest in the region. Too little space and too much abuse only accelerate this negative process. Increasingly violent coastal storms, such as those that took place during the monsoons of 2010, regularly assault coastal areas and send hundreds of thousands fleeing from their homes—to Dhaka. Soon, however, they may have to keep going, past the inhospitable megacity perhaps as migrants before them, all the way to the international borders of India and Myanmar.

BUILDING BARRIERS

The vulnerability of the delta collapsing has the potential to affect up to 35 million, which constitutes almost one in four Bangladeshis. As a result, tensions over the issue of human movement remain high between India and Bangladesh. In 2007 India completed its four-thousand-kilometer, three-meter-high barrier separating the two states. Officially, according to Indian sources, the wall was built to prevent extremists and other criminal elements from crossing into India, but the value of such a wall in keeping huge floods of refugees out of the state figured into calculations.

At the heart of this vulnerable delta—where, according to recent UN IPCC data, temperature variants of two degrees in either direction from "normal" could have catastrophic consequences—Dhaka faces perilous predicaments. The World Bank sees Dhaka facing the triple threat of deteriorating air, land, and water. Air pollution, inadequate solid waste management, and contamination of surface water impact not only human health but industrial and natural resource productivity. Given that the city is on track to become one of the planet's largest by 2015 and that economic activity in Dhaka constitutes one-fifth of the state's gross domestic product, checking environmental constraints to growth should be a critical priority. The compound effect of environmental problems for Dhaka seems, often, too unbearable to consider—particularly in light of how far government has fallen behind in implementing measures of adaptation or mitigation that would have any real impact. The failure to manage different forms of wastes—solid, clinical, human, industrial—is not dealt with seriously. According to A. S. M. Haider, writing in the *Financial Express*, four hundred out of the thirty-five hundred tons of solid waste generated daily in Dhaka in 2010 was left on city roads and in open spaces. The remainder was taken by city vehicles to open surface landfills near the city, contributing to further pollution. Tannery industries in the Hazaribagh and Tejgaon areas leave industrial waste untreated. Experts fear this waste could be seeping underground and contaminating the city's main water sources.

The city generates about 120,000 cubic meters of sewage daily, yet inadequate (and faulty) sewerage networks carry only half of daily totals to the only sewage treatment plant at Pagla in Narayanganj. As Haider notes, vast amounts of sewage ooze out of this faulty network and into the city's canals and the Buriganga River. Untreated sewage is discharged into the river directly.

THE URBAN MANDELBROT

Urban growth and high urban density have made Dhaka more the bull's-eye for human-induced environmental disasters. The rapid influx of people has resulted in growth of slums at shocking speeds. The mass of vehicles crowding Dhaka's streets creates more than air pollution: studies suggest that average noise levels are double what should be considered and rising fast, making an unhealthy environment even worse.

Finally, there is the issue that will challenge Dhaka—and Bangladesh—more than any other: climate change. UN-HABITAT reports that researchers studying the impact of climate change on Dhaka predict the city will be affected in two major ways: flooding and drainage congestion, and heat stress. Given that Dhaka's topography is only a few meters above sea level, even a slight rise in these levels would engulf large swathes of the city. Climate change will devastate the saturated, high-density population, most especially urban poor who live in flood-prone and water-logged areas.[9]

Ultimately, drawing on urban theorist Matthew Grady's concept of urban mandelbrots,[10] Mike Davis suggests in *Planet of Slums* that Dhaka may well come to represent a megacity where all efforts to improve efficiency will fail. Fractal-like, natural and increasingly lethal environmental impacts, combined with urban poverty, anarchic traffic and congestion, failing infrastructures, and toxic waste, will create a lethal mix that does nothing less than "constantly terrorize" city residents. The outlook for Dhaka is not good.

9

CITIES OF FEAR, CITIES OF HOPE

What Could Be Done

The promise is that, again and again, from the garbage the scattered feathers, the ashes and broken bodies, something new and beautiful may be born.

—John Berger, from the preface to Latife Tekin's
Berji Kristin: Tales from the Garbage Hills

We must be careful not to succumb to despair, for there is still the odd glimmer of hope.

—Edouard Saouma

In the final days of completing this work, P. H. Liotta wandered through the fetid stench of the Nairobi slum Kibera. For the most part, residents were friendly and engaging, happy to share ideas and new terms in Kiswahili. Raw sewage ran down the hills and through the narrow lanes that separated flimsy mud and corrugated tin chicken-coop-like shacks. What was most striking was not the deprivation; rather, it was the sense of hope—and purpose—that was present everywhere. What he saw was not anger; what he found was inspiration.

Just as many states across the globe in the "majority world," while certainly not failed states, cling desperately to rapidly fraying threads, so too in slums in so many wretched places on this planet do we rediscover how difficult it is to kill the human spirit. Just as some states are better classified as "parastates," —on permanent life support from international agencies and institutions, akin to George Romero *Night of the Living Dead* zombie-like creations, missing some vital organs and a few limbs, stumbling into the future—so too do we remain astonished at the sheer capacity, and sheer endurance, of so many on this planet. Despite the odds, despite seemingly impossible living conditions in the cities we have considered in this work, they endure.

Population stress, as we have emphasized repeatedly, causes unpredictable, often wrenching, outcomes. Liotta, who has visited the Great Lakes region of Africa numerous times, felt this message keenly on a trip to the Virunga Mountains in the eastern part of the Democratic Republic of the Congo ten years after the Rwandan genocide. (That gross barbarity, in which a million innocent Tutsis and Hutus were slaughtered in one hundred days with horrifying efficiency largely by the use of *panga* [machete]—at a rate five times faster than the Nazis ever achieved—remains a source of international shame.) Rwanda is the most densely populated state in Africa. As we now know, environmental stress, competition viable for too little land with too many people, and struggles for power were all fuses that ignited the disaster. Stopping by a small graveyard framed by stunning peaks on three sides, he asked his guide how many were buried there. The answer he thought he heard was "twenty-seven." He was puzzled, since the graveyard clearly could accommodate more. "No," his guide corrected him, "twenty-seven thousand." The man paused for a long while and then softly murmured, "We only had room for the skulls."

We have no illusions about the solutions we offer. We realize they may be neither feasible nor attainable. But they are issues we must speak to. Over the past ten years, we have discussed, openly debated, and exchanged ideas on these solutions with friends and colleagues with many international perspectives. They include officials from the United Nations (especially UN-HABITAT and the UN Environment Programme); the Woodrow Wilson International Center for Scholars; the RAND Corporation; the Center for Strategic and International Studies; the International Institute for Strategic Studies; the Peace Research Institute, Oslo; the Global Environmental Change and Human Security project; the U.S. State Department; military and government representatives from forty-seven different states, and academics from war colleges and universities around the world.

What is certain is that what has been attempted thus far to address the challenges of new Leviathan megacities is insufficient, sometimes criminally so. Largely we have seen half-measures that inevitably result in failure. The so-called international community is woefully unprepared to take on these challenges. But they must be confronted. Time after time, the clarion cry of "Never Again" becomes "Again and Again." We failed to intervene in Rwanda, even as the butchery splintered into fractured veins spreading from the capital Kigali. We failed to take action effective enough to stop the carnage in Darfur and southern Sudan. When Pakistan or Nigeria or Bangladesh or the Democratic Republic of the Congo collapse, will we stand idle once again? We hope not. The global effects, in these cases, will be intense.

Urban societies in the future might be best described as "large urban agglomerations," a term the UN employs to illustrate how many cities are surrounded by slums and shantytowns, often indistinguishable from the slums and shantytowns inside official city boundaries. These agglomerations can extend over hundreds of square miles. Managing the provision of public services (law enforcement, public health, education, utilities, and public transportation) and expanding and then maintaining a complex, costly infrastructure of roads, hospitals and clinics, school buildings, and water and sewage lines, as well as communication capabilities, present severe challenges.

While recognizing the bleakness of the examples we have provided, we offer here evidence of positive change—from advancing human security in urban environments to vivid signs of change taking root in urban centers that have undergone trauma. From the resurrection from the ashes of Sarajevo to the neighborhood and communal *panchayat* system in Mumbai to efforts to resolve water resource and distribution issues in Israel and the Palestinian Territories, there are—despite the warning signs—reasons for hope.

That there might be neighborhoods in a city in which there is a considerable amount of crime, decaying infrastructure, and inadequate public services is not peculiar to the twenty-first century or to municipalities in the developing world. The 2005 and 2007 riots in Paris, as well as the unrest in 2011 in

Britain, were reminders, after all, that despairing neighborhoods exist in even the most glitteringly successful cities. Leviathan megacities of the twenty-first century will face complex and often overwhelming challenges that cities such as New York and London simply did not have to address as they emerged from semianarchy and rapid population growth.

Part I: What Are the Challenges?

Before presenting our case for solution and resolution, we first wish to present three broad conceptual approaches we must bear in mind as we confront these challenges and seek opportunity. They are realities for human security, response in conditions of decayed urban environments, and resilience that many face living there. And even before presenting these approaches, we must address what we mean by security and distinguish how vulnerabilities differ from threats.

WHAT DO WE MEAN BY SECURITY?

In the classical sense, security—from the Latin *securitas*—refers to tranquility and freedom from care, or what Cicero termed the absence of anxiety upon which the fulfilled life depends. Since the beginning of the twenty-first century, numerous governmental and international reports have focused on the terms "freedom from fear" and "freedom from want," both of which emphasize a pluralist notion that security is a basic, and elemental, need.

Perhaps most widely touted among these reports—and one least put into practice—is the Canadian International Commission on Intervention and State Sovereignty's *Responsibility to Protect* (commonly referred to simply as "R2P").[1] Based on the principle that sovereignty is not a privilege, but a responsibility, R2P focuses on preventing four violations that go beyond the traditional protection of borders: genocide, war crimes, crimes against humanity, and ethnic cleansing. R2P can be broadly broken down into three major conceptual aspects: (1) the state bears responsibility to protect its citizens and population from genocide, war crimes, crimes against humanity, and mass atrocities; (2) if the state fails at this responsibility, the international community must act with capacity-building measures, to include providing early-warning capabilities, mediating conflicts, strengthening security, and mobilizing standby forces; and (3) if the state patently fails to protect its citizens and conflict-avoidance measures are not working, the international community has the responsibility to intervene at first diplomatically, then more coercively, and, as last resort, with military force.[2]

Although the phrase was taken up by the UN secretary-general, it has never been put into action, largely for the failure to answer one essential question: Does the "Responsibility to Protect" mean the indiscriminate right to intervene?

From this general—and Western—understanding of security, the human security concept centers on a concentration on the individual (rather than the state) and that individual's right to personal safety, basic freedoms, and access to sustainable prosperity. In ethical terms, human security is both a "system" and a systemic practice that promotes and sustains stability, security, and progressive integration of individuals within their relationships to their states, societies, and regions. In abstract but understandable terms, human security allows individuals the pursuit of life, liberty, and both happiness and justice.

While one could find little to argue with in these principles—and their relevance to megacities and global insecurity—there are problems nonetheless. On the one hand, all security systems are not equal—or even very similar. Moreover, all such systems collectively involve codes of values, morality, religion, history, tradition, and even language. Any system that enforces human security inevitably collides with conflicting values, which are not synchronous or accepted by all individuals, states, societies, or regions. On the other hand, in the once widely accepted realist understanding, the state was the sole guarantor of security. Realists believe that security necessarily extends downwards from nations to individuals; conversely, the stable state extended upwards in its relationship to other states to influence the security of the international system. This broadly characterizes what is known as the anarchic order. The *responsibility* for the guarantee of the individual good—under any security rubric—has never been obvious.

Essentially cities, states, and regions, in a globalized context, can no longer afford to solely emphasize national security issues without recognizing that abstract concepts such as values, norms, and expectations also influence both choice and outcome. Societies, whether in the majority world or in the developed world see this tension. With expectations that states have to protect citizens, citizens increasingly hold their states—and their major cities—accountable. Thus, despite the "clean" distinctions made in the accompanying graphic, there are dangers in too closely following the precepts of one security concept at the expense of another.

Some brief explanation of the concepts in this graphic might prove useful as well. In essence, these distinctions move from a "top-down" global emphasis to a "bottom-up" individual focus.

Ecological security, as a "mental map" of how one not only views the world but subtly yet vitally determines how one acts in the world, emphasizes the sustained viability of the ecosystem, while recognizing that the ecosystem

ALTERNATIVE "SECURITY" CONCEPTS				
Traditions & Analytic Bases	**Security Type**	**Specific Security Focus**	**Specific Security Concerns**	**Specific Security Hazards (Threats/ Vulnerabilities)**
Nontraditional	**Ecological Security**	The Ecosystem	Global sustainability	Humankind: through resource depletion, scarcity, war, and ecological destruction
Traditional, Realist-Based	**National Security**	The State	–Sovereignty –Territorial integrity	Challenges from other states (and "stateless" actors)
Traditional and Nontraditional, Realist- and Liberal-Based	**"Parasitic" Security**	–Nations –Societal groups –Class/ economic –Political action committees/ interest groups	–Identity/ Inclusion –Morality/Values/ Conduct –Quality of life –Wealth distribution –Political cohesion	–States themselves –Nations –Migrants –Alien culture
Nontraditional, Liberal-, Marxist-Based	**Human Security**	–Individuals –Humankind –Human rights –Rule of law –Development	–Survival –Human progress –Identity and governance	–The State itself –Globalization –Natural catastrophe and change

itself is perhaps the ultimate weapon of mass destruction. In 1556 in China's Shensi Province, for example, tectonic plates shifted and by the time they settled back into place, 800,000 Chinese were dead. Roughly 73,500 years ago, a volcanic eruption on Sumatra was so violent that ash circled the earth for several years, photosynthesis essentially stopped, and DNA samples suggest that only several thousand humans survived worldwide. From an alternative point of view, then, mankind itself is the ultimate threat to the ecosystem. Thus, from a radically extreme perspective, elimination of humanity proves the ultimate guarantee of the ecosystem's survival.

National security represents the traditional understanding of security, to include the protection of territory and citizens from external threats—from other states, and, more recently, "stateless" actors (which range from NGOs to terrorist networks). Hyperemphasis on state security, especially in the emergence of "homeland security," impacts the two following concepts of security, especially regarding the practice of individual liberties and the freedom to participate openly in civil society.

"Parasitic security" is not synonymous with the more commonly used term "societal security." Rather, parasitic security is symbiotically linked to other security concepts. It often represents the narrow interests of specific communities, nations, or political action groups within a state. In its extreme form, it can lead to social stratification, the fracturing of "common" interests, and xenophobia. Certainly, parasitic security played a role in the dismemberment of former Yugoslavia at the end of the Cold War. When "citizens" began to identify with their nations and "nationality" (Croat, Serb, Slovene, Bosniak, Kosovar) rather than with a larger identity, the state itself was doomed.

Human security—or, as we should more appropriately term it, "security with a human face"—retains its focus on the individual, and remains an emerging concept. In a special issue of *Security Dialogue* devoted to the concept, Astri Suhrke pointed to a fundamental ambivalence that human security as conceptual approach and policy principle continues to suffer from: is it related more to long-term "human development," such as was suggested in the 1994 UN *Human Development Report,* or (as a security issue) does it constitute a principle of intervention during immediate crisis, such as Rwanda in 1994 or Kosovo in 1999 or even Iraq in 2003? The answer to either question is "Nes"—a little bit of "no" and a little "yes."

Thus, while some (including Liotta in the past) have argued that there may be a growing convergence between what was traditionally called "national security" and the still developing concept of "human security," there appears to be an even more powerful counterargument in which the opposite trend is apparent. In interventions as disparate as Somalia in 1993, Liberia (at various stages of disintegration), the Balkans, and Iraq in 2003, there emerged an overt dominance of American and British hegemonic behavior, accompanied by an uneven commitment to issues involving human security. While Prime Minister Tony Blair could speak of "universal values" and President George W. Bush proclaim that "freedom is the nonnegotiable demand of human dignity," foreign policy choices regarding intervention were almost exclusively made when such choices satisfied the narrow, selfish, and direct "national security interests" of more powerful states. If such choices also satisfied certain aspects of human security, then all the better.

As the blatant international failure to do anything in Rwanda illustrates—other than a collective international decision to do nothing—human security is hardly proving the trump card of choice in decisions by states to intervene in the affairs of other states, to include violating traditionally respected rights of sovereignty. Taken to extreme forms, both human security and national security can be conceptually approached as antagonistic rather than convergent identities. Each in its exclusive recognition remains problematic. As a basis for international action, we have yet to achieve a consensus on what constitutes "international interests," who should support it, and who should uphold it.

DISTINGUISHING THREATS AND VULNERABILITIES

The following distinctions are contentious, even we are not in complete agreement with each other. In brief, however, we argue that not all security issues involve "threats." Rather, the notion of vulnerabilities is as serious to some peoples—and some cities—as the familiar "threat" of armies massing at the borders, or barbarians at the gates. Admittedly, those who form policy and make critical decisions on behalf of states and peoples will continue to focus on aspects of traditional national security—or "hard" security—in which military forces will play a preeminent role, as well as human security in which "nontraditional" security issues may well predominate.

Commonly, a *threat* is an external cause of harm with identifiable consequences that may be immediate or at least visible on the horizon, which requires near-term tangible response. Military force, for example, has traditionally been sized against threats, to defend a state against an external aggression and to protect vital national interests. In some cases, such as Nigeria and Egypt, the state builds military power against an additional threat: domestic disorder or rebellion. The size of the U.S. and Soviet nuclear arsenals during the Cold War matched the perceived threat of global holocaust in the context of a bipolar, ideological struggle that was far greater then than in today's post-9/11 world. A threat, in short, is either *clearly visible* or *commonly acknowledged*. For policy makers, a threat is something you can target.

Vulnerability, on the other hand, is a weakness or condition that *may* ultimately cause the kind of harm an unattended threat *will* cause. An instructive analogy may be in the field of counterterrorism where the threat is the existence of terrorists plotting to cause damage or kill people and the vulnerabilities are, for example, high-value targets that are not guarded, parts of the telecommunications infrastructure not adequately protected by firewalls and encryption, and critical databases not backed up. This analogy is not exact, since social vulnerabilities such as severe overcrowding may not require an external agent such as a terrorist to call into being the harm that they have the potential to cause.

A vulnerability can be both internal and external in exerting complex influence. Human and economic geographers Hans-Georg Bohle, Karen O'Brien, and Robin Leichenko have addressed this "double bind" of vulnerability in analyses addressing environmental and economic change and its impact on cities in particular. Collectively they suggest that examining and assessing vulnerability is both relevant and necessary for policy issues. Vulnerability approaches can also identify regions and peoples at risk within the seven categories identified in the 1994 UNDP report: economic security, food security, health security, environmental security, personal security, community security, and political security.

In the broadest understanding, vulnerability may not even be recognized or understood—which can be maddeningly frustrating for decision makers. When it is recognized, a vulnerability often remains only an indicator, often not clearly identifiable (such as with population density or rates of poverty), is often linked to a complex interdependence among related issues, and does not always suggest a correct or even adequate response.[3] While disease, hunger, unemployment, crime, socioeconomic conflict, criminality, narco-trafficking, political repression, and environmental hazards are at least somewhat related and do impact security of states, cities, and individuals, the best response to these related issues, in terms of security, is not at all clear.

As stated above, a vulnerability—unlike a threat—is not clearly perceived, often not well understood, and almost always a source of contention among conflicting views. Compounding the problem, the time element in the perception of vulnerability must be recognized. The core identity in a security response to issues involving human or environmental security is of also recognizing a condition of extreme vulnerability. *Extreme vulnerability* can arise from living under conditions of severe economic deprivation, falling victim to natural disasters, or being trapped in the midst of war and internal conflicts.

But there are also cases of long-term vulnerability in which the best response remains uncertain. We term these problematic security concerns "entangled vulnerabilities." Given the uncertainty, the complexity, and the sheer nonlinear unpredictability of entangled vulnerabilities, the frequent—and classic—mistake of the decision maker is to respond with the "gut reaction." The intuitive response to situations of "clear ambiguity" is, classically, to do nothing at all. The more appropriate response is to take an adaptive posture and to avoid the inclination to act on instinct. To be clear here: avoiding disastrous long-term impacts of entangled vulnerabilities (which can evolve over decades) requires strategic planning, investment, and attention. To date, states and international institutions seem woefully unprepared for such strategic necessities. Moreover, environmental and human security issues, since they are contentious, often fall victim to the "do nothing" response because of their vulnerability-based conditions in which the clearly identifiable cause and the desired prevented effect are ambiguous. Plausible entangled vulnerability scenarios might reasonably include the following:

- different levels of *population growth* in various regions, particularly between the developed and the majority world
- outbreak and rapid spread of *disease* among specific "target" populations (such as HIV/AIDS and new strains of emerging contagions such as SARS or H5N1 influenza)
- significant *climate change*
- scarcity of *water* for drinking and irrigation and of other *natural resources* in specific regions
- decline in *food production, access, and availability*, and the need to increase imported goods
- progressing *soil erosion and desertification*
- increased *urbanization and pollution* in megacities around the globe
- and lack of sufficient *warning systems* for natural disasters and environmental impacts—from earthquakes to land erosion.

These emerging vulnerabilities will not mitigate or replace more traditional hard-security dilemmas.

Both middle-power and major-power states, as well as the international community, must increasingly focus on long-term entangled vulnerabilities in order to avoid constant crisis response to conditions of extreme vulnerability. Granted, some have soured on the viability of the concept in the face of recent "either with us or against us" power politics. At the same time, and in a bit more positive light, others have recognized the sheer impossibility of international power politics continuing to feign indifference in the face of moral categories. As PRIO research scholar Peter Burgess writes, "For all its evils, one of the promises of globalization is the unmasking of the intertwined nature of ethics and politics in the complex landscape of social, economic, political and environmental security." While still not feasible to establish a threshold definition, it would be a tragic mistake to assume that national security and human security—both as concepts and as bases for policy decisions—are mutually harmonious rather than more often locked in conflictual and contested opposition with each other in the never-ending competition within governments and international organizations for budgetary resources.

Yet these contradictions are not the crucial recognition. Rather than focusing on the security issues themselves, we should be focusing on the best multidimensional approaches to confronting and solving them. One approach, which might avoid the massive tidal impact of entangled vulnerabilities, is to sharply make a rudder shift from constant crisis intervention toward problem-solving focus. Clearly, the time is now to reorder our entire approach to how we address—or fail to address—security and witness conflict and bloodshed as consequence.

What are the long-term consequences of failing to recognize entangled vulnerabilities? While it may at first seem a stretch, it seems pertinent to recall that the "preservation" of displaced Arabs in refugee camps following the 1967 Arab-Israeli War led to the intifadas of the 1980s, the 1990s, and the twenty-first century. The displacement of Hutus and Tutsis from the Rwanda genocide of 1994 directly impacted the disaster in the Democratic Republic of the Congo—and the 1994 displacement was itself made possible by the earlier expulsion of Tutsi from Rwanda into Uganda where they built the Rwandan Patriotic Front militia. The roots of a potential Balkan conflict twenty years from now can be found in the weak economic conditions, corrupt political institutions, and bands of angry young men with nowhere to go and nothing to look forward to in the streets and ruined foundations of Bosnia-Herzegovina, Kosovo, and Macedonia. Thus, in considering whether such frameworks might be viable for the future, it is important to step away from applying such a template to only crisis response or conditions of extreme vulnerability. Arguably, the roots of the disasters in Bosnia-Herzegovina and Kosovo did not begin in 1998; rather, they began in the aftermath of the Second World War and flared up, again and again, during the 1980s—as illustrations of entangled vulnerability.

We will see the continued reality of threat-based conditions contend with the rise of vulnerability-based urgencies. Entangled vulnerabilities, nonetheless, will receive the least attention from policy makers, as their interdependent complexities grow increasingly difficult to address over time. In making distinctions between threats and vulnerabilities, problematic contradictions will inevitably emerge. Suppositions that insist on a distinction between threat and vulnerability, nonetheless, become suspect in the so-called age of terror.

FACE THE MUSIC: URBAN WARFARE

While no one doubts that certain states and actors are under threat from Al Qa'eda or *Jemaah Islamiyah* or *Lashkar-e-Taiba*, the shadowy nature of such loosely grouped networks defies the traditional sense of "threat." These "networks" operate on the fault line between threat and vulnerability, and too narrow a focus on either "threat" or "vulnerability" will only lead to frustration—and failure. Indeed, most governments focus both on preventing terrorist attacks from occurring through police and military action and on reducing the number and size of the vulnerabilities that the terrorists might try to exploit.

In a piece titled "Feral Cities: Problems Today, Battlegrounds Tomorrow?" written for the inaugural issue of the *Marine Corps University Journal*, Richard Norton asserts that many cities of the future—especially those we have considered—*will* be future battlegrounds. These battlegrounds will not be confined to specific, quarantined locales; to the contrary, effects will be global—and local:

> MS-13, often described as "the most dangerous gang in America," warrants a more detailed examination. MS-13 is involved in a variety of criminal activities from extortion to drug-trafficking and has "a taste for atrocities," according to a recent article. MS-13, with a reported U.S. membership of more than 20,000 individuals, has also reportedly taken on contract work, as Mexican alien smugglers have allegedly hired MS-13 to kill members of the U.S. border patrol.
>
> There has even been speculation that meetings have taken place between leaders of MS-13 and Al-Qa'eda. While the degree of accuracy concerning these reports is open to debate, they do raise the prospect of one of the more chilling potential threats posed by a combination of terrorist organizations, criminal organizations, and feral cities. It is by no means a flight of fancy to envision how a well

financed terrorist organization could contract to load a weapon of mass destruction or mass effect at a feral port, move that cargo to a destination such as Nuevo Laredo, and have that cargo smuggled into the United States. MS-13, which extends its range of operations from El Salvador to Canada, is not the only criminal organization with such an international reach.[4]

Norton acknowledges that state (and, by extension, city) security often begins with human security. While basing his approach on a narrowly defined "freedom from fear" approach, he argues that if the state cannot provision or guarantee essential necessities of life, people will shift their allegiance to those organizations or individuals that can. At the most basic level, obtaining access to drinkable water and breathable air may be difficult. Conditions in some of the world's worst slums today suggest what life may be like for many megacities of the future.

Such recognition is not original, however. Despite the strategic forecasts of the 1990s, where many in the armed forces and defense industries saw battlefields of the future laced with network-centric warfare and high-technology, linked platforms for sensor-to-shooter operations—in essence, distance warfare that relies on superior force—the realities of the post-9/11 world are quite different. Gone are the days when a former U.S. Air Force Chief of Staff could pronounce that, in the future, spaced-based platforms would be able to "track, target, and kill anything on the face of the earth" within a few seconds. In their place, we have seen face-to-face engagements in Somalia, Iraq, and Afghanistan.

It is all the more significant, then, that one study from the Rand Corporation went against the strategic "grain" in 1994. Coauthored by terrorism expert Bruce Hoffman, *The Urbanization of Insurgency: The Potential Challenge to U.S. Army Operations* saw the likelihood of guerrilla-style and criminal warfare in many urban environments of the future. As the dual demographic dynamic of rapid population growth coupled with ever-increasing urbanization in the emerging world, cities were becoming overburdened and overpopulated. As a result, insurgents had entered this "ripe environment." With generations growing up in slums surrounding many states' principal cities, and with governance incapable of providing infrastructure or support for such massive populations, the battleground of the future was being set. Its name was urban warfare.

While in the past, RAND authors claimed, urban insurgencies proved the relatively easiest to defeat, this may no longer be the case in conditions short of traditional, full-scale war between states—in other words, the conditions most likely to confront states in the age of extremism, religious and ethnic insurgencies, and Somalia-like anarchy. Accordingly, governments should move to develop "hybrid strategies": improving tactical capabilities ranging from urban warfare to counterterrorism, improving human intelligence to detect budding insurgencies, jointly training and operating police and military forces with coordinated counterinsurgency strategies, and forcing governments to "face the music"—walk the fine line between overlooking or ignoring developing insurgent movements on one hand, and overreacting with brutal legislation and counterattacks on the other. Echoing these perceptions with a high-technology twist in a 2002 edition of *Aerospace Power Journal*, Troy Thomas saw the sprawling slum peripheries of megacities as "informal, decentralized subsystems . . . where points of leverage in the subsystem are not readily discernible." Citing the "sea of urban squalor" that is Karachi today, he argued that what is commonly called "asymmetric" combat will dictate operations likely to recur again and again in places such as Lagos, Kabul, and Karachi.

We may well be entering an age of continuous conflict—and urban warfare could break out all across the 10/40 Window. While this is unquestionably a worst-case scenario, we critically need increased focus on endemic urban violence. The loose organization and global diffusion of groups such as Al Qa'eda (and its dozens of offshoots, what counterterrorism strategists call its "associated movements") and even *Al Shabaab,* which operates in Somalia but draws recruits from as far away as the American Midwest, suggest a template for armed groups operating in urban environments. Such groups create the conditions for "hydra networks": the ability to operate effectively as a lateral (and noncentralized) entity, to learn, to anticipate, and to "self-organize" or reconstitute after being struck.[5] These ugly truths have created the "new" asymmetry in warfare. We have now entered the netherworld of complex irregular warfare. With these challenges—or more precisely *because* of them—we need to adapt, to experiment, and to network better, faster, sooner.

Unfortunately, international institutions and regimes are not well positioned to address these challenges. As one potential result, political-military alliances such as NATO could either permanently fracture or be permanently drawn in as violence escalates. This potential matters. NATO—often portrayed as the most successful alliance in history and one that has taken a stand on intervention, whether in Kosovo or in Afghanistan—today is almost entirely composed of states with aging, shrinking populations. As Jack A. Goldstone points out in "The New Population Bomb," young and increasingly populous Africa, the Middle East, and Central and South Asia may be able to mobilize insurgents more quickly than NATO could ever mobilize troops. Consider this harsh reality: Afghanistan's current population is 28 million; it will be 45 million by 2025; by 2050 it will be 75 million. We do not need or want these people as our future enemies. But if governments cannot provide adequate services for urban populations, residents are left with few opportunities and little hope, and insurgents can move with impunity in urban centers as well as preserve ties and support operations in the countryside.

While Richard Holbrooke's dying words may well have been, "We have got to stop this war in Afghanistan," the brutal truth is that we must do far more than that. It would be poor strategy to have such a population not only in Afghanistan but even more in the megacities we have addressed in this work, turn against well-intentioned but failed interventions that did nothing more than simply stop the fighting. Interventions must make a difference. NATO's role matters. It must do well by doing good.

AND DESPITE IT ALL, RESILIENCE

The nightmare scenarios of urban warfare do not have to come to pass. Our argument is not whether emphasis should be placed on traditional security issues, which normally derive from relationships among states, or on nontraditional human security issues, which are not confined by national boundaries. Our answer is that the focus must be on both.

Despite the overwhelming challenges megacities and those who live there face, there are still numerous examples of resilience and promise. Given

Liotta's long personal experience in the Balkans, perhaps the most emotional and gratifying example took place during the four-year siege of Sarajevo during the 1990s. The Bosnian War had transformed the city into a war zone, with snipers owning the streets and parks; the soccer stadium had become a cemetery. Yet in an extraordinary act of defiance and of human decency, the Sarajevo Orchestra rehearsed in the rubble of the National and University Library of Bosnia and Herzegovina, which Serb forces had firebombed, destroying its collections. Out of such wreckage, humanity—once again—emerged.

And so it is of this image we must speak. Though time is running out, in these cities of fear there still dwell reasons for hope. While examples of such inspiration could fill an entire volume—and indeed they ought to—we offer a few here.

At the heart of such hope lies the basic sense of community and communal purpose. As Timothy D. Sisk of the University of Denver expressed in *Human Security for an Urban Century*, the cosmopolitan ideal truly exists when polity has global dimensions.[6] In massive cities, the ideal is to have them function as a magnet for education, employment, and public services, with access to justice and civil rights. In so many locales, however, this has failed. Thus, when municipal governance fails, the community must take over. As Sisk writes:

> Resilient urban democracies are more likely to successfully manage and contain inter-group tensions that could lead to violence than are city authorities lacking legitimacy and the consent of the people. Strong systems of urban democracy diffuse values of tolerance, inclusion, accountability and citizen participation, deepening conflict resilience and broadening the basis of human security at the community level. Urban democracy can't be waged as a winner-take-all contest if it is to promote conflict resilience.

Still, we do see cases of resilience. In Mumbai, for example, inadequate and corrupt police forces and inequitable access to policing services for the poor (especially women) has led communities to become directly involved in neighborhood policing through a system of more than two hundred *panchayats* that mediate local disputes and serve as intermediaries between slum residents and police. Before the *panchayat* initiative, relations between the police and settlement inhabitants were almost always negative. Often there was no regular police presence; police entered only when there was a crime or need to arrest suspects. As urban scholar Sheela Patel observes, by harnessing community purpose, *panchayat* representatives help moderate and settle disputes without resorting to a more formal legal system. The *panchayat* has also improved police transparency and accountability, since police and police procedures face more public scrutiny.[7]

UN-HABITAT initiatives, misguided as some of them may be, also point to ways in which improving slums builds human security capacity. Even modest efforts to improve slum conditions can equally improve social capital. In Nairobi's Korogocho slum, the Adopt-a-Light program, which promotes private sector sponsorship of streetlighting in busy areas, has affected public safety perceptions and fostered new relationships among residents, communities, and public institutions. In the bustling city of Durban, South Africa, involving traditional chiefs in policy planning helped defuse potential conflicts during the state's move from apartheid to democratic rule. Jo Beall, director of development studies at the London School of Economics, has suggested that this achievement helped turn what seemed an inevitable descent into conflict into a success story because of the direct participation of the *amakhosi*—the traditional Zulu leaders—some of whom had been involved in violent acts. The *amakhosi* primarily supported the Inkatha Freedom Party, with its mainly rural, Zulu constituency, against the more urbanized African National Congress (ANC). Supporters of the ANC had resisted local political participation by the *amakhosi*. Accommodating the *amakhosi* in governance allowed competing power structures to avoid further escalations—proving that democracy works best not by legislative edict but with participatory involvement.

Perhaps the most positive example of hope where all seemed hopeless is in a state that faces severe challenges: Bangladesh. In the early 1970s, U.S. Secretary of State Henry Kissinger (in)famously referred to Bangladesh as an "international basket case." By all surface appearances today, that condition appears unchanged. But thanks to collaborative international development efforts, coupled with the creative initiative of many who live there, all is not lost. Economist Stephen C. Smith has referred to five separate factors that have helped improve the lives of many Bangladeshis. The Green Revolution, despite the reality it has created by increasing the amount of those impoverished globally, has allowed the country to become self-sufficient in rice production. Family planning, despite cultural and religious restrictions, has helped slow massive population growth. Global partnerships with nongovernmental and development organizations have helped build capacity. The growth (explosion, really) in Bangladeshi textile industries has provided a way out for hundreds of thousands of formerly impoverished women. And remittances—funds transferred back home from Bangladeshis living and working outside of Bangladesh—represent almost 10 percent of gross domestic product and account for half the value of merchandise exports, significantly reducing poverty.[8] As bad as things are for Bangladesh, they could be worse.

In sum, allowing for democratic governance and participation, strengthening social capital and opportunities for access—especially access to scarce resources—and involving residents in municipal governance policy and decision making are crucial components in the quest for urban resilience.

PART II: WHAT CAN WE DO?

Historically, international relations have been a matter for nation-states, and neither the UN nor any of its leading members has fully come to grips with the implications of nonstate entities and substate issues. For decades there have been legitimate concerns that as the power of nongovernmental entities such as multinational corporations and humanitarian agencies grew, as they have been since at least the 1980s, the power of the nation-state would inevitably erode. The concern was that the world would become a more anarchic place as the wings of nation-states were clipped by financial markets that disregarded borders and by humanitarian agencies that could directly lobby at the UN or bypass states by mobilizing public opinion to demand action that the state itself was reluctant to take. The irony is that even as the international community is determining how best to deal with the nonstate actors it wants to include and how best to deal with the ones that it wishes to exclude (such as terrorists and organized crime cartels), it is also now being confronted in international relations with the issue of substate entities, in particular under-governed major cities.

THE HEART AT THE HEART OF THE MATTER

The fundamental issue for substate entities is that, under long-standing norms of international law and diplomacy, the state is the responsible party for most matters of any importance. The relationship between the state and the substate jurisdiction (a province or city) is akin under law and precedent to the relationship between a parent and a child. When the child is hungry or needs attention, the parent is responsible for responding to these needs. Under ordinary circumstances, the parent will rebuff and even resent an attempt by the parents of other children to step in and deal directly with his or her child. Most parents understand and respect this attitude.

So it is under international law. As a basic principle of human security, the parent state is responsible for ensuring that its citizens' needs are addressed and that subnational municipalities and provinces, to which responsibilities are delegated, are functional, if not functioning. In practice, of course, we know that some states make no more than halfhearted gestures at caring for their citizens, and indeed the only concerted efforts that some states rouse themselves to make are military or police campaigns to deprive a domestic minority population of its economic, political, or cultural rights.

TO R2P OR NOT?

Before the end of the Cold War, sovereignty was more or less an inviolate norm. States that oppressed minority populations generally did not have their legal rights to conduct domestic affairs, without outside interference, challenged. That began to change in the 1990s as a consequence of state-perpetrated atrocities such as the genocide in Rwanda and the brutal Balkan wars of the 1990s. The human rights abuses that Rwanda and the former Yugoslavia committed were so egregious that the international community's attention was drawn to both states—and many questioned the inviolate sanctity of sovereignty. After the Cold War fizzled out, there was no longer any balance-of-power reason for one of the five permanent members of the UN Security

Council to veto political, economic, or (on rare occasions) military action against an offending state.

The principle that a state's sovereignty *could* be violated when that state commits atrocities against its citizens or violations of human rights has not been formally adopted in an international convention (the main vehicle for codifying international law), but the precedent has been established. Despite the promise and the moral righteousness of R2P, the principle itself may never become established law. Concerns for potentially destabilizing effects, such as encouraging minority populations to seek UN intervention to address their grievances, still prevail—as if Woodrow Wilson's principles for self-determination in his "Fourteen Points" speech to Congress in 1918 had gone wildly astray. The UN and the rest of the global community continue to take an ad hoc approach to balancing the desire of individual states to preserve their sovereignty and the desire of the community as a whole to prevent and discourage mass violations of human rights by states. The result has led to frequent inconsistency in UN decisions about which abuses in which states warrant intervention.

The halting progress that the international community has made in creating ground rules for intervention in the case of human rights violations by states against their own people provides no guidance for the kinds of problems that we address here. Effective action to manage these problems requires new approaches to state sovereignty. The evolving megacity crises are not the result of the state taking harsh action against a segment of its population—though thousands of residents of Cairo and Lagos who at one point or another were made homeless when authorities bulldozed their shantytowns have been roughly treated. When the UN took notice in Rwanda and the former Yugoslavia, it was only after outrageous atrocities had taken place, atrocities far worse than the heavy-handed eviction of slum dwellers in the name of misguided governments (that never fully implemented urban planning schemes) or the failure to educate slum children. In Rwanda the state attempted to exterminate the entire Tutsi population in an orgy of violence— yet the Security Council emasculated the UNAMIR peacekeeping force. In the former Yugoslavia the state attempted to drive all ethnic Albanians out of

Kosovo—and a UN resolution came about only after NATO's seventy-eight-day bombing campaign forced Belgrade's capitulation.

THE CATEGORY-5 OF MEGACITIES

The problems in some of the world's emerging megacities that we have cataloged are also not the result of aggressive government action such as those that once existed in (the now democratic and pluralistic states of) Rwanda and the former Yugoslavia. These problems are instead the result of inaction or insufficient action. And if we are able to look at ourselves with any honesty, most states would admit to having committed what theologians call "sins of omission"—failing to meet the legitimate needs of much of their citizenry. Every city in the world, after all, has slums and ghettos. The difference, though, is one of scale. The crime, despair, and poverty of a slum in Chicago or Paris are a rain shower; conditions in Leviathan megacities are Category-5 hurricanes.

Given circumstances that the governments of Nigeria, Pakistan, Bangladesh, Egypt, and the DRC have faced during the years before their major cities began to bleed people, it is understandable that their megacity problems have not been effectively addressed. As we have seen, independence came both late and prematurely to these states. Late, in the sense that they have been independent for less than six decades. Prematurely, in the sense that they became independent states before populations secured common national identities and safe borders. Each of these states spent too much of its first decades of independence suppressing domestic insurgencies, fighting separatist movements, and attempting to fend off neighbors who were unsatisfied with the borders drawn by retreating Western colonialists. Forced by circumstances to invest in building national institutions, primarily armed forces, these states neglected the critical need to develop institutions of governance at the municipal level—a failing of perhaps minor consequence until cities metastasized into megacities no longer effectively governable.

WHAT MEGACITIES NEED

At a minimum, we will need more intrusive and directive forms of technical assistance, humanitarian aid, and economic development programs than ones traditionally deployed to poor and disaster-stricken states such as Haiti,

Tanzania, and Sri Lanka. In extreme cases, a form of municipal trusteeship may be required. Under such an approach, the UN or a coalition of states would do for a megacity what the UN did for the entire countries of Cambodia and East Timor: temporarily but directly manage and develop some or all of the institutions of government. The analogy here is to a failing school district in the United States that is temporarily taken over and administered by the state department of education. While we will address the idea of municipal trusteeships later, it is important to concede here that this would inevitably undermine the principle of sovereignty. If successful, the trusteeship could create public expectations of good governance and effective public services that would continue to influence the affected state's policy making for years after the expiration of the trusteeship. In other words, affected states may, if they are shortsighted, view the prospect of international efforts to improve the functioning of megacity governments as both a blessing and a curse.

WHERE THE MONEY GOES: DISASTER RESPONSE

UN organizational structures make it difficult for the international community to fully appreciate the nature of emerging megacity problems. The greater problem, however, is in the organization's composition. The UN is made up of states that determine with their votes *and* financial contributions what the organization's agencies do and where they do it. Many of these states, especially those newly independent, have historically been unenthusiastic about UN actions that create precedents that could later be used as justification for a subsequent violation of sovereignty. At the same time, more established and wealthy states have traditionally been unenthusiastic about major new international efforts that are expensive and do not respond to an immediate crisis that might not garner support from their respective citizenries. There has been a subtle, but very important, trend in the attitudes of donor countries toward UN programs. This is not merely what some have called donor fatigue—the reluctance of donor countries to cough up money in response to seemingly never-ending UN appeals for support for worthy project after worthy project. With mounting economic problems proliferating in the early twenty-first century, donations for UN humanitarian and economic development projects have been declining. But what could be as significant is that donations for severe natural disasters have increased. Countries are choosing to spend relatively more on natural disaster responses than on long-term economic development and nonemergency humanitarian programs. There are two reasons for this and both could be crucial with respect to the megacity challenge.

One reason is that disasters are becoming more severe because of climate change *and* overcrowding in environmentally precarious cities. As climate shifts cause more severe cycles of storms and other weather conditions, continued increase in disaster response funding and decrease in funding for nonemergency programs (such ones that would address urban infrastructure and economic development) will take place. This will produce negative effects on efforts to raise money to address underlying problems of the world's megacities.

A second reason is that disasters are more politically marketable to the citizens of wealthy European, North American, and East Asian states than traditional foreign aid. Televised images of families made homeless by cyclones or entire villages flattened by earthquakes or swept away by raging floodwaters resonate with voters. As a result, disaster relief expenditures, often in the form of donations to the UN, are comparatively easy to justify to budget-conscious voters. Images of squalor in Karachi or Lagos do not have as powerful an effect on would-be donors precisely because the images are of conditions that are the usual responsibility of municipal and state governments.

The fact remains: what is going on in certain megacities is a disaster—one that clearly needed to be understood in the corridors of the UN and on main streets across the economically developed world. The millions living in Cairo cemeteries or on the streets of Karachi and Lagos are suffering as much as disaster victims, and the global rescue missions launched after major earthquakes or tsunamis should not be mistaken for being enough. After the hundreds of thousands of victims of the 2010 floods in Pakistan are resettled (if they ever are), Karachi and Lahore will still be seething pots of violence and grim living conditions. Floods will cause conditions in these two cities to worsen if large numbers of flood victims decide to give up hardscrabble lives in the countryside and move to the city. Disaster relief aims at—but rarely accomplishes—the restoration of the status quo ante, yet in many megacities and slums in smaller cities the status quo ante is already grim and becoming more dangerous.

MACRO-STEPS: CREATING THE "TWELVE-STEP SOLUTION"

As daunting as problems appear to be, megacities are not lost causes—yet. But they will become desperate if steps are not taken to improve governance, infrastructure, and the delivery of essential services such as law enforcement, education, and public health.

Our concerns about the dangers of ungoverned megacities should not be dismissed as mere "predictions." The trends and events we describe are already taking place and have begun to sculpt the future. The question cannot be whether these things will actually happen; it is already too late for that. As consequences take hold, we may well enter an ecology of urban ruin in some of the most fragile, yet connected (by globalized trade and migration), locales in the world.

While terrorism, homelessness, poverty, and failure of government to provide support are not one and the same, they often coexist and collectively are symptomatic of a severe "dis-ease" within the system—one with which the system in many countries is demonstrably unable to cope. There are practical applications, nevertheless, that the larger international structure can and should take on to strengthen governance in states most directly threatened by the challenges that new, urban Leviathans pose.

What we offer here are hardly panaceas for seemingly insurmountable problems; equally, these actions cannot be taken in isolation from each other. As practical means to achievable ends, they should be symbiotically applied to deal with specific environments as well as common symptoms. Foremost among these deep-rooted problems is an element common to many states and urban Leviathans within the 10/40 Window: corruption. Without dealing with this cancerous reality, any instrument or idea to address these challenges, no matter how worthy, will be dead on delivery.

The first steps on the Long March towards meeting the challenges of megacities require recognizing the nature and severity of the problems. Naturally, we hope to contribute to this recognition. But recognition is not enough. Actions need to be taken, and they need to be soon. In the following pages we offer initiatives that the international community and individual donor nations should consider. We have grouped our recommendations into two categories: broad policy prescriptions and narrowly focused policies that address a specific issue. The recommendations are listed in a general priority order, reflecting the fact that the first few recommendations listed are likely to have the most dramatic impact or should be acted upon earliest because they will create a base upon which the other recommended actions might be built.

In brief, we must generate awareness, mobilize it, and marshal action on the part of international system actors in order to

1. take on the politics of plunder;
2. invest in regional organizations;
3. broker cooperative ventures for transnational missions;
4. launch centers of excellence for operations;
5. target "intelligent" aid;
6. make aid work best, by bringing governments and NGOs together;
7. mobilize and coordinate private sector contributions;
8. craft strategies that work for megacities;
9. harness remittances and microcredits and avoid their dangers;
10. promote megacity-oriented civil society and civil-human security;
11. recognize human impact; and
12. establish "charter cities."

More extensively, and in order, we address these twelve steps here.

1. The Politics of Plunder

A basic first step must be taken and not just with respect to megacities. That step is to address corruption. Governments and megacity leaders themselves—not foreign donors—should design projects and set agendas that focus on both physical and social infrastructure improvement and urban design and planning, as well as health and education improvement. Political leaders must be held accountable.

Corruption, of course, is a human condition and can never be completely eradicated, but UN, donor nations, and nongovernmental organizations must demand accountability and must condition future economic assistance on adherence to accountability standards. During the Cold War, accountability was not required, and corrupt countries continued to receive aid because there was a strategic reason for not rocking the boat. The Soviet Union and the United States judged that corruption was a small price to pay for a client state's continued political support. When the Cold War ended, the political value of client states diminished, as did the toleration of their corruption, which clients such as Mobutu learned to their dismay.

One unfortunate side effect of the "long war" against violent extremism is renewed tolerance for corruption in some states. What was once tolerated because of the strategic calculus of the political balance of power between the United States and the Soviet Union is now tolerated to secure cooperation on the counterterrorism front or to promote stability in countries where the United States is "nation-building," a misnomer to be sure since what is really being built is the rudimentary apparatus of a modern state.

Pakistan is a poster child for tolerated corruption. Because it is a major player in the "long war," there are few alternatives to gently prodding the government to remove corrupt office holders and prosecute the occasional scapegoat. A more serious effort to actually root corruption out of the Pakistani government would antagonize many of the influential people who could undermine political support for the state's cooperation with the United States in suppressing Islamist extremists.

Corruption exists not only in donor countries but in humanitarian organizations and UN agencies, so addressing corruption requires reform all around—not just in recipient countries. Yet by far the most serious problem is with corruption in countries such as Pakistan and Nigeria, where civil servants are poorly paid, bribes are virtually standard operating procedure, and a culture of unaccountability and impunity for well-connected individuals and families flourishes.

Corruption does more than raise the cost of providing humanitarian aid or technical assistance; it erodes the faith of populations in institutions of government, which in turn makes it ever harder for institutions to function effectively. Pervasive corruption can also have a cost in terms of lost direct investment by foreign corporations. Private sector investment is an important complement to UN or government efforts to pump life into a downtrodden community—but when investors are put off by additional burdens that corruption imposes, foreign corporations will not provide enough fishing poles, nets, and boats for the people who may have been fed and then taught to fish by UN or other programs.

2. Heavy Investment in Regional Organizations

Within the 10/40 Window, in particular, regional organizations have begun to play an important role in peacekeeping—for example, the African Union and the Economic Community of West African States. These organizations offer better prospects for more effective action than global organizations, such as the UN.

We should increase reliance on regional organizations to reduce the burden on the UN and delegate greater responsibilities to organizations that are closer to the scene than New York or Geneva. Regional organizations *can* play a crucial role in promoting economic growth among neighboring states and *can* promote stability through peacekeeping missions to member states. Regional organizations *can* be important sources of assistance in matters such as law enforcement or with problems such as natural disasters, pollution, and disease that knows no borders.

We emphasize "can" when referring to the capabilities of regional organizations because not all regional organizations were created equal. The most successful and enduring regional organizations have for obvious reasons taken root in the fertile soil of economically advanced parts of the world, specifically Western Europe and North America. The advanced states in these regions have the wherewithal to invest in regional organizations and the economic incentive for cooperation and mutual defense. The North Atlantic Treaty Organization is, by any measure, the apotheosis of an effective intergovernmental regional security organization. In existence since 1949, and despite its sometimes cumbersome processes, NATO has long experience in joint planning and cooperative decision making. The organization has the benefit of decades of investment in interoperable hardware and exercises which military forces of member states practice common functions together. Though no other organization approaches NATO in terms of its capability, less capable organizations can make estimable contributions to international stability and to social and security challenges posed by megacities that have sprouted in weak or struggling states.

The European Union is new in comparison to NATO but has demonstrated effectiveness in a number of political, economic, and even military areas.[9] Unfortunately, other long-standing structures such as the League of Arab States, the Organization of American States, and, to a lesser degree, the African Union (formerly the Organization of African Unity) have proven ineffective at organizing action much beyond the expression of their membership's collective political position on a particular policy issue at the UN. The League of Arab States, for example, has been widely criticized for building layers of committees that do little beyond endlessly discussing minor issues and for not developing effective mechanisms to address issues affecting Arab states—one of the main ones being overcrowding in Cairo. The League has also failed to rouse itself to condemn genocide in Sudan, a member state that has allowed atrocities in Darfur to continue for years.

The African Union, nonetheless, has begun to take its security responsibilities more seriously and has developed standby military brigades that can be dispatched to help stabilize a crisis situation until the UN is able to generate a full-scale peacekeeping mission. There are several subregional organizations on the continent that show promise for contributing to economic growth and security. The two farthest along in terms of tangible capability are the Economic Community of West African States (ECOWAS) and the South African Development Community (SADC). Both started life as economic associations, designed to promote trade among member states and thereby improve regional economies, and both have expanded their charters to include defense and security. ECOWAS was founded in 1975 and is the most experienced regional peacekeeping organization, having conducted missions in Liberia and Sierra Leone.[10] ECOWAS has also developed a central bureau to coordinate regional approaches to terrorism and cross-border criminal activity. This is a development that should be fostered and expanded to other organizations.

Models for these structures exist in Europe and North America, where law enforcement agencies have long cooperated with each other and shared intelligence. The European Law Enforcement Agency is a prime example and has heightened cooperation among law enforcement and intelligence agencies worldwide as a result of the "long war." But there are gaps. Some of the most important gaps relate to the ungoverned megacities where police presence is minimal and police reputation for arbitrariness and corruption may well cost authorities their most crucial source of information about terrorist and criminal plots: tips from compliant residents. More gaps are likely to develop as national governments struggle (and largely fail in some states) to provide services and develop infrastructures in grossly overcrowded cities, leaving remote rural provinces more or less to their own devices. Monitoring criminal, terrorist, and separatist group activity in these remote locations will be beyond the capability of governments stressed by urban nightmares. Relying upon cooperative efforts with neighboring states to keep these areas under surveillance may be the only practical approach.

There are legitimate concerns about subregional organizations that one or two members dominate (as with Nigeria in the case of ECOWAS) and who are able to tilt peacekeeping operations away from strict neutrality, as well as about the professionalism and preparedness of the subregional military forces. These are not insurmountable obstacles, however, and the UN and its leading members ought to invest in equipping and training subregional forces such as those in ECOWAS.

There is ample precedent for such a program. The United States has operated three programs since the late 1990s to provide this training: the African Contingency Operations Training and Assistance program, the African Crisis Response Initiative (ACRI), and the Global Peace Operations Initiative. More than fifteen thousand African troops have been trained for peacekeeping under these programs. In addition, the United States has donated equipment and supplies to African peacekeeping missions. Several other states, notably European ones that once controlled African colonies and Canada, have also contributed funds for the training and equipping of African peacekeeping units.

A third and more important form of assistance to regional organizations is to oversee peacekeeping operations. Oversight ensures adherence to UN standards regarding respect for existing borders, as well as for human rights and the protection of noncombatants. If there is a credible process for monitoring regional peacekeeping operations, confidence in the regional organization doing the peacekeeping will grow across the region and with it the organization's soft power.

3. Cooperative Ventures for Transnational Missions

New regional organizations or subcomponents of existing organizations should also address specific transnational concerns such as crime, pollution, climate change, and terrorism. Criminal and terrorist activity in ungoverned rural areas, for example, is related to the question of weak or nonexistent border controls. The ability of armed groups to move freely in neighboring states in some regions (such as the Afghanistan-Pakistan border; the Yemen–Saudi Arabia border; the eastern borders of the DRC; the triangle where Paraguay, Argentina, and Brazil meet; and Colombia's borders with Venezuela, Ecuador, and Brazil) reduces what little incentive there is for national governments to invest scarce resources in enforcing laws and asserting government control. The Afghanistan-Pakistan border is an extreme example and one in which there simply may be no practical solution because terrain is so rugged and has little inherent economic or strategic value.

But in some areas, where border control and customs inspection are a shared bilateral function, regional organizations could offer a less expensive, practical approach to the problem: cooperative ventures for surveillance over remote areas and for improving border control. For all their practical appeal, states may resist such ideas and remain more concerned about national sovereignty or about their neighbors' ulterior motives. Oversight of these functions by a credible third party, such as a special UN commission or monitoring body, might make these options more palatable and perhaps more effective as well.

4. Centers of Excellence

A worthy complement to establishing cooperative ventures for transnational concerns would be to increase international assistance for the recruitment, training, and equipping of police units that would be attached to peacekeeping missions or deployed separately, and to support the development of permanent training institutes in the region for peacekeepers. This could be a major step in the right direction when it comes to rebuilding (or building in the first place) competent and honest police forces in troubled and ungoverned sections of megacities. This is something that the UN and at least three regional organizations already do. They need to do more of it. The UN mission in the DRC, for example, included about twelve hundred police personnel—many contributed by states that are also members of the African Union or the Arab League. In a state as large as the DRC, twelve hundred police officers may not be enough, but a force that large could make an important difference in a single city where its mission was to help build up the local police force. The Organization for Security and Cooperation in Europe (OSCE) and the European Union have also made valuable efforts to help improve law enforcement in Afghanistan, Albania, Belarus, Bosnia-Herzegovina, Ukraine, and Tajikistan. Generally speaking, the OSCE and EU efforts are small-scale operations and usually involve the provision of some training or technical assistance to local police authorities.

There is a global shortage of capable police officers available for deployment to another state. In countries with a federal system, such as the United States, most police officers are employed at the state and local levels, and often those jurisdictions cannot afford to spare officers for overseas missions—although recent pressures on state and local budgets may create a temporary surplus as officers are laid off. More generally, though, the UN has experienced significant difficulties filling quota requirements for peacekeeping missions, even as authorizations are never enough. We need an international effort to recruit and train police reserves composed globally of retired peace officers who would be on call for peacekeeping missions or the municipal trusteeships touched upon earlier.[11]

There already is a Center of Excellence for Stability Police Units in Italy, where police officers from around the world receive general training on operations in the context of peacekeeping, but enrollment is relatively small and the focus is on "training the trainers." Graduates are expected to go back to their home countries and help establish police units that could be deployed in UN peacekeeping missions.

Over time this center could have significant impact. Much like senior military war colleges in the United States and elsewhere, Center of Excellence graduates are future leaders who make a difference over time. The time factor is key, as the need is now and there are no guarantees that, unless large numbers of up-and-coming officers from a given state are trained, there will be a critical mass among the rising leaders for establishing "police stability units" that would be deployed as components of UN peacekeeping missions.

The Center for Excellence in Disaster Management and Humanitarian Assistance (COE) is another principal agency whose mission promotes disaster preparedness and societal resiliency in the Asia-Pacific region, and has undertaken operations in Europe and North and South America as well. As part of its mandate, COE takes on education, training, and research in disaster preparedness, consequence management, international disaster preparedness, disaster mitigation, disaster management, disaster response, health security, and humanitarian assistance. Under the inspiring leadership of retired lieutenant general John F. Goodman (who, as commanding general of U.S. Marine Corps Forces, Pacific, led the highly charged and politically sensitive American relief effort in Myanmar in response to Cyclone Nargis in 2008), COE partners with a wide variety of national and international governmental, nongovernmental, and international organizations—including multiple agencies of the United Nations—to provide relevant education, training, interagency coordination, and research.

Regional centers (as these examples illustrate) could be established in the most distressed megacities to train officers from regional states for missions other than peacekeeping. These officers could be trained not for UN missions, but for the provision of assistance to law enforcement authorities in neighboring countries. The focus here is really on two issues. One is to increase the number of trained, capable police available for UN missions. The other is to build cadres of law enforcement personnel who can be employed by regional/subregional organizations or by agreement among neighboring states to improve the provision of law enforcement in troubled areas, most notably undergoverned megacities.

5. "Intelligent" Aid

The United States and the major donor nations of the world must reprioritize how they allocate foreign aid. This is hardly a new issue, as there have been numerous calls for the United States to change its approach. Many of those calls have been for the United States to change by spending less, or by spending less through UN channels and more through direct aid to the recipient state. We recommend none of the above. Rather, we argue that foreign aid should be increased and redirected away from traditional programs and clients toward the small number of megacities that can severely, and devastatingly, impact respective states and regions.

We suggested one form of reprioritization in an earlier policy choice proposal: regional organizations should be given higher priority in government foreign aid programs. Aid should also be prioritized in terms of the types of aid provided. Focus should be broadened to enable the orchestration of all of the efforts of governmental and nongovernmental donors toward common goals in the megacities.

Many governments, including of course the U.S. government, routinely earmark foreign aid. That is to say, they allocate a portion of their foreign aid budget to states that are allies or that they want to influence. Foreign aid serves foreign policy purposes, and these purposes do not always align with objective assessments of where "need" is greatest. Often, earmarking results in resources that could otherwise be used on infrastructure upgrades, economic development, or the provision of social services being expended instead upon the acquisition of military hardware. For these reasons, we believe the United States and other donor countries should either earmark a portion of their foreign aid budgets for megacity issues or substantially cut back on earmarks and allow for a more objective balancing of the national interests of donors and humanitarian needs. Indeed, we have sought to make the point that humanitarian conditions in a handful of important but decrepit cities and states are affecting and will increasingly affect traditional national security interests of donor states.

6. Governments, Nongovernmental Organizations, and Aid

A recent World Bank study made the case that aid works best when donors work together for common long-term goals, instead of as competitors for political advantage or, in the case of private organizations, for fundraising publicity. Nongovernmental organizations and private sector foundations also earmark aid—in the sense that they maintain ongoing humanitarian operations in the same countries for extended periods of time, in some cases several decades. For example, Catholic Relief Services has been operating in Sierra Leone and the DRC for five decades. This is not to say that the humanitarian needs in these countries are not real or deserving of attention. The point instead is that decades of humanitarian operations in a particular state bespeaks a form of earmarking. Because an interruption in humanitarian aid could set back improvements in living conditions that have been carefully built over time, Catholic Relief Services is, in an admirable way, earmarking funds to Sierra Leone and the Democratic Republic of the Congo—and continues operations there in part because it wants to make sunk costs good. Nongovernmental organizations also execute something akin to earmarking on a functional basis.

Many NGOs have charters or mission statements that limit their activities to specific functions or geographic environments. These charters also inform the individuals and corporations who donate money to the NGO that the funds will be spent on those functions or in those exact locales. One of the most notable organizations for achieving results in places others avoid, for example, is the Aga Khan Foundation, which focuses on a small number of specific development problems by forming intellectual and financial partnerships with those that share in its objectives. With a small staff, a host of cooperating agencies, and thousands of volunteers, the foundation reaches out to vulnerable populations irrespective of race, religion, political persuasion, or gender.[12]

Equally, groups such as *Médecins Sans Frontières* (Doctors without Borders), target spending on meeting the medical needs of populations distressed by conflict or disaster, and Greenpeace International on protecting the environment. In these cases, donors, in effect, earmark funds for particular functions as they decide for whatever reason which organization to support. This form of earmarking is constructive because NGOs can become ever more proficient through specialization; moreover, donors receive some assurance that donations are spent on things that they wanted money to be spent on. The result is that NGOs continue to focus on functions and regions that might not be as important or compelling as others. Admittedly, this can self-correct to some extent if donors recognize that there are higher priorities, but it is not always in the interest of NGOs already receiving donations to educate donors about greater needs in their standard "haunts."

Governments also vary considerably in how they distribute aid. In some countries, much of the aid is delivered outside government channels, through NGOs. Most also distribute aid bilaterally on a government-to-government basis, as well as through multilateral organizations such as the EU's humanitarian office or one of the UN's agencies. This adds to administrative overhead and makes coordination for maximal effect considerably more complex. States vary considerably as well in the extent to which they offer official development assistance (ODA), the term for foreign aid that is not emergency relief. According to statistics compiled by the Organization of Economic Cooperation and Development (OECD), for example, almost three fourths of Italy's ODA is distributed through multilateral organizations such as the UN or the World Bank. Only one-fourth of Italian ODA is "invested" bilaterally—that is to say, given directly by Italy to another state. Many other states invest 50 to 60 percent of their ODA funds bilaterally. The largest ODA investors in terms of absolute dollars spent are the United States and Japan. Both invest almost three-fourths bilaterally and only one-fourth multilaterally.

A more effective approach would be to orchestrate a global approach to foreign aid that targets greater levels of foreign aid at the burgeoning urban populations of emerging megacities and on states attempting to govern them. This is not only considerably easier said than done—it is unrealistic to believe perfect coordination of effort will ever be achieved. Official foreign aid has traditionally reflected the national interests and domestic political pressures of donating states and will continue to do so as long as the world is organized around states. Improvements in the targeting and coordination of all forms of public and private foreign aid, nevertheless, are both warranted and possible. The community of donor states, international organizations, and NGOs should start now to focus on ways of improving coordination of aid programs with respect to emerging megacities.

7. Private Sector Contributions

A considerable amount of aid—and investment—comes from the private sector. For the United States alone, the dollar value of American "foreign aid" that citizens, corporations, and foundations provide through private sector channels ranks in the many billions. Private donations to support relief for the 2010 Haitian earthquake alone exceeded $2 billion. There is no question that this aid could be more effectively spent. One area where more funds should be spent is municipal governance in megacities.

Overall the total value of all private donations is larger than the total value of all bilateral and multilateral official aid, combined. We must mobilize a coordinated targeting of private investment, remittances, and donations. In addition to foreign aid by governments, a considerable amount of aid—and of course, investment—is contributed by the private sector outside government channels. For example, citizens, corporations, and foundations in the United States and other countries routinely donate funds directly to nongovernmental organizations, such as the aforementioned Catholic Relief Services and *Médecins Sans Frontières*, for expenditure in underdeveloped and/or disaster-afflicted states in Eastern Europe, Africa, Asia, and Central and South America. These donations are substantial.

Yet there are many states in which private donations are small relative to the size of national economies and in comparison to official aid amounts. This suggests untapped private sector resources that could be mobilized through concerted efforts to educate about and provide access opportunity to nongovernment channels. Foreign aid by governments is not enough to cope with the problems many in the world face. Educational efforts should highlight the serious problems that some megacities present to their millions of residents, to weak states theoretically parent to the megacities, and to the rest of the globe. As we saw in our discussion of Cairo, the UN has already held a conference on the challenges of urban growth. Yet that conference did not spark the kind of human (or security) concerns that other conferences have achieved.[13] Perhaps it is time for the UN to try again with a conference dedicated to the megacity challenge.

Private sector contributions are by nature outside the ambit of governments and, in theory, are made wherever the individual donor or investor chooses. This makes coordination and orchestration of overall efforts difficult, as donors and investors may be reluctant to agree on a set of common priorities and policies. Education will be crucial.

The challenge then is to encourage individuals and other private sector entities (social clubs, religious organizations, corporations, and foundations), once again, to realize the target value of their contributions and at the same time energize donors to target more donations to NGOs whose charters commit them to taking on megacity challenges.

8. Megacity Strategies

While previous strategy papers have addressed emerging nations—such as the 2003 Goldman Sachs report on the four emerging major BRIC (Brazil, Russia, India, and China) economies and the "N-11" states (which include Bangladesh, Egypt, Nigeria, and Pakistan)—few analyses focus on megacities.[14] While we previously saw the efforts of World Bank studies, the OECD has created a Development Co-operation Directorate and a Development Assistance Committee whose jobs are to coordinate the aid strategies of the most economically advanced countries in the world. The directorate and committee are focused on achieving "millennium development goals" to substantially reduce poverty, unemployment, and child mortality, and to increase gender equality and widen the availability of primary education by 2015.[15] The question arises: what next?

The OECD took the early lead in pushing for such goals and for an international effort to achieve them. Its 1996 strategy paper, *Shaping the 21st Century*, called for realistic but measurable foreign aid goals and was instrumental in creating the momentum that ultimately led to the UN's adoption of the Millennium Development Goals. The OECD should consider further strategies to address the myriad and compelling challenges that emerging megacities pose now and will pose to even greater extent in coming years. Such strategies will chart the course as effective resources to educate donors, as well as serve as clarion call for NGOs to place greater emphasis on megacities. These efforts create vehicles by which donors can channel donations to programs and projects that improve megacity conditions.

9. Remittances and Microcredits

Our next macro-level choice is to establish mechanisms that harness the effects of remittances—funds "remitted" or transferred from individuals in one state to individuals in another state. Typically, they are sent by expatriate workers who support their families back home by sending them some of the money they earn. Internationally the sheer volume of remittances migrants send has grown at astonishing rates—outstripping foreign aid and *all* global foreign direct investment. Since 1995, as the World Bank data in the table below indicates, the value of remittances overall has been significantly greater than the total value of the traditional economic development form of foreign aid.

In 2005 officially recorded remittances worldwide reached an astounding $232 billion, with "emerging" states receiving $167 billion—more than twice the level of development aid from all sources. In 2012 the combined total of officially and unofficially tracked flows for remittances may well exceed $400 billion worldwide.[16]

Remittances form a major source of income to states in Africa, the Middle East, South Asia, and Southeast Asia—the very regions that face the most dire security, economic, and environmental challenges.[17] According to World Bank and other prominent studies, India's economy gained an estimated $11.5 billion in 2002 from remittances and Egypt's $3.7 billion. The Egyptian total was larger than the amount the state received in both foreign direct investment and foreign aid.

GLOBAL REMITTANCES (World Bank data)

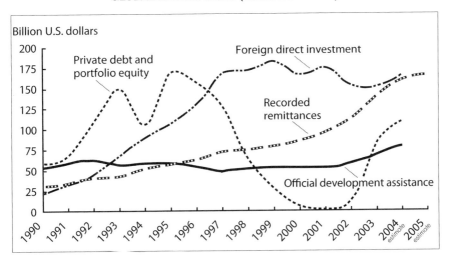

Remittances are almost always spent by family members still in the home country on food, clothing, and other forms of consumption. As such they increase economic activity, but they do not by themselves contribute directly to infrastructure development. There are, however, mechanisms established in Mexico and some South American countries to increase the impact of remittances on development and, indirectly, on governance. For example, the Organization of American States has sponsored a Pan-American Development Foundation to help expatriate workers invest in economic and infrastructure development in Mexico and El Salvador. There is also a Transnational Community Development Fund that enables expatriates in the United States to donate funds for development projects back home. The United States supports this program by allowing tax-deductible donations; under some conditions, the U.S. government and home countries match these donations. Similar programs should be expanded to other regions and to other wealthy countries beyond the United States, with community development funds for West Africa, the Middle East, and South Asia. Ideally these funds would target expenditures on infrastructure improvements in the most overcrowded cities.

It would also be prudent for clerics in Muslim states, particularly wealthy Persian Gulf states, to consider whether contributions to these community development funds could be considered religiously acceptable as the tithe Islam requires all Muslims to pay. This "tax" is technically intended as alms for the poor, and infrastructure improvements in the wretched slums of Karachi, Lahore, and Cairo would certainly benefit impoverished urban neighborhoods. Given the wealth in the Persian Gulf states, a favorable ruling could result in a substantial amount of funding.

A further step that could increase the positive impact of remittances on the home country is to establish better banking systems in the developing countries, so that expatriates would be able to send money home through banks that would then have larger reserves and could lend more money to development projects. Not only would this introduce greater transparency and regulation into local financial institutions—itself a valuable contribution to governance—but it might also elicit greater investments from overseas workers.

There are dangers, of course, in attempting to "harness" the power of re-mittances, which could lead to overcontrol and even less efficient functioning of this important practice that fills a crucial socioeconomic need. But abuses, especially in the charging of exorbitant rates to transfer remittances from country to country, are already taking place. We can do better.

We should recognize the immense value—and dangers—in microlend-ing. In 2006 the relatively unknown Bangladeshi economist Muhammad Yunus received the Nobel Peace Prize for his successful implementation of an extraordinarily sensible—and extraordinarily effective—idea. Through his founding of the Grameen Bank and its innovative use of microlending—giving numerous, high-risk loans to people of extremely limited means—dramatic changes took place in Bangladesh. The cumulative effect of microcredit prac-tice successfully lifted many out of poverty.[18] Grameen made a difference for the overcrowded, ecologically vulnerable state. Citizens—not only in urban centers but in nearly eighty thousand Bangladeshi villages (90 percent of the total)—received the benefits and opportunities that microlending provides. Notably, the vast majority of these loan recipients were women. Microlending led to dramatic changes in numerous locales throughout the 10/40 Window. Now, there should be a particular focus on urban microlending.

Inevitably there have been critics of microcredits—and the most power-ful have been those who articulate how such programs manage to tread water but fail at overall poverty reduction. Jaime Joseph, a community organizer in Lima, Peru, points out in *Development and Cities* that "[t]here has been much emphasis placed on small or micro-enterprises as the magic solution in offering economic development for the urban poor. Our work over the last 20 years with some small businesses, which are multiplying in the megacity, shows that most of them are simply survival tactics with little or no chances for accumulation."

The increasing use of microfinancing has led to recent ominous outcomes as well. In India it has become patently evident that a number of creditors are far more interested in "loot and scoot" schemes than in actually providing assistance. While microcredits have for decades now provided a path out of poverty for millions—with the World Bank and venture capitalists using India as a kind of petri dish for improving social capital while fulfilling human needs—some lenders have more than doubled revenues annually and used coercive methods to collect. Admitting that a loan of as little as $50—whether for the purchase of a sewing machine or a cellular telephone—can literally change a life, there are dark sides to this reality. With mounting suicides and the fleeing from native homes of those inexperienced at lending practices, some India officials fear that the microfinance debacle could become India's equivalent of the subprime mortgage collapse, where profit-at-any-cost lending practices and devious investment swaps threatened the global banking system.

Perhaps most ominous of all: A recent *New York Times* headline read, "Can Microlending Save Haiti?"

10. Megacity Civil Societies and Civil-Human Security

Civil society organizations perform useful functions and can help overwhelmed municipal and national governments provide essential services, as well as aid in educating urban populations on community self-help and neighborhood-level political organization. New means and measures for civilian groups in megacities to interact with security organizations—most importantly civilian-police task forces—will improve law enforcement and public safety and help achieve truly organic civil-human security.

The UN, the United States, and members of the OECD promote civil society as an essential contribution to urban infrastructure and governance. Civil society organizations include a wide range of entities: labor unions, professional and trade associations, values-oriented organizations (such as environmental and human rights advocacy groups), and nongovernmental organizations that provide humanitarian and other services. They can be valuable sources of technical assistance and advice about infrastructure construction and maintenance and the reorganization of municipal agencies. They can also help educate urban populations about community self-help and neighborhood-level political organization.

To some extent this is happening already. The Muslim Brotherhood, for example, provides important medical and educational services in many poor, underserved Cairo neighborhoods and isolated villages outside the metropolis. In many of the communities in which it operates, the Brotherhood provides far more services than the Egyptian government. As constructive as those services are, the Brotherhood's ideology and political objectives have put it at odds with the Egyptian government and in bad odor with the West.[19] Control of student and professional associations further placed it in the position where the Cairo government sees the Brotherhood as its main opposition. Its ideological reputation in official Egyptian circles and elsewhere undoubtedly limits its effectiveness as an agent of governance reform and economic development. It is, nevertheless, an example of a civil society organization that fills the gaps in public services created by an incompetent or indifferent government.

Prospects for developing indigenous civil society organizations to assist municipal governments will improve naturally as more funds become available through grants from the UN, from UN members states, and from older, more established NGOs. This is another reason why it is important that the UN and OECD become "seized" with the megacity issue.

Concomitant with civil society enhancements is the recognition that some aspects of security assistance programs that the United States and some of its allies administer could be reoriented toward police and court reform. Security assistance programs involve various forms of assistance to the armed forces of other nations. Under these programs African peacekeeping forces have been supplied with communications equipment, and military officers from many states have received training or education at U.S. military schools.

Support for peacekeeping should be continued. But other aspects of programs should be transformed to support police and court reform. There are several reasons for this. One is that the signal national security threat of the era is terrorism, and effective police forces overseas can be the first line of defense against terrorist plots. Another important reason is that economic growth and domestic stability—two things that megacities desperately need—depend in no small measure on the rule of law. Establishing confidence in the administrative competence and integrity of governmental organs charged with executing the law is a key challenge facing many countries in less developed areas of the world.

In many of the states where the most overburdened megacities exist, incompetence, corruption, and arbitrariness are notoriously characteristic of police; immigration, customs, licensing, and taxing agencies; as well as court systems. In some states, private militias and undisciplined regular military forces intervene in domestic affairs, further complicating matters. Until such time as these "security sector" organizations and systems are reformed and public confidence in them established, maintaining progress on other fronts will be difficult. Vital long-term foreign and domestic investment in infrastructure and commercial ventures will remain limited as long as investors lack confidence in the predictability and competence of regulatory authorities, the integrity of law enforcement authorities, and their ability to get a fair hearing in court.

Unstable security conditions in postwar Iraq and in the territory of the Palestinian Authority show difficult security sector reform. In these and other locations, efforts to establish control over multiple security sector organizations (Hamas and the Palestinian Authority, for example, in Gaza) amount to a small-scale civil war among domestic factions with sharply divergent political agenda. The situation in Iraq also demonstrates that security sector reform may be more important over the long term than elections or the erection of checks and balances between legislative and executive branches of government and between central and regional authorities. No government can succeed over the long haul without ability to provide security or without minimum levels of confidence that security sector agencies have ceased to be predatory.

The issue is how the international community can constructively promote and assist security sector reform. Because security assistance is consensual—the recipient's desires should be taken into account—it may not be possible for any one state to unilaterally reorient security assistance away from the hardware that the recipient state's military wants to obtain. In some cases there may well be a legitimate need for traditional military hardware to suppress an internal uprising or to maintain the balance of power against a regional adversary. What is needed is dialogue and greater understanding among all parties about what the most pressing, long-term challenges are.

11. Human Impact: From Dependency Ratios to
"Geomechanical Pollution"

Our final two macro-level proposals qualify, to put it mildly, as controversial. Yet recognizing that human impacts and global responses necessary to address the megacity test are symbiotic, we want to first consider two disparate aspects that portray the array of effects that can and have taken place.

First: take "dependency ratios." Among demographers, the dependency ratio is an uncomplicated, powerful tool to help explain how societies succeed or fail. Simply put, it is the relation between the number of people not of working age and the number of people who are. As Malcolm Gladwell observed in an extraordinary (and now ironically titled) piece written for the *New Yorker*, "The Risk Pool: What's Behind Ireland's Economic Miracle—and GM's Financial Crisis," dependency ratios help explain East Asia's financial miracle and Africa's continuing quagmire. Even as East Asia has seen its dependency ratio decline by 35 percent over the past three and a half decades, the high point—where people of working age supported those not of working age (either because the latter were pensioners or youth still enrolled in the educational system)—allowed extraordinary economic growth to occur.

The People's Republic of China, the most strategically future-focused of all states, is in the midst of its demographic "sweet spot." In the 1960s at the height of the Cultural Revolution, replacement fertility rates for families approached 8.0; now, as a result of the "One Child Policy," China has dramatically dropped its birth rate.[20] Children are now grown up and in the workforce, and there is no similarly sized class of dependents behind them. China will peak with a 1:2.6 dependency ratio by 2015. By 2050 China will have a 1:1.5 dependency ratio, with over 30 percent of Chinese over sixty—a spectacular shift in dependency ratio. The bottom line: China is in a race to get rich before it gets old.

India, by contrast—which abruptly terminated its forced sterilization program of the 1970s as in the world's largest democracy—has reduced its birth rate more slowly and has yet to hit the sweet spot. Its best years are ahead. Equally, as Gladwell notes, Africa has a major dependency ratio crisis:

> People have talked endlessly of Africa's political and social and economic shortcomings and simultaneously of some magical cultural

ingredient possessed by South Korea and Japan and Taiwan that has brought them success. . . . But the truth is that sub-Saharan Africa has been mired in a debilitating 1-to-1 ratio for decades, and that proportion of dependency would frustrate and complicate economic development anywhere.

Recent data also indicate that even the United States has dropped below the "replacement fertility rate" (RFR) of 2.0. Notably, RFR is 1.8 for non-Hispanic Caucasians and 2.75 for Hispanics in the United States. In Europe, with an RFR of 1.75, 80 million fewer Europeans will exist over the next decades—a decline greater than the "Black Death." Numbers that make the dependency ratio shifts even more significant for industrialized states suggest that in 1945, each retiree in America was supported by forty-two workers; today, each retiree in America is supported by three workers. In Europe today there are also three workers for every retiree. By 2050 in Europe—if immigration rates remain unchanged—we will be seeing one worker for each retiree.

One obvious solution would be for industrialized states to encourage families to have more children, as well create policies more family friendly. France, Finland, and Sweden already provide incentives: child care, generous leave, financial allowances. But immigration helps as well, for both industrialized and emerging states. As Jack A. Goldstone asks: Why not encourage "reverse flow" of older immigrants from developed to developing countries such as in the southern Mediterranean, Latin America, or Africa? Doing so would reduce elder-care costs at home and provide employment and training to young, growing populations in the majority world. And it would help break the dependency ratio trap.

China in particular faces daunting demographic urban challenges. For the People's Republic, which has rapidly extended its strategic reach and massive investment in South Asia and in Africa, challenges "at home" are frightening. More than one hundred Chinese cities have populations over one million, as opposed to only nine cities in the United States. Many of these cities are new creations. The megacity of Shenzhen in southeastern China (on the mainland facing Hong Kong), for example, *did not even exist* prior to 1979 except as a simple fishing village; today its population is over 14 million. The movement of peasant populations from the west to the megacities of eastern China represents the largest—and most rapid—migration in human history.

While China certainly has the capacity to deal with such cataclysmic socio-economic shifts, it may also contribute to adverse effects through inattention or simply bad practices—especially in relation to human impact. Specifically, through what we term "geomechanical pollution"—whether through large-scale geoengineering activities such as mining, creation and use of water reservoirs, or even sequestration of CO_2 into the Earth's crust (especially close to industrial plants and factories)—such activity might advance natural earthquake cycles or trigger seismic events.

Yes, humans may be causing earthquakes. Since 1900 more than two hundred damaging earthquakes associated with industrialization and urbanization have been documented. These events produced not only regional but sometimes global economic impacts. The 1989 Newcastle earthquake caused thirteen deaths and $3.5 billion worth of damage—3.4 percent of Australia's gross domestic income. Far more devastating was the 2008 seismic shocker in Sichuan, China, an 8.0 magnitude quake that left more than five million homeless and ninety thousand dead. It may have been unleashed by the huge Zipingpu Dam through reservoir-induced seismicity. The 511-foot-high dam holds 315 million tons of water and is 500 meters from the fault line and three miles from the epicenter of the quake—and was known to shift water levels as much as 150 meters in a single year.

Some scientists, both in China and the United States, believe the weight of water and penetration into rock could have affected pressure on the fault line underneath, unleashing ruptures. Fan Xiao, chief engineer of the Sichuan Geology and Mineral Bureau in Chengdu, claimed it was "very likely" that construction and filling of the reservoir led to the disaster: "This earthquake was very unusual for this area. There have been no seismic activities greater than a magnitude seven quake along this particular seismic belt before." Christian Klose, a scientist at Columbia University, argued there had been no "major seismic activity" on that fault line for millions of years. He suggested that the sudden shift of huge water quantity could have simultaneously relaxed tension between the two sides of the fault, allowing them to move apart, and also increased direct pressure enough to cause a violent rupture. The effect was "25 times more" than a year's worth of natural stress from tectonic movement.

Needless to say, wherever we have spoken globally about such human impact possibility, we are greeted with outraged protests. All these "foul play" cries originate with natural scientists, who counter that the proof, and data, are not yet sufficient. We are, of course, reminded of our favorite Einstein adage: "If at first, the idea is not absurd, then there is no hope for it." Drawing on earlier concepts and through the validation of zebra-like magnetic striping on the ocean floors, the theory of tectonic plates and the Vine-Matthews-Morley hypothesis received similar claims of scoffing rejection in 1963. What a pity skeptics were wrong.

12. Establish "Charter Cities"

Our most controversial proposal is also the last in our "twelve-step solution": that the UN, a regional organization, or an ad hoc coalition be given temporary responsibility for administering and reforming failed municipal agencies in select megacities. We spoke of this earlier as a municipal trusteeship, but it could equally be compared to a rescue mission after a natural disaster. Restoring damaged infrastructure is high priority after disasters, so improving inadequate infrastructure in locations where people routinely suffer as badly as many disaster victims is not too great a reach.

This is an approach that would presumably only be taken as a last resort, when other options have failed. Clearly it is not an approach that a proud state such as Pakistan, Egypt, or Nigeria would willingly agree to if forced upon them. But states overwhelmed by the task of managing a megacity could see that it would be in their interest to request international assistance before their jurisdictions spin off into anarchy. Municipal authorities in many states already accept help from the U.S. Agency for International Development (USAID), the UN, and NGOs in improving ability to govern and provide public services. USAID has had governance programs under way in Karachi since 2005. Through these programs, USAID has helped Karachi modernize its system for maintaining voter rolls and also provided technical assistance to municipal authorities on ways to improve the delivery of education and health services. Worthy as this is, the USAID program is too marginal to make a significant difference for the city's massive population.

Collectively the UN, the EU's many states, and the NGO community have most of the skills, capabilities, and resources to reorganize a municipal government, identify and help build critical infrastructure, train local staff, and arrange for more effective delivery of public services. But these skills and capabilities have not been organized into a coordinated single package or set of capabilities that could be deployed on request.

If such a set of capabilities were to exist—perhaps under the direction of an urban affairs equivalent to the League of Nations Trusteeship Council, with a centralized planning staff such as the UN Department of Peacekeeping Operations—it might well do more than provide a useful tool to correct hazards in megacity Leviathans. An established organization at the UN with real capacity and capability would draw more attention to megacity issues and could thereby inspire states to dedicate energy and resources to managing major cities.

Paul Romer, distinguished Stanford University economist, has done the most to advance this radical proposal through his "charter cities" approach. Highlighted in the subversively titled *Atlantic Monthly* piece "The Politically Incorrect Guide to Ending Poverty," written by Sebastian Mallaby (himself a distinguished economist at the Council on Foreign Relations), Romer has addressed the chief source of legitimate coercion that exists today: governments that preside over the world's more successful states. To launch charter cities, poor states would lease chunks of territory to enlightened foreign powers, which would preside over a kind of imperial protectorate. As Mallaby notes, "Romer's prescription is not merely neo-medieval, in other words. It is also neo-colonial."

Romer certainly has his share of critics. Elliott Sclar, professor of urban planning at Columbia, declared to Mallaby that "Romer makes it sound as though setting up a charter city is like setting up a fairground. . . . We take a clear piece of land, we turn on the bright lights, and we create this separate environment that will stand apart from everything that's around it. I wish it were that simple." The reality, however, while not perhaps simple, is clear. Many states have failed managing their cities. In presentations Romer often illustrates this poignantly with a photograph of Guinean teenagers doing their homework under streetlights. Mallaby describes the contradictions in this image perfectly:

> The line of hunched, concentrating figures presents a mystery, Romer says; from the photo it is clear that the teens are not dirt poor, and youths like these generally own cell phones. Yet they evidently have no electric light at home, or they would not be studying by the curb-side. "So here is the puzzle," Romer declares. "Why do these kids have access to a cutting-edge technology like the cell phone, but not to a 100-year-old technology for generating electric light in the home?" The answer, in a word, is rules. Because of misguided price controls in the teenagers' country, the local electricity utility has no incentive to connect their houses to the power grid. Their society lacks the rules that make technological advance meaningful.

To date, no state has truly taken on the charter cities approach—although one came close. In 2008 Romer began visiting Madagascar and eventually convinced then president and former businessman Marc Ravalomanana of the concept's potential. If Romer could convince at least two rich states to play the role of trustee, Ravalomanana suggested launching two initial parallel experiments on the island state. The implications were revolutionary: "a nation of 20 million people was about to embrace a neo-medieval, neo-colonial scheme untested in the modern history of development," says Mallaby. In the end, and for different circumstances, Ravalomanana was forced from office.

Then, too, there is the question of why a wealthy state would be willing to undertake such a mission. Any government in a state with pockets of poverty, high unemployment, disease, and crime—in other words, just about every state—might have a hard time convincing its citizens that it would be a good idea to undertake such a project without having first cured its own domestic ills. To date, charter cities have not found a home—or sponsors. But it is an idea whose time may well have come.

MICRO-STEPS: CREATING THE CHANGE

Although we have discussed micro-level issues and potential solutions throughout this work, we propose them here in a collective form—though not as extensively as our consideration of macro-level approaches. But, once again, we must generate awareness, mobilize it, and marshal action on the part of international system actors in order to

1. recognize human rights as the cornerstone of security;
2. aggregate human rights as a collection of "rights"—defecation rights, water distribution, women's rights, access and land rights;
3. widen the use of microcredits and monitor implementation;
4. establish mechanisms to measure community-level progress;
5. monitor macro-level efforts to improve micro-level conditions;
6. contrast violence levels and economic improvement efforts;
7. draw on community organizers and local NGOs as mediators or negotiators;
8. improve education for children and community-level training for police; and
9. enhance civil-police cooperation, such as the *panchayat* system in Mumbai.

WHAT WE CAN DO RIGHT NOW

Land Reform

Securing land reform in shantytowns and slums that so dominate the urban landscape in megacities is possible. In almost all megacities, slums are illegal settlements on public and, in some cases, private land, and the slum dwellers have no right to their ramshackle homes. Three things happen as a result. First, residents invest little in improving property since they cannot sell what they do not own. This obviously contributes to poor living conditions in the community. Second is that, as economist Hernando de Soto discovered in his studies of illegal settlements in Peru, opportunities for capital formation are lost when residents do not own their land or buildings they erect on it. Because they do not own the land, they cannot obtain mortgages they might use to invest in small businesses or education for their children. Third, the illegal status of neighborhoods gives municipal authorities an excuse not to invest in building infrastructure there. It also gives municipal authorities freer rein in terms of bulldozing neighborhoods in the name of urban planning— considerably more risky politically and legally if landowners were the ones being driven from their homes.

Some form of land reform, under which residents could acquire titles to land they reside on, would stabilize communities and promote socioeconomic growth. Residents would have more of a stake in the status quo and possess the incentive to improve properties as they become more active citizens.

Move Toward "Bottom-up" Change

By establishing systems and mechanisms that promote bottom-up change in megacities, real change would happen. Some of this can be achieved by improving education and transportation systems so that residents acquire wider skills and manage to get to where the jobs actually are. Land reform could provide access to capital. Honest and equitable microlending regimes would help. NGOs can help organize cooperatives, unions, and grassroots political movements such as the environmental NGO Green Belt Movement established in Kenya in the 1970s. To date the organization has planted over 30 million trees across Kenya to prevent further soil erosion and reduce air pollution—and works today to save the endangered Mau Forest, whose disappearance could make the legendary wildebeest migration from Masai Mara to the Serengeti a thing of the past as crucial water sources evaporate.

All these groups should receive support—and protection when necessary— because their collective, long-term impacts on society are considerable. The International Republican Institute (IRI) based in Washington, D.C., has designed and implemented a number of mechanisms that foster bottom-up change. IRI operates so-called transparency salons, which provide access to official records about the local government plans and budgets, and collect complaints and requests that are in turn relayed to municipal authorities. Because travel can be difficult in communities without mass transit, some of these "salons" are mobile—going into communities to learn what needs exist and to give disconnected residents a chance to influence what their governments do. IRI assists municipal governments in formulate transparent budgets that can be shared with and understood by residents—a major improvement in places where populations view government as dishonest, rapacious, and venal. IRI also runs programs that create public information campaigns to educate national leaders and the population in general about successes achieved in individual communities. Such programs educate people at the top about innovations by people at the bottom.

Judicious Force

The use of force, or rather the threat of force to impose order in the most unruly neighborhoods in megacities, is difficult for local and national governments for a variety of reasons. But it needs to be done. The costs of operations with poorly trained and equipped police forces could be substantial. There is no guarantee that anything other than a professionally planned and executed operation will succeed in imposing order. Unless carefully conducted, the operation will be perceived as yet another example of heavy-handedness on the part of an uncaring government.

Brazil continues the attempt to assert control over its notoriously ungoverned *favelas* in Rio de Janeiro and São Paulo—sending what amounts to massive force into neighborhoods to establish order and then set up what might, and perhaps should, be permanent outposts to maintain an effective presence. After decades of neglecting the violence, crime, and wretched living conditions in *favelas*, Brazil has begun taking these actions to prepare for hosting the 2014 World Cup and the 2016 Summer Olympics. Brazil has also been fortunate to enjoy dramatic economic growth in recent years and can now afford to confront social problems more seriously than it has in the past. While touting a "successful" outcome during interventions in a weeklong pitched battle in Rio slums in late 2010—especially in the explosive *favela* of Alemão—the real successful outcomes remain, sadly, to be seen.

States with the most worrisome megacities do not have the same incentives or economic resources as Brazil has with respect to Rio or São Paulo, but they possess the need—and perhaps desire—to address ungoverned neighborhoods. The international community might consider reviewing Brazil's actions and consider whether its current model can be usefully applied—or radically avoided—in other megacities; determine what international resources training, equipping, and police units that intervene in the neighborhoods should play; and examine whether or not international oversight is necessary to ensure citizens' rights are upheld. Military force, in some cases, may well have to remain until such time as police units are ready to step in and maintain peace.

This may sound like harsh prescription. It is. But establishing security and the rule of law inside megacities is crucial to addressing dangers residents face and the stability national governments might lose—not to mention the stability of sometimes fragile neighboring states.

PART III: MOVING FORWARD: REDRAWING THE MAP OF THE FUTURE

We must generate awareness of these problems to the actors who matter in the international system: the UN, its leading members, regional and economic organizations such as the AU and the OECD, and major NGOs. Next, we must mobilize awareness into action and then marshal action into ways that secure results. We recognize this requires larger budgets—when global purse strings are drawn tightly—but additional resources can and should come through reallocation of funds from other areas. We acknowledge that across-the-board success cannot be guaranteed; there are too many moving pieces in this puzzle. Even the best orchestration of international effort will come up short in some locations.

All of these difficult choices cannot—and must not—be left to political leaders alone. Politicians are driven by pressing, near-term issues and are never renowned for attention to the future—or even the not-so-distant future megacity scenarios looming before us. But a bottom-up–driven revolution in ideas to redraw and reshape the map of the future is the only path we have. Success requires combined, concerted actions of powerful governments, international agencies, nongovernmental organizations, and corporations—and peoples themselves. Right decisions will focus on the long view and not just the *next* crisis. To do this wisely requires strategic attention, strategic planning, and strategic investment. But by doing this, we provide the best hope for addressing problems that megacities of the emerging world—and through them, the rest of the world—face as the new Leviathans arise.

We cannot fail at this. The future is waiting.

NOTES

Chapter 1. Introduction

1. Onookome Okome, "Writing the Anxious City: Images of Lagos in Nigerian Home Video Films," in *Under Siege: Four African Cities—Freetown, Johannesburg, Kinshasa, Lagos: Documenta11_Platform4*, moderated by *Okwui Enwezor* (Ostfildern, Germany: Hatje Cantz Verlag, 2003). Program outline and speakers are available in pdf form at: http://www.radio bridge.net/www/folder.pdf.

2. Image source: *The Joshua Project*, http://www.joshuaproject.net/10-40-window.php. Previously referred to as the "resistant belt," the 10/40 concept was coined by Christian strategist Luis Bush in 1990. It highlights three aspects: as an area of great poverty, low quality of life, and lack of access to Christian resources.

3. We should stress that massive population does not necessarily spell disaster for a city. Tokyo, for example, will remain the world's largest city—with a population already exceeding 35 million—but it possesses the capacity, the infrastructure, and the socioeconomic resiliency to support such population and to prosper.

4. Robert Neuwirth, *Shadow Cities: A Billion Squatters, A New Urban World* (New York: Routledge, 2006), xiii.

5. Although Rio de Janeiro is well removed geographically from the 10/40 Window, its significance as a city intimately linked to globalization—as well as a city plagued by violence, criminality, and growing slum populations—warrants serious attention.

6. Jakarta is also ecologically vulnerable. During the wet season, clogged sewer pipes and waterways cause the city to flood rapidly, creating a massive impact on an increasingly frequent scale. This vulnerability is further aggravated by deforestation in the surrounding highlands areas south of Jakarta. The floods of 2007 impacted 70 percent of the city, forced 350,000 from their homes and by some estimates caused losses exceeding a half a billion dollars in infrastructure and lost state revenues. The island of Java, where Jakarta is located, ranks among the highest "danger zones"

in the world for natural disasters. In 1997 wildfires in Indonesian peat bogs placed a chokehold on all air traffic in Southeast Asia and released 2.6 billion tons of CO_2 into the atmosphere—amounting to 40 percent of total global emissions that year. Another (bizarre) example of ecological imbalance: according to seismological data, over the recent past mud has been erupting from the ground in eastern Java—at the rate of 37 million gallons per day.

7. John Bresnan, "Indonesia," *In Pivotal States: A New Framework for U.S. Policy in the Developing World*, edited by Robert Chase, Emily Hill and Paul Kennedy (New York: W. W. Norton, 2000), 15.
8. Steve Coll, "Flood Tides," *The New Yorker*, September 6, 2010, 20.

Chapter 2. Too Far, Too Fast

1. Neuwirth, *Shadow Cities*, 16–17.
2. This claim is extremely conservative and likely outdated—U.S. oil consumption is likely much, much higher than this. United States oil production peaked in 1970 and began to significantly decline; by 2005 imports were twice as great as production. In 2010, oil consumption globally exceeded production by over five million barrels per day for the first year ever. Sources: "Oil Production and Consumption: Running Dry," *Economist Online*, June 9, 2011, http://www.economist.com/blogs/daily chart/2011/06/oil-production-and-consumption; *Annual Energy Review 2010, Independent Statistics & Analysis*, U.S. Department of Energy Information Administration, http://www.eia.gov/totalenergy/data/annual/pdf/aer.pdf; James Jordan and James R. Powell, "After the Oil Runs Out," *Washington Post,* June 6, 2004, B07: http://www.washingtonpost.com/wp-dyn/articles/A17039-2004Jun4.html; Kathleen Kingsbury, "After the Oil Crisis, A Food Crisis?" *Time,* November 16, 2007: http://www.time.com/time/business/article/0,8599,1684910,00.html?iid=sphere-inline-sidebar.
3. Paul Goldberger, "Shelter and Style," *The New Yorker* (October 2, 2010), http://www.newyorker.com/online/blogs/festival/2010/10/paul-goldberger.html.
4. Debra Davis and Paulo Saldiva, "Urban Air Pollution Risks to Children: A Global Environmental Health Indicator," World Resources Institute, September 1999.
5. Robert O. Paxton, *Europe in the Twentieth Century* (Belmont, CA: Thomson Wadsworth, 2005), 8.
6. Not coincidentally, the boulevards of Paris were broad enough to make it almost impossible for angry residents to throw up spur-of-the-moment barricades to protest government policies and social conditions.
7. Tunde Agbola, *The Architecture of Fear: Urban Design and Construction Response to Urban Violence in Lagos* (Ibadan, Nigeria: ABB, 1997), 51.

8. A 2002 study showed that residents of Kibera pay up to five times more for a liter of water than an average American citizen does. Considering the gross disparity in relative incomes, such costs lead to desperate measures. Some residents use sewage water, rely on rainwater, or draw their water from broken pipes.

9. Kiberans, as with all Kenyans, are endlessly creative. From the hordes of sewage pits that run throughout the slum, residents have been able to tap into naturally created methane gas—and use it for heating community showers, providing warm water otherwise not available.

10. Mike Davis, *Planet of Slums* (London: Verso, 2007), 139. Also drawn from Liotta's personal observations and interviews conducted in country.

11. Ayşe Yönder, "Implications of Double Standards in Housing Policy: Development of Informal Settlements in İstanbul," in *Illegal Cities: Law and Urban Change in Developing Countries*, eds. Edésio Fernandes and Ann Varley (London: Zed Books, 1998), 62.

12. This may also be an overly simplistic, even optimistic, assessment. In Latife Tekin's classic and brutally realistic novel, *Berji Kristin: Tales from the Garbage Hills*—where the unemployed, the homeless, the elderly, and the bereft scavenge for food and fight against impossible odds in their *gecekondu* literally built from refuse—the squatters of "Flower Hill" build and rebuild their shanties by night, even as the authorities destroy them each morning. As Mike Davis notes in *Planet of Slums* (page 39), "Only after a Homeric siege of 37 days does the government finally relent and allow the new *gecekondu* to take root on a garbage mountain."

13. Neuwirth, *Shadow Cities*, 153–54.

14. Mumbai became the official name of the city formerly known as Bombay in 1995, after the Hindu Nationalist Shiv Sena party won elections in the state of Maharashtra that year. The port city was renamed after a combination of the Hindu goddess Mumbadevi, the city's patron deity, and *Aai*, which means "mother" in Marathi. Shiv Sena claimed that "Bombay" was a corrupted English version of "Mumbai" and an unwanted legacy of British colonial rule. Notably, Shiv Sena wanted to also change the name of the "Bollywood" film industry, but that proved a bridge too far, and the name has stuck.

15. Dharavi is commonly called *the* world's largest slum in *the* world's largest city. Neither claim is true. Mexico City's Neza-Chalco-Itza barrio has four times as many people. Karachi's Orangi Township has also now surpassed Dharavi.

16. As with most population estimates for megacity slums, this is a claim that cannot be stated with any accuracy. We have found data, for example, that argues that Dharavi's population in 2004 was 2.8 million people—suggesting figures well above 3 million today.

17. Neuwirth, *Shadow Cities*, 129.

18. In a disgusting replication of this effort, Zimbabwean president Robert Mugabe attempted to evict seven hundred thousand residents from the capital, Harare, in June 2005 in Operation Murambastvina—Operation Drive Out Trash.

19. Kalpana Sharma, *Rediscovering Dharavi: Stories from Asia's Largest Slum* (New York: Penguin Books, 2000); For further background on Arjun Appadurai, see http://www.arjunappadurai.org/.

20. Anand Giridharadas, "Mumbai: City of Heavens and Hells," *International Herald Tribune*, November 6, 2008. http://www.nytimes.com/2008/11/06/world/asia/06iht-letter.1.17579250.html?scp=1&sq=%22Mumbai:%20City%20of%20heavens%20and%C2%A0hells%22&st=cse.

21. The Kiswahili word for government is *serikali,* a combination of words *siri* (secret) and *kali* (fierce).

22. Uhuru is Kiswahili for "freedom." Jomo Kenyatta was born with the Kikuyu name Kamau; after converting to Christianity he eventually took the name Johnstone Kamau. "Kenyatta" is a synonym for "light of Kenya." (Kenya itself is an Akamba word, *Kiinya,* meaning "Mountain of the Ostrich"—referring to how the Batian and Nelion peaks of Mount Kenya, sacred to Kikuyu, Meru and Akamba, resemble black and white ostrich tail feathers.)

23. In what may well be a surprise, the fastest-growing African city is in one of Africa's smallest states: Kigali, Rwanda.

24. Remarks made by Sir Edward Clay, "Address of High Commissioner Clay to the British Business Association of Kenya, *Daily Nation*, July 14, 2004. Most editorials that appeared in media following High Commissioner Clay's address were highly critical, even indignant, that a "foreigner" would criticize the government of Mwai Kibaki, despite obvious problems. The *Nation*, long an independent source and one quite happy to resist government pressure, took a different stance. Subsequent editorials supported Clay, noting, "Britain, in any case, is not just any country with which Kenya has diplomatic relations. It has huge property here. How it acquired that property, of course, is a matter which political activists will always raise." Since the *Nation* is under the ownership of His Royal Highness Aga Khan IV, a major development benefactor in Kenya through the Aga Khan Development Network, Kenya remains reluctant to confront him or his holdings in any direct way.

25. "Where Graft is Merely Rampant, *Economist*, December 18, 2004, 65.

26. In 2010, legislation passed declaring that no new *matatus* would be allowed in Nairobi and that older vehicles would not be replaced when they came out of service. This effort sought over time to replace *matatu* transportation (often controlled by criminal gangs) with official public transportation. Earlier efforts dropped the number of passengers for *matatu* from an astonishing twenty-four per vehicle (which meant that some riders had to hang on to the vehicle standing in an open doorway) to fourteen—still a tight fit.

27. Police have also recently been videotaped using handheld devices such as smartphones to transfer bribes directly to their banking accounts while on duty.

28. The previous embassy was destroyed by a terrorist bombing in August 1998. An architect who had worked on other embassies in the country confided the new embassy structure—which looks like a maximum-security prison—could withstand a nuclear impact.

29. Liotta has regularly seen families lock themselves behind barriers when retiring to sleeping quarters for the night—in both South Africa and Kenya.

30. Having visited Nairobi and Kibera numerous times, Liotta finds this census data impossible to accept.

31. In Kikuyu, *Mungiki* means "multitude" or "united people." Although we can identify no central doctrine, the Mungiki reject all things Western, including Christianity, as trappings of colonialism, favoring Kikuyu tradition over Kenya's modernization.

32. The average rent for a Kiberan resident is 600 Kenyan shillings a month—roughly $7.50. To move into high-rise Kiberan apartments is a considerable expense. While some single-bedroom housing in the Karanja Estates costs 2,000 Kenyan shillings a month, rents can go as high as 15,000 shillings for a three-bedroom in Kibera housing—an increase of 2,500 percent from average rent and the equivalent of six months' salary for many. As of late 2010, construction had ceased, and it was unclear whether or not Kiberan apartment dwellers were paying any rent at all.

33. To be sure, Kenya ethnic identities can become so bewildering—and mixed—that not even Kenyans can fully agree on who belongs where: Masai; Kalenjin; Kikuyu; Gujarasomalis; Turkopokotomarkweiyo; Arabogiriamas; Maagikumerumbians; Kisiis; or Luos, Luhyias, and Abagusii (which some argue could collectively be synthesized as Abagusiluohyias).

34. In a flagrant violation of two International Criminal Court arrest warrants for genocide and crimes against humanity, the Kenyan government refused to arrest Sudanese president Omar Hassan al-Bashir when he attended ceremonies in Nairobi celebrating Kenya's new constitution. Claiming that honoring the ICC arrest warrants might upset "regional stability," Kenyan authorities also attempted to block the ICC prosecution of Kenyan political leaders who organized the violence that convulsed the country after its disputed 2007 election.

35. Jack A. Goldstone, "The New Population Bomb: The Four Megatrends That Will Change the World, " *Foreign Affairs* vol. 89, 1 (January/February 2010): 43.

36. Richard Manning, "The Oil We Eat: Following the Food Chain Back to Iraq," *Harper's* (February 2004): 37–43, http://www.harpers.org/archive/2004/02/0079915.

37. There are dangers in hyper-emphasizing the "youth bulge" concept.

Some analyses such as the National Intelligence Council's *Global Trends 2025: A Transformed World* counter-pose the advantages that surplus youth populations could offer societies in the future, noting that three of every four youth-bulge countries will be located in sub-Saharan Africa, while the remainder will be located in the Middle East, scattered through South and Central Asia, and in the Pacific Islands. The open source intelligence document thus focuses on positive aspects that could emerge. In Iran, for example, the state's politically restless, job-hungry youth bulge may dissipate, yielding a more mature population and workforce growth rates. This could be a "demographic bonus," with a more educated and developed Iran of 2025, where young adults find careers and consumption more attractive than extremist politics. http://www.dni.gov/nic/PDF_2025/2025_Global_Trends_Final_Report.pdf.

38. Barack Obama, *National Security Strategy of the United States*, Washington, DC, The White House, May 2010, http://www.whitehouse.gov/sites/default/files/rss_viewer/national_security_strategy.pdf.

39. Originally published as an essay in the *New York Review of Books*, Buruma and Margalit set forth "Four features of Occidentalism [that] can be seen in most versions of it; we can call them the City, the *Bourgeois*, Reason, and Feminism. Each contains a set of attributes, such as arrogance, feebleness, greed, depravity, and decadence, which are invoked as typically Western, or even American, characteristics." "Occidentalism," *New York Review of Books* vol. 49, 1 (January 17, 2002). *Occidentalism: The West in the Eyes of Its Enemies* (New York: Penguin: 2005).

40. Oswald Spengler, *The Decline of the West*, vol. 1 (New York, 1926), 107.

Chapter 3. Canary in the Coal Mine

1. It is intriguing that Hamas militias—instigators of earlier violence—patrolled the Gaza border for security in 2011, ensuring that the deadlocked peace with Israel continued.

2. Program on Humanitarian Policy and Conflict Research (HPCR), *Human Security for Gaza in 2010: An HPCR Research and Policy Initiative, Project Synopsis* (Boston: Harvard School of Public Health, June 2004).

Chapter 4. Triumphant Failure

1. Tony Horowitz, *Baghdad without a Map* (New York: Plume, 1992).

2. John Walsh, "Understanding Centrist Islam," *Harvard International Review* (May 2006).

3. Sarah Sabry, *Poverty Lines in Greater Cairo: Underestimating and Misrepresenting Poverty, Poverty Reduction in Urban Areas Series*—Working Paper 21 (London: Human Settlements Programme—International Institute for Environment and Development (IIED), May 2009).

4. United Nations, "Report of the International Conference on Popula-
    tion and Development," October 1994, http://www.un.org/popin/icpd/
    conference/offeng/poa.htm.

Chapter 5. The Most Dangerous Place

1. J. A. Aziz, "Towards Establishing Air Quality Guidelines for Pakistan,"
    Eastern Mediterranean Health Journal, 12, no. 6 (World Health Organi-
    zation, November 2006), http://www.emro.who.int/publications/emhj
    /1206/Article21.htm.
2. World Wildlife Fund, *Water Pollution Factsheet*, http://wwfpak.org/fact
    sheets_wps.php.
3. UN Habitat, "Cities Must be Empowered to Tackle Climate Change,"
    December 2009, http://www.unhabitat.org/content.asp?cid=7680&
    catid=5&typeid=6.
4. Asian Development Bank, "Development Effectiveness Brief Pakistan:
    Making a Difference in the Fight Against Poverty" 2009, http://www.adb.
    org/Documents/Brochures/Development-Effectiveness-Country-Briefs/
    decb-pak.pdf.
5. Arif Hasan, "Introduction," in Akhtar Hameed Khan, *Orangi Pilot Proj-
    ect: Reminiscences and Reflections* (New York: Oxford University Press,
    2005), xxxiv.
6. Murtaza Haider, *Urbanization Challenges in Pakistan: Developing Vision
    2030* (McGill University, Canada, and National Institute of Infrastructure
    Planning, Peshawar, Pakistan: January 30, 2006), 2. http://www.docstoc.
    com/docs/50551493/URBANIZATION-CHALLENGES-IN-PAKISTAN.
7. Jane Perlex and Pir Zubair, "In Violent Karachi, Insurgency Finds a Haven,"
    New York Times, May 21, 2010, http://www.nytimes.com/2010/05/22/world
    /asia/22karachi.html?scp=4&sq=Taliban%20Karachi&st=cse.
8. Sebastian Junger, *War* (New York: Twelve Books, 2011), 201–2.
9. Ismail Khan, "Pakistani Outposts Struck by Large Taliban Assault," *New
    York Times*, December 24, 2010, http://www.nytimes.com/2010/12/25
    /world/asia/25pstan.html?scp=1&sq=Mohmand%20region&st=cse.

Chapter 6. Oil, Guns, and Corpses

1. U.S. State Department, "Background Note: Nigeria," 2011, http://www.
    state.gov/r/pa/ei/bgn/2836.htm.
2. Lagos was the capital of Nigeria from 1914 to 1991 but was stripped of its
    status when government offices began transitioning to Abuja, which was
    intentionally built for such purpose.
3. While difficult, if not impossible, to claim with certainty, estimates of
    the deaths that have occurred in eastern Congo since the overthrow of
    Mobutu Sese Seko in 1997 have ranged as high as 8 million—described as
    Africa's first world war.

4. *Report of the Panel of Experts on the Illegal Exploitation of Natural Resources and Other Forms of Wealth of the Democratic Republic of the Congo* (United Nations, April 12, 2001), http://www.un.org/news/dh/latest/drcongo.htm.

5. The *Economist* reports that Rwanda is extracting as much as $12 million a month of precious resources (largely coltan), while other sources report on the movement of diamonds—which are not found in Rwanda—through the small state. Notably, Rwandan president Paul Kagame—and not Laurent-Désiré Kabila, who became leader of the DRC—led the forces of the Rwandan Patriotic Front through a thousand miles of dense jungle to prove the determining force in overthrowing Mobutu and taking Kinshasa in 1997. Kagame, for his strategic brilliance both in turning the tide against the largely Hutu-led government during the 1994 Rwandan genocide and after, has been called "the Napoleon of Africa."

6. Bruce Einhorn, "The Hardest Hardship Posts," *Business Week* (April 2009), http://images.businessweek.com/ss/09/03/0304_difficult_cities/1.htm.

7. Jeffrey Taylor, "Worse Than Iraq? Nigeria's president and onetime hope for a stable future is leading his country toward implosion—and possible U.S. military intervention," *Atlantic Monthly* (April 2006), 33–34, http://www.theatlantic.com/magazine/archive/2006/04/worse-than-iraq/4707/?single_page=true.

8. The 2009 UN report was based on 2007 data.

9. While about the same percentage as states in central and southern Africa, in advanced economies a newborn has more than a 90 percent chance.

10. UNICEF, "At A Glance: Nigeria," http://www.unicef.org/infobycountry/nigeria_statistics.html.

11. United Nations Department of Economic and Social Affairs, Population Division, http://www.un.org/esa/population/publications/wup2001/WUP2001_CH6.pdf

12. Davis, *Planet of Slums*, 97.

13. Quoted in Voice of America, "Clinton: Nigerian Corruption, Poor Governance Foster Radicalization," January 26, 2010, http://www.voanews.com/english/news/africa/Clinton-Nigerian-Corruption-Governance-Foster-Radicalization--82706067.html.

14. Davis, *Planet of Slums*, 191.

15. Filip De Boeck, "Kinshasa: Tales of the 'Invisible City' and the Second World," in *Under Siege: Four African Cities—Freetown, Johannesburg, Kinshasa, Lagos: Documenta11_Platform4,* moderated by *Okwui Enwezor* (Ostfildern, Germany: Hatje Cantz Verlag, 2003). Program outline and speakers are available in pdf form at: http://www.radiobridge.net/www/folder.pdf.

16. Theodore Trefon, Introduction: Reinventing Order, in Theodore Trefon, ed., *Reinventing Order in the Congo: How People Respond to State Failure* (London: Zed Books, 2005), 1.

17. Davis, *Planet of Slums*, 146.
18. See the "Reading On and Looking Forward" section of this book for extended excerpts from Nlandu's work in *Kinshasa Symphony*.
19. Davis, *Planet of Slums*, 195. This phenomenon, of course, is hardly exclusive to Kinshasa or the DRC. In East Africa in the more "developed" state of Kenya, posted advertisements are not uncommon in the wealthy and exclusive Nairobi neighborhood of Karen for various *Mutaigha*—or witch doctors—with Internet links. One practitioner, a certain Dr. Khalifu, assists with any ailment, from bankruptcy to impotence.
20. Vincent Beeckman, "Growing Up on the Streets of Kinshasa," *The Courier ACP-EU: The Magazine of Africa* (September/October 2001): 63–64.
21. U.S. Energy Information Administration, "Country Analysis Brief: Nigeria," August 2011, http://www.eia.gov/cabs/Nigeria/Full.html.
22. Harry Goldstein, "How Not to Make a Megacity: Some Cities Are Littered with Garbage. Lagos Is Littered with Corpses," June 2007, *IEEE Spectrum: Inside Technology—Special Report: A How-To Manual for the Megacity*, 58, http://spectrum.ieee.org/energy/environment/how-not-to-make-a-megacity. Goldstein is senior associate editor at IEEE Spectrum.

Chapter 7. Cities of God
1. Matthew Harwood, "Gang Violence in Rio Poses Security Questions for 2016 Summer Games," http://www.securitymanagement.com/news/gang-violence-rio-poses-security-questions-2016-summer-games-006318.
2. The practice of burning public buses may have several explanations. Aside from obvious intimidation, which makes life more difficult for those who work outside the *favela*, these incidents also force customers to rely on semilegal small van operators who proliferate in the rapidly expanding city. Criminal networks are known to be involved in the running of these transport operations.
3. By the use of "parallel power structure," we mean to suggest that, within *favelas*, municipal governance has no effective meaning; community governance runs parallel to, or in place of, outside influence.
4. Monte Reel, Special Series: "Life in Rio's *Favelas:* Youth Torn Between Gangs and the Government," *Washington Post & Foreign Policy*, N.d. http://www.washingtonpost.com/wp-srv/world/specials/favelas/dividedcells.html.
5. In the brutal carjacking in which the boy's body was left hanging from his seatbelt, the gang leader, twenty-three-year-old Carlos Eduardo Toledo Lima, was incarcerated under such an open regime. When he failed to return to prison in late December 2006, no action was taken to locate him.
6. "'We Have Come to Take Your Souls': The *Caveirão* and Policing in Rio de Janeiro," Amnesty International, March 2006: AI Index: AMR 19/007/2006,

http://www.amnesty.org/en/library/asset/AMR19/007/2006/en/1327a7a0-d454-11dd-8743-d305bea2b2c7/amr190072006en.pdf.

7. A YouTube video of BOPE operations in *favelas* is available at: http://www.youtube.com/watch?v=0hPYBF_5f8w. As one observer notes: "They don't arrest; they kill."

8. Brett Forrest, "The Battle of Rio: With the 2016 Olympics Looming, the City's Embattled Police Invade the *Favelas*," *Atlantic Monthly*, December 2010, http://www.theatlantic.com/magazine/archive/2010/12/the-battle-of-rio/8297/

9. Andrew Downie, "Brazil Vows Olympic Security after Rio Violence: At Least 14 People Were Killed in Rio de Janeiro This Weekend, Including Two Policemen Who Died When Their Helicopter Was Brought Down by Warring Drug Gangs," October 18, 2009, *Christian Science Monitor*, http://www.csmonitor.com/World/Americas/2009/1018/p06s07-woam.html.

10. A useful informational website: http://rioradar.com/upp.

11. Suzana Taschner, "Squatter Settlements and Slums in Brazil," in Brian C. Aldrich and Ravinder S. Sandhu, eds., *Housing the Urban Poor: A Guide to Policy and Practice in the South* (London: Zed, 1995), 196, 219.

Chapter 8. The Most Vulnerable Megacity

1. http://www.youtube.com/watch?v=sMg9Ly9nKog.

2. The Goldman Sachs report was a follow-up to the 2003 paper on the four emerging major BRIC (Brazil, Russia, India, and China) economies. The "N-11" states, candidates to emerge as major twenty-first-century economic forces, are Bangladesh, Egypt, Indonesia, Iran, Mexico, Nigeria, Pakistan, the Philippines, South Korea, Türkiye, and Vietnam.

3. Jane A. Pryer, *Poverty and Vulnerability in Dhaka Slums: The Urban Livelihood Study* (London: Ashgate, 2003).

4. Global Integrity, *The 2010 Global Integrity Report*, http://www.globalintegrity.org/report/Bangladesh/2010/.

5. To hyper-emphasize this pervasiveness, Khaleda Zia, a former prime minister of Bangladesh, was arrested in 2007 on charges of corruption in Dhaka.

6. Reported by the Internet resource service, *Strategic Foresight Group*, May 2009.

7. Robert D. Kaplan, "Waterworld: With rising Islamic fundamentalism, weak government, and not enough dry land for its 150 million people, Bangladesh could use a break. Instead, it must face the catastrophic threat of climate change," *Atlantic Monthly* (January/February 2008), http://www.theatlantic.com/magazine/archive/2008/01/w terworld/6583/.

8. *National Security and the Threat of Climate Change* (Alexandria, VA:

CAN Corporation, 2007), http://www.cna.org/sites/default/files/news/FlipBooks/Climate%20Change%20web/flipviewerxpress.html.
9. The situation is mirrored in Lagos, which lacks adequate infrastructure to cope with flooding. Lagos lies less than two meters above sea level. Yet poor residents build homes (often on stilts) in areas at high risk of flooding simply because these are the only affordable sites. The expected increase and intensity of violent storms will further compound an already severe problem.
10. So named by Grady as homage to Benoît Mandelbrot, the father of fractal geometry. Grady suggests that these urban complexities, much like the Mandelbrot mathematical set, can be visualized as infinitely complex and infinitely mutating.

Chapter 9. Cities of Fear, Cities of Hope
1. *The Responsibility to Protect: Report of the International Commission on Intervention and State Sovereignty* (Ottawa: International Development Research Centre, 2001), http://responsibilitytoprotect.org/ICISS%20Report.pdf.
2. The brutally ugly—and brutally honest—response to the *Responsibility to Protect* can be found in "The Sovereignty Solution," written by Anna Simons, Don Redd, Joe McGraw, and Duane Lauchengco, and originally published in the *American Interest*. The authors contend that strengthening sovereignty ought to be *the* bedrock principle for U.S. national security strategy. States—especially "rogue" states—must be held accountable for their behavior. Sovereignty implies that every state has the right to order its society according to its own preferences. In return, every state bears the responsibility to prevent its citizens from transgressing the sovereignty of others. With an overarching strategy that promises strategic clarity and operational ambiguity, backed by the assurance that those who transgress will feel the weight of a massive military counterblow, the proposal is simple and controversial. In the author's own words: "If we excel at breaking but not at fixing, and if as a people we prefer straight talking and straight shooting, why not build U.S. strategy around these traits? Or, to come at this from a slightly different angle: We are the world's dominant power. Why not use that power for the ultimate liberation? You want to be treated as head of a sovereign state? Fine: Then act like one. But if you or your citizens violate U.S. sovereignty, the response will be destruction, not defeat. If this sounds ruthless, it's meant to."
3. Even more frustrating for decision makers, vulnerability may not reveal itself until *after* impact has occurred.
4. Richard J. Norton, "Feral Cities: Problems Today, Battlegrounds Tomorrow?" *Marine Corps University Journal* (Spring 2010): 69.

5. The mythological chthonic beast that Hercules was sent to kill, the Hydra displayed the unfortunate ability to sprout two new heads whenever one of its many heads was cut off.

6. *Human Security for an Urban Century: Local Challenges, Global Perspectives,* http://www.eukn.org/E_library/Security_Crime_Prevention/ Security_Crime_Prevention/Human_security_for_an_urban_century_ local_challenges_global_perspectives.

7. Ibid.

8. Stephen C. Smith, "The Miracle of Bangladesh: From Basket Case to Case in Point, *World Ark* (Summer 2009): 12–19.

9. To the EU's credit, forces were deployed to the northeastern DRC under the EU flag in 2003 in Operation Artemis, successfully stabilizing the situation in the city of Bunia and shoring up the security environment as an interim multinational presence until transition back to the United Nations Mission in the Democratic Republic of the Congo (MONUC) could be assured. Operation Artemis was the first autonomous EU military mission outside Europe.

10. Of significant importance, ECOWAS—unlike the UN, which chose to invoke the diplomatic practice of "shaming" to denounce the failed 2010 elections in Côte d'Ivoire—took a stand. Announcing their intention to use all available measures, including military intervention, ECOWAS leaders demanded that Laurent Gbagbo cede power to his rival, Alassane Ouattara, widely credited with winning the election—or face forcible ouster. This declaration was widely seen as a demonstration of international and African solidarity, as well as a test of African unity.

11. Thanks to European initiatives, these templates are already being set. In September 2004 the European Union released *A Human Security Doctrine for Europe,* which detailed the scope, organization, and intent that the EU "should build its security policy on a 'human security doctrine,' aimed at protecting individuals through law-enforcement, humanitarian assistance with the occasional use of force." Taking into account the need for complementarities in civil and military operations for EU missions in the Balkans, in the Great Lakes region of sub-Saharan Africa, and in the South Caucasus, the document proposed the development of a civil-military force of fifteen thousand personnel (roughly the size of one division), to include one-third civilian professionals who would support crisis management operations and would be able to deploy to locales as disparate as Macedonia, Kosovo, and the Democratic Republic of the Congo. The force itself would be tiered, drawing first on staff and headquarters capabilities from Brussels, with a secondary force of five thousand personnel able to deploy in ten days. The final tier of five thousand personnel would remain at lower levels of readiness but would periodically train and exercise together. The force would also draw from a professional core,

with a civilian component of doctors, medical personnel, legal specialists, human rights monitors, and those who "straddle" the military/police divide such as *carabinieri* or *gendarmes*. The final aspect of this organization would be the "Human Security Volunteer Service." All would be expected to be culturally aware, multinational, attuned to the multiple dimensions of conflict and intervention, and imbued with a specific, dedicated ethos. Nongovernmental organizations and private corporations might also form part of the "Human Security Volunteer Service." This represents an ambitious initiative to respond to crisis challenges.

12. While serving in Tajikistan during its horrendous civil war of the late 1990s, P. H. Liotta quickly saw that the only organization that provided meaningful support and aid—and that refused to leave despite the dangers—was the Aga Khan Foundation.

13. A counterexample with positive consequence is the UN Conference on the Human Environment (also known as the Stockholm Conference), convened in Sweden in June 1972. The first major conference on international environmental issues, it marked a turning point in the development of international environmental politics. Founded as a direct result of the Stockholm Conference and headquartered in Nairobi, the UN Environment Programme (UNEP) coordinates UN activities and assists emerging states with crafting and implementing environmentally sound policies and practices. Despite UNEP's relatively small budget and constant struggles for funds, the organization's activities involve work that concentrates on the atmosphere as well as marine and terrestrial ecosystems. UNEP is engaged with international environmental conventions, promoting environmental science, funding and implementing environmentally related development projects, and promoting coordinated policy with national governments, regional institutions, and NGOs. It has also engaged international trade issues that involve harmful chemicals and transboundary concerns (whether they be water or pollution issues). The UN's World Meteorological Organization and UNEP established the Intergovernmental Panel on Climate Change in 1988.

14. A useful exception is the Mega-Cities Project, a transnational, nonprofit network of leaders from grassroots groups, nonprofits, government, business, academia, and the media interested in innovative solutions to the problems cities face in common. http://www.megacitiesproject.org/.

15. Worthy as the UN's Millennium Development Goals are, they were always unachievable. A success story does exist: Ghana is set before 2015 to become the first country in Africa to halve its rates of poverty and hunger.

16. Global Commission on International Migration (GCIM), *Migration in an Interconnected World: New Directions for Action. Report of the Global Commission on International Migration* (October 5, 2005), http://www.unhcr.org/refworld/docid/435f81814.html.

17. In what has become a form of dependency syndrome, some states rely heavily on remittances for socioeconomic survival. The tiny Pacific island-state of Tonga, for example, claims 30 percent of its gross domestic product in the form of remittances, whereas both Haiti and Lebanon claim 22 percent each. A powerful interactive *New York Times* graphic by Farhana Hossain and Shan Carter that shows effects and impacts of global migration is available at http://www.nytimes.com/ref/world/20070622_CAPE-VERDE_GRAPHIC.html#.

18. It is also possible to microfinance loans online. Kiva.org—"Loans That Change Lives"—is the best-known source for such individual decisions.

19. While perhaps a "blip" on Egyptian political radar, it is worth noting how poorly the Muslim Brotherhood fared in late 2010 elections. Despite deep community roots, eloquent spiritual leaders, and sheer determination, the Muslim Brotherhood (and other grassroots movements such as *Kefaya*) lost ground as citizens went online to debate difficult political issues such as regime change, gender and political life, and transnational Islamic identity. It was these disparate and disaffected voices that created the revolution of 2011 in Cairo—not the Muslim Brotherhood. The echoes that rippled off and eventually became a tsunami that engulfed the Arab world from "the slap heard 'round the world"—the public humiliation of twenty-six-year-old fruit vendor Mohamed Bouazizi in Tunisia that led to his self-immolation—proved both unstoppable and a complete surprise. We argue that the Muslim Brotherhood was caught off guard almost as much as the Mubarak regime.

20. "Replacement fertility rate" (RFR) is also a simple equivalent that measures the replacement population that must exist in order for a state to continue growth. The standard RFR is 2.1: 2.1 children per woman includes two children to replace the parents, with one-tenth of a child extra to make up for the mortality of children who do not reach the age of fifteen. Consider this: In the United States—which is the only country among "developed" states to continue population growth, largely due to immigration—eight people are born and four people die every minute; someone immigrates every two minutes. In India, forty-eight are born and seventeen die every minute.

READING ON & LOOKING FORWARD

This list is eclectic but provides a sense of direction for those who might like to further examine how and where demographics and security intersect. Some of these works we never referred to during the writing of this book—but their voices were there. Many authors, scholars, and filmmakers contributed to our understanding, and we are grateful.

Barcott, Rye. *It Happened on the Way to War: A Marine's Path to Peace.* London: Bloomsbury, 2011.

Barcott is a terrible writer but a master storyteller. *It Happened on the Way to War* recounts his trials and triumphs as cofounder of the NGO Carolina for Kibera. First visiting the Kibera megaslum of Nairobi in 2000, Barcott tells how he successfully built a network of human inspiration, even as he later serves as a Marine in Iraq and then completes business studies at Harvard. The real heroes of this book, nonetheless (and the author clearly admits it), are the nurse Tabitha Atieno Festo and the community organizer Salim Mohamed. Despite many setbacks that ensue, Barcott's is an optimistic work, in useful contrast to many of the bleaker assessments found in this list.

Barnett, Thomas. *The Pentagon's New Map: War and Peace in the Twenty-first Century.* New York: G.P. Putnam's Sons, 2005.

This bestselling work proved influential in the halls of the Pentagon— the Chief of Naval Operations called it "mind-bending" in a navy-wide message—and instrumental in the disastrous and costly Iraq intervention. Ever the eternal optimist, Barnett argued that the U.S. had a moral responsibility to shape a "future worth creating" for the world and in radically restructuring the U.S. Departments of Defense and State. Though Barnett would never claim himself a Marxist, his work draws consistently on economic determinism, particularly his conceptual approach to the "Functioning Core" of economically developed, politically stable states integrated into global systems set against the "Non-Integrating Gap," the most likely source of threats to U.S. and international security. Barnett's assertion, nonetheless, that those most disconnected from the flows of globalization are where we will be most likely to intervene is flawed. Notably, Liotta clashed with Barnett in the pages of *Esquire*—where Barnett is now a contributing editor.

Blade Runner. DVD. Directed by Ridley Scott, 2007. Los Angeles, CA: Time Warner.

Using *Blade Runner* as one of several Hollywood films—*Chinatown* and *Lost in Translation* are two other different but intriguing examples—Homay King argues in *Lost in Translation: Orientalism, Cinema, and the Enigmatic Signifier* that Hollywood has embedded the "Shanghai gesture" that has shaped its core: the trope of "otherness," where there is endless fascination with an Orient that shrouds itself in mystery and always looming menace. Yet this reality obscures the truth that *Blade Runner* is *the* dystopian urban masterpiece: the city has become Moloch and ravenously devours its inhabitants. Despite his many critics, Ridley Scott remains Hollywood's best and most visionary director, delivering films on time and under budget—from *Gladiator* to *Hannibal* to *Black Hawk Down*.

Buruma, Ian, and Margalit, Avishai. *Occidentalism: The West in the Eyes of Its Enemies*. New York: Penguin Press, 2004.

A seminal work, the first to recognize that the impulses that led to the 9/11 attacks and the persistent hatred of the West cluster around four central images: the sinfulness, rootlessness, and "evil" of urban life; the corruption of the human spirit in a materialistic, market-driven society; the loss of organic community and the rise of the rule of law over faith; and the glory of heroic self-sacrifice in overcoming the shallow blankness of *bourgeois* life. The role of women, needless to say, is subjugated as well. In short, Western liberalism is a threat.

Chomsky, Noam. *How the World Works*. Interviewed by David Barsamian and edited by Arthur Naiman. Berkeley, CA: Soft Skull Press, 2011.

Named by the *New York Times* as "arguably the most important intellectual alive," Chomsky never fails to provoke—actually *inflame* is a more accurate phrasing. But his ideas have become only more prescient over time. He—along with his close friend and colleague, the Marxist historian Howard Zinn (with whom Liotta was also close)—has made a deep impact on American political culture and thought.

City of God. DVD. Directed by Fernando Meirelles, 2002. Los Angeles, CA: Miramax Lions Gate, 2011.

Based on Bráulio Mantovani's 1997 novel of the same name, the film depicts real characters and actual events. Meirelles went on to create the *City of Men* television series using many of the same characters. Nominated for four Academy Awards, including best director and best screenplay, the film was an international sensation and gave the harsh reality of *favela* life global attention.

City of God, Guns, and Gangs. New York: Vanguard Documentary, 2011.

Useful update as Rio prepares for the World Cup and the Olympic Games and attempts to deal with high crime rates, rampant corruption, and *favela* pacification. Journalist Mariana van Zeller interviews multiple participants from drug lords to preachers to BOPE officers and sociologists, detailing how government plans to pacify forty of Rio's six hundred *favelas* by the time the games begin. Of interest: Cidade de Deus—the *City of God*—is now one of these pacified neighborhood communities where police walk the streets unchallenged and are welcomed.

Collapse. DVD. Washington, DC: National Geographic Video, 2010.

A much narrower and more sensational interpretation than Diamond's book—though it does includes extended comments from Diamond and Joseph Tainter—the documentary focuses on a group of burlap-clad archaeologists who set out in the year 2210 to determine what brought us down. Largely focusing on the Mayan and Roman empires—Diamond barely mentions the Romans in his book—the video posits the ecological disasters we are creating to bring about our own demise.

The Cove. DVD. Directed by Louie Psihoyos, 2009. Los Angeles, CA: Lions Gate, 2009.

Shocking, stunning, superb—no descriptor is adequate to describe this Academy Award–winning film. Call it propaganda if you like but you would be a fool to ignore it. This film is a riveting narrative of how one man's ignorant mistake led to a lifelong crusade to change the world. One might reasonably ask how this film links to the issue of megacities and urbanization. The answer is clear: Just as with *Darwin's Nightmare,* the threads and the consequences of actions we take through the complex web of globalization can and do have devastating impact.

Darwin's Nightmare. Directed by Hubert Sauper, 2004. Homevision Studio: 2007.

With the introduction of the Nile Perch to Lake Victoria five decades ago as a "little scientific experiment," this voracious predator has long since depleted the entire stock of native fish and now cannibalizes its own. The Nile Perch, however, remains prized for its tender, plump fillets, and remains much sought after in European markets. Thus, the push of free market trade and the pull of the European city make Thomas Friedman's seemingly absurd suggestion that globalization is the integration of everything with virtually everything else begin to make weird sense. In this stark documentary, we see cargo planes fly out daily from Mwanza airfield in Tanzania with 55 tons of processed fish daily (while any number of them fly in with smuggled arms on-board). Meanwhile, starving villagers at the edge of a ruined ecosystem that was a pristine and thriving natural wonder scrounge for food from discarded fish heads and rotting carcasses. We see disease, war, crime, homelessness, and children addicted to sniffing glue. The picture is bleak—for both humans and fish.

Davis, Mike. *Planet of Slums.* London: Verso, 2007.

Davis is a hard-nosed scholar and MacArthur "genius" recipient. This book, certainly not without controversy, provides a wealth of often devastating insight into the squalid conditions many urban dwellers are forced to live with in some of the most tenuous locations on earth.

Diamond, Jared. *Collapse: How Societies Choose to Fail or Succeed.* New York: Viking, 2005.
———. *Guns, Germs, and Steel: The Fates of Human Societies.* New York: Norton, 1999.

Jared Diamond is a master of narrative, and his broad sweep of history and human geography is powerful. The chapter titled "Malthus in Africa: Rwanda's Genocide" in *Collapse* gives particular insight on how environmental and socioeconomic stressors lead to sometimes horrific outcomes.

Earth 2100: The Final Century of Civilization? DVD. Michael Bicks, Executive Producer. New York, NY: ABC News, 2009.

Because *Gaia's Revenge: Climate Change and Humanity's Loss* was the first work to draw on alternate futures and scenarios with multi-variate aspects of security from national to human security, P. H. Liotta and Allan W. Shearer were the original creative consultants for this project. In this instance, the scenario is pretty miserable: in the not-too-distant future we have created the "perfect storm" where population growth, resource depletion, and climate change have all converged—with catastrophic results. In executive producer Michael Bicks' note to the production, he made clear that "the scenarios in *Earth 2100* are not a prediction of what will happen but rather a warning about what might happen. They are based on the work of some of the world's top scientists and experts, as well as peer-reviewed articles from publications around the world. These notes are just a glimpse of the wide and diverse sources used to develop this program. . . . This program was developed to show the worst-case scenario for human civilization. Again, we are not saying that these events will happen—rather, that if we fail to seriously address the complex problems of climate change, resource depletion and overpopulation, they are much more likely to happen."

Ehrlich, Paul R. *The Population Bomb: Population Control or Race to Oblivion?* New York: Ballantine, 1970.

Ehrlich has been much maligned for the failure of predictions made in *The Population Bomb* to have ever materialized. In its time, nonetheless, this work had seminal impact and brought the issue of exploding demographics to the forefront of debate. Critics mistook, as always, *projections* for predictions. As we discuss in this work, the influence of technology—particularly the "Green Revolution—radically altered events in the near term. Ehrlich's ideas mattered. His concept of "inalienable rights"—given increased stratification between rich and poor, and majority world and economically sheltered states—is more relevant today than ever before. Our book, clearly, is titled as homage.

Ehrlich, Paul R., and Anne H. Ehrlich. *One with Nineveh: Politics, Consumption, and the Human Future.* Washington: Island Press, 2005.

Girardet, Herbert. *Gaia Atlas of New Cities: New Directions of Sustainable Urban Living.* Nairobi, Kenya: UN-HABITAT, 1996.

Relating to what would become the United Nations Habitat II (Second UN Conference on Human Settlements) in İstanbul in 1996, this work provided ideas and strategies on how to make cities more ecologically sustainable—perhaps more interesting today for where and why we have largely failed.

Junger, Sebastian. *War.* New York: Twelve Books, 2011.

A work of stunning integrity, Junger best illustrates through powerful examples the links between Pakistani urban militants and insurgents in the Korengal Valley of northeastern Afghanistan. Between June 2007 and June 2008,

Junger—bestselling author of *The Perfect Storm* and contributing editor for *Vanity Fair*—redefined the term "embedded" reporter as he lived in hellish conditions where a fifth of the combat that 70,000 NATO troops engaged in was fought by the 150 men of Battle Company with whom he lived; 70 percent of the bombs dropped in Afghanistan were dropped in and around the Korengal Valley. Dubbed the "Valley of Death" by American forces, forty-two service members died and hundreds of others were wounded there. (Staff Sergeant Salvatore Augustine Giunta also became the first living recipient of the Medal of Honor since Vietnam for his efforts to rescue Sergeant Joshua Brennan from Taliban captors in the Korengal during Operation Rock Avalanche.) U.S. forces permanently withdrew from the Korengal in April 2010. Junger and photojournalist Tim Hetherington, nonetheless, created 150 hours of videotape, segments which aired on ABC News and became the basis of their Academy Award–nominated film *Restrepo*. Junger's reporting is meticulous: with the advantage of video recording, he uses direct quotation marks only when the person speaking makes comments on camera or Junger writes down directly in his notebook as the person is speaking. In a cruelly ironic twist, Junger ended the 2011 edition of *War* with an acknowledgment to Hetherington for the extraordinary success of their collaboration, hoping there would be "many more": On April 20, 2011, Tim Hetherington was killed by mortar shells fired by Muammar Gaddafi's forces while covering the 2011 Libyan civil war.

Kaplan, Robert D. *The Coming Anarchy: Shattering the Dreams of the Post Cold War.* New York: Vintage, 2001.

Rising out of an essay titled "The Coming Anarchy," originally published in the *Atlantic Monthly* in 1994, this book of nine provocative essays collectively argues that we have reach a "bifurcated world" where hazards in some of the world's most dangerous places will bleed over in contagion effect. Kaplan is not without his share of critics and naysayers. Combining skills as a travel writer with the insights of a foreign policy expert, Kaplan is controversial—and he means to be. One would be foolish to simply dismiss his arguments.

Khanna, Parag. *How to Run the World: Charting a Course to the Next Renaissance.* New York: Random House, 2011.

Praise and dispraise for this book tend toward polar extremes, but Khanna does present a sweeping view of how—with the end of the American Century—we have entered a Middle Ages of decentralization where individuals, organizations (particularly NGOs), radicals, and even mercenaries wield influence in unprecedented ways. Arguing for a fresh dance among these elements to solve global problems on a local scale in a "fractured, fragmented, multi-polar" (11) world, Khanna covers a wide range of topics. His work on the Age of the City excerpted in *Foreign Policy* is especially useful.

Kinshasa Symphony. DVD, 2010. Directed by Claus Wischmann and Martin Baer. http://www.kinshasa-symphony.com/index.php?id=43.
 Not just a documentary but an organic project with global performances ongoing in 2011 from "L'Orchestere Symphonique Kimbanguiste." The project describes itself as showing "how people living in one of the most chaotic cities in the world have managed to forge one of the most complex systems of human cooperation ever invented: a symphony orchestra. It is a film about the Congo, about the people of Kinshasa and about music." The film offers a three-way perspective of 1) The City: Kinshasa, one of the fastest growing, most chaotic megacities, a veritable Moloch. Poet Thierry Mayamba Nlandu describes the city as "beyond chaos." 2) The People: Various *Kinois* include bread salesgirl Chantal Ikina, electrician and hairdresser Joseph, artisan Albert Matubenza, and preacher Armand Diangienda. 3) The Music: *Kinois* converge at the rehearsal venue of the only symphony orchestra not only in Kinshasa or the Congo, but in all sub-Saharan Africa.

Koyaanisqatsi: Life Out of Balance. DVD, 1983. Los Angeles, CA: MGM, 2002.
 Punctuated with Philip Glass' ghostly, lyrical (some might also call it maddening) music, first-time filmmaker Godfrey Reggio's experimental documentary from 1983—filmed in the desert Southwest and New York City on basically no budget with no script. Now known as the first of the *Koyaanisqatsi Trilogy,* it was never meant as such at the time and remains a stand-alone film on the isolation and deprivation urbanization can induce.

Liotta, P. H., and Allan W. Shearer. *Gaia's Revenge: Climate Change and Humanity's Loss.*
 In Greek mythology, Gaia is Mother Earth. Her revenge for human accumulation of greenhouse gasses, the authors contend, is climate change and human impacts. While maintaining a strategic perspective on the implications of environmental effects, they are the first to examine this challenge through futures scenario planning and the various lenses of security—national, international, and human. Dr. Geoffrey Dabelko, director of the Woodrow Wilson International Center for Scholars' Environmental Change and Security Program, singled out this work as the first to address the critical need "for the science-policy interface."

Malthus, Thomas Robert. *An Essay on the Principles of Population,* 2nd ed. New York: Norton, 2003.

First published in 1798, Malthus described how population would grow exponentially, outstripping food production and securing of critical natural resources. Malthus's theory has to date not come to pass, thanks in part to emerging technologies and human ingenuity over the past centuries. This Norton edition has commentaries from a number of sources, including Lester R. Brown, Paul and Anne Ehrlich, Garrett Hardin, Julian Simon, and Pope Paul VI.

Meadows, Donella H., Jorgen Randers, and Dennis L. Meadows. *The Limits to Growth: The 30-Year Update.* White River Junction, VT: Chelsea Green, 2004.

Admittedly a pessimistic work that warns of the danger of human "overshoot"—drawing down natural resources without sufficient replenishment. Twice-updated since its original publication in 1972, the authors provide computer modeling to illustrate how "profound correction" is needed to prevent serious consequence in the coming decades.

Metropolis. DVD. Directed by Fritz Lang, 1927—re-issue, 2010. Los Angeles, CA: KINO International.

Although frequently boring to watch, there are scenes of such fierce hallucinatory, hypnotic intensity—the Tower of Babel, the sea of lusting eyes— they confirm the Occidentalist's worst paranoid fantasies of the city turning its residents into automatons and the muse of the city, the siren-like robot, as automaton-ic whore.

Miskel, James F., and P. H. Liotta. *A Fevered Crescent: Security and Insecurity in the Greater Near East.* Gainesville, FL: University Press of Florida, 2006.

Drawing on work that appeared in the *New York Times, Newsweek, Parameters, Naval War College Review, Security Dialogue, Orbis: A Journal of World Affairs, and World Policy Journal,* this is a more formal, academic work than *The Real Population Bomb*—but remains its precursor. Ambassador Peter Galbraith, author of *Unintended Consequences: How War in Iraq Strengthened America's Enemies,* described this work as "an original and exceptionally well written analysis of what the authors rightly describe as the central challenge of our time: the problem of depopulating rural areas and megacities that no one governs. This is the proverbial swamp that stretches in a crescent from Lagos to Jakarta and must be drained if we are to win the war on terror, as well as cope with challenges ranging from pandemics and organized crime to drug smuggling and migration. Liotta and Miskel convincingly demonstrate that governments are largely clueless about the nature of the problem and that much of current analysis, both in the policy and academic community, is way off base. This groundbreaking book also discusses policies that developed countries might pursue in meeting the challenge from the fevered crescent. There are no panaceas but at least Liotta and Miskel point us in plausible directions."

Myers, Norman. *The Gaia Atlas of Future Worlds: Challenges and Opportunities in an Age of Change.* New York: Anchor, 1991.

This is, to say the least, a quirky book. Yet Myers provides a fascinating look forward from several decades back—often proving as interesting where shown to be wrong, as when he is right.

Naqoyqatsi: Life as War. DVD. Directed by Godfrey Reggio. Los Angeles, CA: Miramax, 2003.

The final film in the *Koyaanisqatsi Trilogy,* Reggio sees daily life as open warfare in an age of advanced technology: bombarded by constantly shifting, updating, newly archival images, solarization, digital enhancements, thermal effects, 2-D and 3-D animation, athletic and military regimentation, and the blooming of weapons of mass destruction. Indeed, the trilogy itself takes the view that extreme ecologists take: humanity is the ultimate threat to Gaia—and must be removed.

Neuwirth, Robert. *Shadow Cities: A Billion Squatters, A New Urban World.* New York: Routledge, 2006.

Using the resources of a MacArthur fellowship, Neuwirth writes an optimistic assessment of his time living in the slums of İstanbul, Mumbai, Nairobi, and Rio de Janeiro. Describing the hardships and challenges residents of major urban slums must daily endure, Neuwirth's book is a testament to the true resilience of the human spirit.

Planet of the Apes. Directed by Franklin Schaffner, 1968. Los Angeles, CA: Fox.

Schaffner, who won an Academy Award as Best Director for *Patton,* made a minor masterpiece with this film—unequalled by any to follow until 2011's prequel, *Rise of the Planet of the Apes.* The synopsis is deliciously simple and cruel: A U.S. spacecraft lands on a desolate planet where astronauts discover a world where apes rule and humans drool. Only until much later does the lead character—Charlton Heston, of course—discover that they in truth returned to Earth where mankind first destroyed its cities and then destroyed itself.

Powwaqatsi: Life in Transformation. DVD. Directed by Godfrey Reggio. Los Angeles, CA: MGM, 2002.

With a different director (a former Christian brother), the second film of the *Koyaanisqatsi Trilogy* takes a more passionate polemic: displacement, pollution, alienation. But he spends as much time beautifully depicting what various cultures have lost—cooperative living, a sense of joy in labor, and religious values—as he does confronting viewers with trains, airliners, coal cars, and loneliness.

Pryer, Jane A. *Poverty and Vulnerability in Dhaka Slums: The Urban Livelihood Study*. Hampshire: Ashgate Publishing, 2003.

In this thorough volume, Pryer examines the social and economic effects of the rapid formation of slums in Dhaka, identifies the coping strategies of slum dwellers, and recommends policies that could alleviate poverty and other social problems in the slums.

Silver, Christopher. *Planning the Megacity: Jakarta in the Twentieth Century*. New York: Routledge, 2008.

Soylent Green. DVD. Los Angeles, CA: Warner Home Video, 2008.

Yes, it's corny, creepy, and confusing. But it's also provocative and way ahead of its time. A small science-fiction apocalyptic masterpiece: in the year 2022 overcrowding, pollution, and resource depletion have forced society's leaders to find food for the masses in a miracle product named Soylent Green. We promise that the final lines of the film—just as Charlton Heston's final lines in *Planet of the Apes*—are ones you'll never forget.

Tainter, Joseph A. *The Collapse of Complex Societies*. Cambridge: Cambridge University Press, 1990.

Providing one of the more intriguing perspectives in the ABC News documentary, *Earth 2100: The Final Century of Civilization?*, the archaeologist Tainter offers a wealth of detail and background on how and why empires from the Roman to the Mayan and many others abruptly disappeared. Suggesting that collapse is perhaps a return to normalcy, Tainter lays the foundation that Jared Diamond covers in later books such as *Guns, Germs, and Steel* and *Collapse*.

United Nations, *International Conference on Population and Development*. Cairo, 1994. http://www.un.org/popin/icpd2.htm.

United Nations, Department of Economic and Social Affairs. *World Urbanization Prospects: The 2009 Revision*. http://esa.un.org/unpd/wup/index.htm.

———. *World Population Prospects: The 2010 Revision*. http://esa.un.org/unpd/wpop/index.htm.

———. *Population Information Network*. http://www.un.org/popin/.

———. *Demographic and Social Statistics*. http://unstats.un.org/unsd/demographic/.

Verma, Gita Dewan. *Slumming India: A Chronicle of Slums and their Saviours*. Delhi: Penguin Books, 2003.

Verma's study assigns the lion's share of blame for proliferating slums in India to the government itself, which failed to monitor and enforce grand plans for land development. While criticized for over-emphasizing the significance of various master plans, this work offers insight into the impacts that occur when governance is deficient.

INDEX

ABOUT THE AUTHORS

P. H. Liotta is the Thomas Hawkins Johnson Visiting Scholar at the United States Military Academy, West Point, New York.

He served for three decades in the U.S. Air Force, and piloted T-38, KC-135, UV-18, and C-12 aircraft, as well as (with the Hellenic Air Force) the Mirage 2000. He was a Fulbright lecturer and poet-in-residence *(slobodan umjetnik,* 1988–1989) in former Yugoslavia and has traveled widely throughout the former Soviet Union and border regions, particularly the Caucasus and Central Asia—to the Altai region of Siberia, Tajikistan, the Afghan front, Uzbekistan, Turkmenistan, Georgia, and Iran—as well as throughout Asia, Africa, and South America.

The author of eighteen books and numerous articles, Liotta has also published a novel, *Diamond's Compass*, about Iran. His research interests focus on environmental, human, and demographic security issues in the contemporary environment.

Since 2004, he has been senior lecturer in demographics, migration, and global security at the NATO Defense College in Rome, Italy. In 2005, he joined Working Group II (Impacts, Adaptation and Vulnerability of Climate Change) of the United Nations Intergovernmental Panel on Climate Change (IPCC). He recently served as expert consultant on endemic urban violence for the Canadian government and Department of Foreign Affairs and International Trade's Human Security and Cities Initiative. He is active on the international boards of both the (Robert) Frost Place and the Anthony Quinn Foundation. He was also original creative consultant for the ABC News documentary *Earth 2100: The Final Century of Civilization?*

In 2007, as a member of the IPCC, he shared the Nobel Peace Prize.